Unconditional Parenting

Unconditional Parenting

MOVING FROM

REWARDS AND PUNISHMENTS

TO LOVE AND REASON

Alfie Kohn

ATRIA BOOKS

NEW YORK   LONDON   TORONTO   SYDNEY

ATRIA BOOKS

1230 Avenue of the Americas
New York, NY 10020

Library of Congress Cataloging-in-Publication Data
Kohn, Alfie.
Unconditional parenting : moving from rewards and punishments to love
and reason / Alfie Kohn.
p. cm.
Includes bibliographical references.
ISBN 0-7434-8747-8 (alk. paper)
1. Parenting 2. Parent and child. 3. Parental acceptance. 4. Child rearing. I. Title.
HQ755.8.K65 2005
649'.1—dc22   2004062371

First Atria Books hardcover edition March 2005

10 9 8 7 6 5 4 3 2

ATRIA BOOKS is a trademark of Simon & Schuster, Inc.

Manufactured in the United States of America

For information regarding special discounts for bulk purchases,
please contact Simon & Schuster Special Sales at 1-800-456-6798
or business@simonandschuster.com

How much more precious is
a little humanity than all the rules in the world.

—JEAN PIAGET

CONTENTS

INTRODUCTION   1

1: CONDITIONAL PARENTING   10

2: GIVING AND WITHHOLDING LOVE   24

3: TOO MUCH CONTROL   46

4: PUNITIVE DAMAGES   63

5: PUSHED TO SUCCEED   74

6: WHAT HOLDS US BACK?   93

7: PRINCIPLES OF UNCONDITIONAL PARENTING   117

8: LOVE WITHOUT STRINGS ATTACHED   140

9: CHOICES FOR CHILDREN   167

10: THE CHILD'S PERSPECTIVE   191

APPENDIX • *Parenting Styles: The Relevance of Culture, Class, and Race*   212

NOTES   222

REFERENCES   243

ACKNOWLEDGMENTS   255

INDEX   257

INTRODUCTION

Even before I had children, I knew that being a parent was going to be challenging as well as rewarding. But I didn't *really* know.

I didn't know how exhausted it was possible to become, or how clueless it was possible to feel, or how, each time I reached the end of my rope, I would somehow have to find more rope.

I didn't understand that sometimes when your kids scream so loudly that the neighbors are ready to call the Department of Child Services, it's because you've served the wrong shape of pasta for dinner.

I didn't realize that those deep-breathing exercises mothers are taught in natural-childbirth class don't really start to pay off until long after the child is out.

I couldn't have predicted how relieved I'd be to learn that other people's children struggle with the same issues, and act in some of the same ways, that mine do. (Even more liberating is the recognition that other parents, too, have dark moments when they catch themselves not liking their own child, or wondering whether it's all worth it, or entertaining various other unspeakable thoughts.)

The bottom line is that raising kids is not for wimps. My wife says it's a test of your capacity to deal with disorder and unpredictability—a test you can't study for, and one whose results aren't always reassuring. Forget "rocket science" or "brain surgery": When we want to make the point that something isn't really all that difficult, we ought to say, "Hey, it's not parenting. . . ."

One consequence of this difficulty is that we may be tempted to focus our energies on overcoming children's resistance to our requests and getting them to do what we tell them. If we're not careful, this can become our primary goal. We may find ourselves joining all those people around us who prize docility in children and value short-term obedience above all.

Several years ago, while on a lecture trip, I was sitting in an airplane that had just landed and taxied to its gate. As soon as the *ding!* signaled that we were free to stand up and retrieve our carry-on bags, one of my fellow passengers leaned into the row ahead of us and congratulated the parents of a young boy sitting there. "He was so good during the flight!" my seatmate exclaimed.

Consider for a moment the key word in that sentence. *Good* is an adjective often laden with moral significance. It can be a synonym for *ethical* or *honorable* or *compassionate*. However, where children are concerned, the word is just as likely to mean nothing more than *quiet*—or, perhaps, *not a pain in the butt to me*. Overhearing that comment in the plane, I had a little *ding!* moment of my own. I realized that this is what many people in our society seem to want most from children: not that they are caring or creative or curious, but simply that they are well behaved. A "good" child—from infancy to adolescence—is one who isn't too much trouble to us grown-ups.

Over the last couple of generations, the strategies for trying to produce that result may well have changed. Where kids were once routinely subjected to harsh corporal punishment, they may now be sentenced to time-outs or, perhaps, offered rewards when they obey us. But don't mistake new means for new ends. The goal continues to be control, even if we secure it with more modern methods. This isn't because we don't care about our kids. It has more to do with being overwhelmed by the countless prosaic pressures of family life, where the need to get children into and out of the bed, bathtub, or car makes it hard to step back and evaluate what we're doing.

One problem with just trying to get kids to do what we say is that this may conflict with other, more ambitious, goals we have for them.

This afternoon, your primary concern for your son may be for him to stop raising a ruckus in the supermarket and accept the fact that you're not going to buy a big, colorful box of candy disguised as breakfast cereal. But it's worth digging a little deeper. In the workshops I conduct for parents, I like to start off by asking, "What are your *long-term* objectives for your children? What word or phrase comes to mind to describe how you'd like them to turn out, what you want them to be like once they're grown?"

Take a moment to think about how you would answer that question. When I invite groups of parents to come up with the most important long-term goals they have for their kids, I hear remarkably similar responses across the country. The list produced by one audience was typical: These parents said they wanted their children to be happy, balanced, independent, fulfilled, productive, self-reliant, responsible, functioning, kind, thoughtful, loving, inquisitive, and confident.

What's interesting about that collection of adjectives—and what's useful about the process of reflecting on the question in the first place—is that it challenges us to ask whether what we're doing is consistent with what we really want. Are my everyday practices likely to help my children grow into the kind of people I'd like them to be? Will the things I just said to my child at the supermarket contribute in some small way to her becoming happy and balanced and independent and fulfilled and so on—or is it possible (gulp) that the way I tend to handle such situations makes those outcomes *less* likely? If so, what should I be doing instead?

If it's too daunting to imagine how your children will turn out many years from now, think about what really matters to you today. Picture yourself standing at a birthday party or in the hall of your child's school. Around the corner are two other parents who don't know you're there. You overhear them talking about . . . your child! Of all the things they might be saying, what would give you the most pleasure?[1] Again, pause for a moment to think of a word or sentence that you would be especially delighted to hear. My guess—and my hope—is that it wouldn't be, "Boy, that child does everything he's told and you never hear a peep out of him." The crucial question, there-fore, is whether we sometimes act as though that *is* what we care about most.

Almost twenty-five years ago, a social psychologist named Elizabeth Cagan reviewed a bushel of contemporary parenting books and con-cluded that they mostly reflected a "blanket acceptance of parental prerogative," with little "serious consideration of a child's needs, feel-ings, or development." The dominant assumption, she added, seemed to be that the parents' desires "are automatically legitimate," and thus the only question open for discussion was how, exactly, kids could be made to do whatever they're told.[2]

Sadly, not much has changed since then. More than a hundred par-enting books are published in the United States every year,[3] along with countless articles in parenting magazines, and most of them are filled with advice about how to get children to comply with our expecta-tions, how to make them behave, how to train them as though they were pets. Many such guides also offer a pep talk about the need to stand up to kids and assert our power—in some cases explicitly writ-ing off any misgivings we may have about doing so. This slant is reflected even in the titles of recently published books: *Don't Be Afraid to Discipline; Parents in Charge; Parent in Control; Taking Charge; Back in Control; Disciplining Your Preschooler—and Feeling Good About It; 'Cause I'm the Mommy, That's Why; Laying Down the Law; Guilt-Free Parenting; "The Answer Is No";* and on and on.

Some of these books defensively stand up for old-fashioned values and methods ("Your rear end is going to be mighty sore when your father gets home"), while others make the case for newfangled tech-niques ("Good job! You peed in the potty, honey! Now you can have your sticker!"). But in neither case do they press us to be sure that what we're asking of children is reasonable—or in their best interests.

It's also true, as you may have noticed, that many of these books offer suggestions that turn out to be, shall we say, not terribly helpful, even though they're sometimes followed by comically unrealistic parent-child dialogues intended to show how well they work.[4] But while it can be frustrating to read about techniques that prove to be ineffective, it's much more dangerous when books never even bother to ask, "What do we mean by *effective?*" When we fail to examine our objectives, we're left by default with practices that are intended solely to get kids to do what they're told. That means we're focusing only on what's most convenient for us, not on what they need.

Another thing about parenting guides: Most of them offer advice based solely on what the author happens to think, with carefully chosen anecdotes to support his or her point of view. There's rarely any mention of what research has to say about the ideas in question. Indeed, it's possible to make your way clear across the child-care shelf of your local bookstore, one title at a time, without even realizing that there's been a considerable amount of scientific investigation of various approaches to parenting.

Some readers, I realize, are skeptical of claims that "studies show" such-and-such to be true, and understandably so. For one thing, people who toss that phrase around often don't tell you what studies they're talking about, let alone how they were conducted or just how significant their findings were. And then there's that pesky question again: If a researcher claims to have proven that doing x with your kids is more effective than doing y, we'd immediately want to ask, "What exactly do you mean by *effective?* Are you suggesting that children will be better off, psychologically speaking, as a result of x? Will they become more concerned about the impact of their actions on other people? Or is x just more likely to produce mindless obedience?"

Some experts, like some parents, seem to be interested only in that last question. They define a successful strategy as anything that gets kids to follow directions. The focus, in other words, is limited to how children *behave,* regardless of how they feel about complying with a given request, or, for that matter, how they come to regard the person who succeeded in getting them to do so. This is a pretty dubious way of measuring the value of parenting interventions. The evidence suggests that even disciplinary techniques that seem to "work" often turn out to be much less successful when judged by more meaningful criteria. The child's commitment to a given behavior is often shallow and the behavior is therefore short-lived.[5]

But that's not the end of the story. The problem isn't just that we miss a lot by evaluating our strategies in terms of whether they get kids to obey; it's that obedience itself isn't always desirable. There is such a thing as being too well behaved. One study, for example, followed toddlers in Washington, D.C., until they were five years old and found that "frequent compliance [was] sometimes associated with maladjustment." Conversely, "a certain level of resistance to parental authority" can be a "positive sign." Another pair of psychologists, writing in the *Journal of Abnormal Child Psychology*, described a disturbing phenomenon they called "compulsive compliance," in which children's fear of their parents leads them to do whatever they're told—immediately and unthinkingly. Many therapists, too, have commented on the emotional consequences of an excessive need to please and obey adults. They point out that amazingly well-behaved children do what their parents want them to do, and become what their parents want them to become, but often at the price of losing a sense of themselves.[6]

We might say that discipline doesn't always help kids to become *self*-disciplined. But even that second objective isn't all it's cracked up to be. It's not necessarily better to get children to internalize our wishes and values so they'll do what we want even when we're not around. Trying to foster internalization—or self-discipline—may amount to an attempt to direct children's behavior by remote control. It's just a more powerful version of obedience. There's a big difference, after all, between a child who does something because he or she believes it's the right thing to do and one who does it out of a sense of compulsion. Ensuring that children internalize our values isn't the same thing as helping them to develop their own.[7] And it's diametrically opposed to the goal of having kids become independent thinkers.

Most of us, I'm convinced, do indeed want our children to think for themselves, to be assertive and morally courageous . . . when they're with their friends. We hope they'll stand up to bullies and resist peer pressure, particularly when sex and drugs are involved. But if it's important to us that kids not be "victims of others' ideas," we have to educate them "to think for themselves about all ideas, including those of adults."[8] Or, to put it the other way around, if we place a premium on obedience at home, we may end up producing kids who go along with what they're told to do by people outside the home, too. Author Barbara Coloroso remarks that she's often heard parents of teenagers complain, "He was such a good kid, so well behaved, so well mannered, so well dressed. Now look at him!" To this, she replies:

> From the time he was young, he dressed the way you told him to dress; he acted the way you told him to act; he said the things you told him to say. He's been listening to somebody else tell him what to do. . . . He hasn't changed. He is still listening to somebody else tell him what to do. The problem is, it isn't you anymore; it's his peers.[9]

*   *   *

The more we ponder our long-term goals for our kids, the more complicated things become. Any goal might prove to be objectionable if we consider it in isolation: Few qualities are so important that we'd be willing to sacrifice everything else to achieve them. (On the subject of happiness, for example, see p. 239n1. Maybe it's wiser to help children strike a balance between opposing pairs of qualities, so that they grow up to be self-reliant *but also* caring, or confident *yet still* willing to acknowledge their limitations. Likewise, some parents may insist that what matters most to them is helping their children to set and meet their own goals. If that makes sense to us, then we have to be prepared for the possibility that they'll make choices and embrace values that aren't the same as ours.

Our thinking about long-term goals may lead us in any number of directions, but the point I want to emphasize is that however we think about those goals, we ought to think about them a lot. They ought to be our touchstone, if only to keep us from being sucked into the quicksand of daily life with its constant temptation to do whatever it takes to get compliance. As the parent of two children, I am well acquainted with the frustrations and challenges that come with the job. There are times when my best strategies fall flat, when my patience runs out, when I just want my kids to do what I tell them. It's hard to keep the big picture in mind when one of my children is shrieking in a restaurant. For that matter, it's sometimes hard to remember the kind of people *we* want to be when we're in the middle of a hectic day, or when we feel the pull of less noble impulses. It's hard, but it's still worthwhile.

Some people rationalize what they're doing by dismissing the more meaningful goals—such as trying to be, or to raise one's child to be, a good person—as "idealistic." But that just means having ideals, without which we're not worth a hell of a lot. It doesn't necessarily mean "impractical." Indeed, there are pragmatic as well as moral reasons to focus on long-term goals rather than on immediate compliance, to consider what our children need rather than just what we're demanding, and to see the whole child rather than just the behavior.

In this book, I'll be talking about why it makes good sense to shift away from the usual strategies for doing things *to* kids, and toward ways of working *with* them. It's true that plenty of people, adults as well as children, are subjected to "doing to" tactics. But it won't do to respond, "Well, that's just the way the world is" when presented with a case against, say, using punishments and rewards to get people to fall into line. The critical question is what kind of people we want our children to be—and that includes whether we want them to be the kind who accept things as they are or the kind who try to make things better.

This is subversive stuff—literally. It subverts the conventional advice we receive about raising kids, and it challenges a shortsighted quest to get them to jump through our hoops. For some of us, it may call into question much of what we've been doing—and perhaps even what was done to us when we were young.

The subject of this book is not merely discipline but, more broadly, the ways we act with our children, as well as how we think about them and feel about them. Its purpose is to help reconnect you with your own best instincts and to reaffirm what really matters—after the pajamas are on, after the homework is done, after the sibling squabbles have finally been quieted. It asks you to reconsider your basic assumptions about parent-child relationships.

Most important, it offers practical alternatives to the tactics we're sometimes tempted to use to make our kids behave, or to push them to succeed. I believe these alternatives have a reasonable chance of helping our kids to grow up as good people—*good,* that is, in the fullest sense of that word.

1

CONDITIONAL PARENTING

I have sometimes derived comfort from the idea that, despite all the mistakes I've made (and will continue to make) as a parent, my children will turn out just fine for the simple reason that I really love them. After all, love heals all wounds. All you need is love. Love means never having to say you're sorry about how you lost your temper this morning in the kitchen.

This reassuring notion is based on the idea that there exists a thing called Parental Love, a single substance that you can supply to your children in greater or lesser quantities. (Greater, of course, is better.) But what if this assumption turns out to be fatally simplistic? What if there actually are different ways of loving a child, and not all of them are equally desirable? The psychoanalyst Alice Miller once observed that it's possible to love a child "passionately—but not in the way he needs to be loved." If she's right, the relevant question isn't just whether—or even how much—we love our kids. It also matters *how* we love them.

Once that's understood, we could pretty quickly come up with a long list of different types of parental love, along with suggestions about which are better. This book looks at one such distinction—namely, between loving kids for *what they do* and loving them for *who they are*. The first sort of love is conditional, which means children

must earn it by acting in ways we deem appropriate, or by p
ing up to our standards. The second sort of love is *un*conditi
doesn't hinge on how they act, whether they're successful c
behaved or anything else.

I want to defend the idea of unconditional parenting on the basis
of both a value judgment and a prediction. The value judgment is, very
simply, that children shouldn't have to earn our approval. We ought
to love them, as my friend Deborah says, "for no good reason." Furthermore, what counts is not just that we believe we love them unconditionally, but that *they feel* loved in that way.

The prediction, meanwhile, is that loving children unconditionally
will have a positive effect. It's not only the right thing to do, morally
speaking, but also a smart thing to do. Children need to be loved as
they are, and for who they are. When that happens, they can accept
themselves as fundamentally good people, even when they screw up
or fall short. And with this basic need met, they're also freer to accept
(and help) other people. Unconditional love, in short, is what children
require in order to flourish.

Nevertheless, we parents are often pulled in the direction of placing conditions on our approval. We're led to do so not only by what
we were raised to believe, but also by the way we were raised. You
might say we're conditioned to be conditional. The roots of this sen-
sibility have crept deep into the soil of American consciousness. In fact,
*un*conditional acceptance seems to be rare even as an ideal: An Inter-
net search for variants of the word *unconditional* mostly turns up discussions about religion or pets. Apparently, it's hard for many people
to imagine love among humans without strings attached.

For a child, some of those strings have to do with *good behavior*
and some have to do with *achievement*. This chapter and the following three will explore the behavioral issues, and in particular the way
many popular discipline strategies cause children to feel they're
accepted only when they act the way we demand. Chapter 5 will then
consider how some children conclude that their parents' love depends
on their performance—for example, at school or in sports.

In the second half of the book, I'll offer concrete suggestions for how we can move beyond this approach and offer something closer to the kind of love our kids need. But first, I'd like to examine the broader idea of conditional parenting: what assumptions underlie it (and distinguish it from the unconditional kind), and what effects it actually has on children.

Two Ways to Raise Kids: Underlying Assumptions

My daughter, Abigail, went through a tough time a few months after her fourth birthday, which may have been related to the arrival of a rival. She became more resistant to requests, more likely to sound nasty, scream, stamp her feet. Ordinary rituals and transitions quickly escalated into a battle of wills. One evening, I remember, she promised to get right into the bath after dinner. She failed to do so—and then, when reminded of that promise, she shrieked loudly enough to wake her baby brother. When asked to be quieter, she yelled again.

So here's the question: Once things calmed down, should my wife and I have proceeded with the normal evening routine of snuggling with her and reading a story together? The conditional approach to parenting says no: We would be rewarding her unacceptable behavior if we followed it with the usual pleasant activities. Those activities should be suspended, and she should be informed, gently but firmly, why that "consequence" was being imposed.

This course of action feels reassuringly familiar to most of us and consistent with what a lot of parenting books advise. What's more, I have to admit that it would have been satisfying on some level for me to lay down the law because I was seriously annoyed by Abigail's defiance. It would have offered me the sense that I, the parent, was putting my foot down, letting her know she wasn't allowed to act like that. I'd be back in control.

The unconditional approach, however, says this is a temptation to be resisted, and that we should indeed snuggle and read a story as usual. But that doesn't mean we ought to just ignore what happened. Unconditional parenting isn't a fancy term for letting kids do whatever they want. It's very important (once the storm has passed) to teach, to reflect together—which is exactly what we did with our daughter after we read her a story. Whatever lesson we hoped to impart was far more likely to be learned if she knew that our love for her was undimmed by how she had acted.

Whether we've thought about them or not, each of these two styles of parenting rests on a distinctive set of beliefs about psychology, about children, even about human nature. To begin with, the conditional approach is closely related to a school of thought known as behaviorism, which is commonly associated with the late B. F. Skinner. Its most striking characteristic, as the name suggests, is its exclusive focus on behaviors. All that matters about people, in this view, is what you can see and measure. You can't see a desire or a fear, so you might as well just concentrate on what people *do*.

Furthermore, all behaviors are believed to start and stop, wax and wane, solely on the basis of whether they are "reinforced." Behaviorists assume that everything we do can be explained in terms of whether it produces some kind of reward, either one that's deliberately offered or one that occurs naturally. If a child is affectionate with his parent, or shares his dessert with a friend, it's said to be purely because this has led to pleasurable responses in the past.

In short: External forces, such as what someone has previously been rewarded (or punished) for doing, account for how we act—and how we act is the sum total of who we are. Even people who have never read any of Skinner's books seem to have accepted his assumptions. When parents and teachers constantly talk about a child's "behavior," they're acting as though nothing matters except the stuff on the surface. It's not a question of who kids are, what they think or feel or need. Forget motives and values: The idea is just to change what they do. This, of course, is an invitation to rely on discipline techniques whose only purpose is to make kids act—or stop acting—in a particular way.

A more specific example of everyday behaviorism: Perhaps you've met parents who force their children to apologize after doing something hurtful or mean. ("Can you say you're sorry?") Now, what's going on here? Do the parents assume that making children speak this sentence will magically produce in them the feeling of *being* sorry, despite all evidence to the contrary? Or, worse, do they not even care whether the child really is sorry, because sincerity is irrelevant and all that matters is the act of uttering the appropriate words? Compulsory apologies mostly train children to say things they don't mean—that is, to lie.

But this is not just an isolated parental practice that ought to be reconsidered. It's one of many possible examples of how Skinnerian thinking—caring only about behaviors—has narrowed our understanding of children and warped the way we deal with them. We see it also in programs that are intended to train little kids to go to sleep on their own or to start using the potty. From the perspective of these programs, *why* a child may be sobbing in the dark is irrelevant. It could be terror or boredom or loneliness or hunger or some other reason. Similarly, it doesn't matter what reason a toddler may have for not wanting to pee in the toilet when his parent asks him to do so. Experts who offer step-by-step recipes for "teaching" children to sleep in a room by themselves, or who urge us to offer gold stars, M&Ms, or praise for tinkling in the toilet, are concerned not with the thoughts and feelings and intentions that give rise to a behavior, only with the behavior itself. (While I haven't done the actual counting that would be necessary to test this, I would tentatively propose the following rule of thumb: The value of a parenting book is inversely proportional to the number of times it contains the word *behavior*.)

Let's come back to Abigail. Conditional parenting assumes that reading her a book and otherwise expressing our continued love for her will only encourage her to throw another fit. She will have learned that it's okay to wake the baby and refuse to get in the bath because she will interpret our affection as reinforcement for whatever she had just been doing.

Unconditional parenting looks at this situation—and, indeed, at human beings—very differently. For starters, it asks us to consider that the reasons for what Abigail has done may be more "inside" than "outside." Her actions can't necessarily be explained, in mechanical fashion, by looking at external forces like positive responses to her previous behavior. Perhaps she is overwhelmed by fears that she can't name, or by frustrations that she doesn't know how to express.

Unconditional parenting assumes that behaviors are just the outward expression of feelings and thoughts, needs and intentions. In a nutshell, *it's the child who engages in a behavior, not just the behavior itself, that matters.* Children are not pets to be trained, nor are they computers, programmed to respond predictably to an input. They act this way rather than that way for many different reasons, some of which may be hard to tease apart. But we can't just ignore those reasons and respond only to the effects (that is, the behaviors). Indeed, each of those reasons probably calls for a completely different course of action. If, for example, it turned out that Abigail was really being defiant because she's worried about the implications of our paying so much attention to her baby brother, then we're going to have deal with that, not merely try to stamp out the way she's expressing her fear.

Alongside our efforts to understand and address specific reasons for specific actions, there is one overriding imperative: She needs to know we love her, come what may. In fact, it's *especially* important tonight for her to be able to snuggle with us, to see from our actions that our love for her is unshakable. That's what will help her get through this bad patch.

In any case, imposing what amounts to a punishment isn't likely to be constructive. It probably will start her crying all over again. And even if it did succeed in shutting her up temporarily—or in preventing her from expressing whatever she's feeling tomorrow night for fear of making us pull away from her—its overall impact is unlikely to be positive. This is true, first, because it doesn't address what's going on in her head, and, second, because what we see as teaching her a lesson will likely appear to her as though we're withholding our love.

In a general sense, this will make her more unhappy, perhaps cause her to feel alone and unsupported. In a specific sense, it will teach her that she is loved—and lovable—only when she acts the way we want. The available research, which I'll review shortly, strongly suggests that this will just make things worse.

As I've thought about these issues over the years, I've come to believe that conditional parenting can't be completely explained by behaviorism. Something else is going on here. Once again, imagine the situation: A child is yelling, obviously upset, and when she quiets down her daddy lies in bed with his arm around her and reads her a *Frog and Toad* story. In response, the proponent of conditional parenting exclaims, "No, no, no, you're just reinforcing her bad behavior! You're teaching her that it's all right to be naughty!"

This interpretation doesn't merely reflect an assumption about what kids learn in a given situation, or even *how* they learn. It reflects an awfully sour view of children—and, by extension, of human nature. It assumes that, given half a chance, kids will take advantage of us. Give 'em an inch, they'll take a mile. They will draw the worst possible lesson from an ambiguous situation (not "I'm loved anyway" but "Yay! It's okay to make trouble!"). Acceptance without strings attached will just be interpreted as permission to act in a way that's selfish, demanding, greedy, or inconsiderate. At least in part, then, conditional parenting is based on the deeply cynical belief that accepting kids for who they are just frees them to be bad because, well, that's who they are.[1]

By contrast, the unconditional approach to parenting begins with the reminder that Abigail's goal is not to make me miserable. She's not being malicious. She's telling me in the only way she knows how that something is wrong. It may be something that just happened, or it may reveal undercurrents that have been there for a while. This approach offers a vote of confidence in children, a challenge to the assumption that they'll derive the wrong lesson from affection, or that they'd always *want* to act badly if they thought they could get away with it.

Such a perspective is not romantic or unrealistic, a denial of the fact that kids (and adults) sometimes do rotten things. Kids need to be guided and helped, yes, but they're not little monsters who must be tamed or brought to heel. They have the capacity to be compassionate or aggressive, altruistic or selfish, cooperative or competitive. A great deal depends on how they're raised—including, among other things, whether they feel loved unconditionally. And when young children pitch a fit, or refuse to get in the tub as they said they would, this can often be understood in terms of their age—that is, their inability to understand the source of their unease, to express their feelings in more appropriate ways, to remember and keep their promises. In important ways, then, the choice between conditional and unconditional parenting is a choice between radically different views of human nature.

But there's one more set of assumptions that we should lay bare. In our society, we are taught that good things must always be earned, never given away. Indeed, many people become infuriated at the possibility that this precept has been violated. Notice, for example, the hostility many people feel toward welfare and those who rely on it. Or the rampant use of pay-for-performance schemes in the workplace. Or the number of teachers who define anything enjoyable (like recess) as a treat, a kind of payment for living up to the teacher's expectations.

Ultimately, conditional parenting reflects a tendency to see almost every human interaction, even among family members, as a kind of economic *trans*action. The laws of the marketplace—supply and demand, tit for tat—have assumed the status of universal and absolute principles, as though everything in our lives, including what we do with our children, is analogous to buying a car or renting an apartment.

One parenting author—a behaviorist, not coincidentally—put it this way: "If I wish to take my child for a ride or even if I wish to hug and kiss her, I must first be certain that she has earned it."[2] Before you dismiss this as the view of a lone extremist, consider that the eminent psychologist Diana Baumrind (see pp. 104–5) made a similar argument against unconditional parenting, declaring that "the rule of reciprocity, of paying for value received, is a law of life that applies to us all."[3]

Even many writers and therapists who don't address the issue explicitly nevertheless seem to rely on some sort of economic model. If we read between the lines, their advice appears to be based on the belief that when children don't act the way we want, the things they like ought to be withheld from them. After all, people shouldn't get something for nothing. Not even happiness. Or love.

How many times have you heard it said—emphatically, defiantly—that something or other is "a privilege, not a right"? Sometimes I fantasize about conducting a research study to determine what personality characteristics are generally found in people who take this stance. Imagine someone who insists that everything from ice cream to attention should be made conditional on how children act, that these things should never simply be given away. Can you picture this person? What facial expression do you see? How happy is this person? Does he or she really enjoy being with children? Would you want this person as a friend?

Also, when I hear the "privilege, not a right" line, I always find myself wondering what the speaker *would* regard as a right. Is there anything to which human beings are simply entitled? Are there no relationships we would want to exempt from economic laws? It's true that adults expect to be compensated for their work, just as they expect to pay for food and other things. But the question is whether, or under what circumstances, a similar "rule of reciprocity" applies to our dealings with friends and family. Social psychologists have noticed that there are indeed some people with whom we have what might be called an exchange relationship: I do something for you only if you do something for me (or give something to me). But they quickly add that this is not true, nor would we want it to be true, of all our relationships, some of which are based on caring rather than on reciprocity. In fact, one study found that people who see their relationships with their spouses in terms of exchange, taking care to get as much as they give, tend to have marriages that are less satisfying.[4]

When our kids grow up, there will be plenty of occasions for them to take their places as economic actors, as consumers and workers, where self-interest rules and the terms of each exchange can be precisely calculated. But unconditional parenting insists that the family ought to be a haven, a refuge, from such transactions. In particular, love from one's parents does not have to be paid for in any sense. It is purely and simply a gift. It is something to which all children are entitled.

If that makes sense to you, and if any of the other underlying assumptions of unconditional parenting ring true as well—that we ought to be looking at the whole child, not just at behaviors; that we shouldn't assume the worst about children's inclinations; and so on— then we need to call into question all the conventional discipline techniques that are based on the opposites of these assumptions. Those practices that define conditional parenting tend to be ways of doing things *to* children to produce obedience. By contrast, the suggestions offered in the latter half of this book, which flow naturally from the idea of unconditional parenting, are variations on the theme of working *with* children to help them grow into decent people and good decision-makers.

Thus, we might summarize the differences between these two approaches as follows:

	UNCONDITIONAL	CONDITIONAL
Focus	Whole child (including reasons, thoughts, feelings)	Behavior
View of Human Nature	Positive or balanced	Negative
View of Parental Love	A gift	A privilege to be earned
Strategies	"Working with" (Problem solving)	"Doing to" (Control via rewards and punishments)

The Effects of Conditional Parenting

Just as it's possible for our practices to be at odds with the long-term goals we hold for our children (see Introduction), so there might be an inconsistency between the methods associated with conditional parenting and our most basic beliefs. In both instances, it may make sense to reconsider what we're doing with our kids. But the case against conditional parenting doesn't end with its connection to values and assumptions that many of us will find troubling. That case becomes even stronger once we investigate the real-world effects such parenting has on children.

Nearly half a century ago, the pioneering psychologist Carl Rogers offered an answer to the question "What happens when a parent's love depends on what children do?" He explained that those on the receiving end of such love come to disown the parts of themselves that aren't valued. Eventually they regard themselves as worthy only when they act (or think or feel) in specific ways.[5] This is basically a recipe for neurosis—or worse. A publication by the Irish Department of Health and Children (which has been circulated and adopted by other organizations all over the world) offers ten examples to illustrate the concept of "emotional abuse." Number two on the list, right after "persistent criticism, sarcasm, hostility, or blaming," is "conditional parenting, in which the level of care shown to a child is made contingent on his or her behaviours or actions."[6]

Most parents, if asked, would insist that of *course* they love their children unconditionally, and that this is true despite their use of the strategies that I (and other writers) have identified as problematic. Some parents might even say that they discipline their children in this way *because* they love them. But I want to return to an observation that so far I've made only in passing. *How we feel about our kids isn't as important as how they experience those feelings and how they regard the way we treat them.* Educators remind us that what counts in a classroom is not what the teacher teaches; it's what the learner learns. And so it is in families. What matters is the message our kids receive, not the one we think we're sending.

Researchers trying to study the effects of different styles of discipline have not had an easy time trying to figure out how to identify and measure what actually goes on in people's homes. It's not always possible to observe the relevant interactions firsthand (or even to videotape them), so some experiments have been done in laboratories, where a parent and a child are asked to do something together. Sometimes parents are interviewed, or asked to fill out a questionnaire, about their usual parenting styles. If the children are old enough, *they* may be asked what their parents do—or, if they're grown, what their parents used to do.

Each of these techniques has its drawbacks, and the choice of method can affect a study's results. When parents and children are asked separately to describe what's going on, for example, they may offer very different accounts.[7] Interestingly, when there is some objective way to get at the truth, children's perceptions of their parents' behaviors prove to be every bit as accurate as the parents' reports of their own behaviors.[8]

But the important question is not who's right, which, where feelings are concerned, is usually unanswerable. Rather, what matters is whose perspective is associated with various consequences to the children. Consider one study that investigated a version of conditional parenting. Kids whose parents said they used this approach weren't in any worse shape than kids whose parents said they didn't. But when the researcher separated the kids on the basis of whether *they* felt their parents used this technique, the difference was striking. On average, children who said they experienced conditional affection from their parents weren't doing as well as children who didn't report receiving conditional affection.[9] The details of this study will be discussed later; my point here is simply that what we think we're doing (or would swear we're not doing) doesn't matter as much, in terms of the impact on our kids, as *their* experience of what we're doing.

There has been a small surge in research on conditional parenting over the last few years, and one of the most remarkable examples was just published in 2004. In that study, information was collected from more than a hundred college students, each of whom was asked whether the love offered by his or her parents tended to vary depending on any of four possible conditions: whether the student as a child had (1) succeeded in school, (2) practiced hard for sports, (3) been considerate toward others, or (4) suppressed negative emotions such as fear. The students were also asked several other questions, including whether they did, in fact, tend to act in those ways (that is, hide their feelings, study hard for tests, and so on) and how they got along with their parents.

It turned out that the use of conditional love seemed to be at least somewhat successful at producing the desired behaviors. Children who received approval from their parents only if they acted in a particular way were a bit more likely to act that way—even in college. But the cost of this strategy was substantial. For starters, the students who thought their parents loved them conditionally were much more likely to feel rejected and, as a result, to resent and dislike their parents.

You can easily imagine that, had they been asked, each of those parents would have declared, "I don't know where my son gets that idea! I love him no matter what!" Only because the researchers thought to interview the (now grown) children directly did they hear a very different—and very disturbing—story. Many of the students felt they had consistently received less affection whenever they failed to impress or obey their parents—and it was precisely these students whose relationships with their parents were likely to be strained.

To drive home the point, the researchers conducted a second study, this one with more than a hundred mothers of grown children. With this generation, too, conditional love proved damaging. Those mothers who, as children, sensed that they were loved only when they lived up to their parents' expectations now felt less worthy as adults. Remarkably, though, *they tended to use the identical approach once* they *became parents.* The mothers used conditional affection "with their own children in spite of the strategy['s] having had negative effects on them."[10]

Although this is the first study (as far as I know) to show that conditional parenting styles can be passed on to one's children, other psychologists have found similar evidence about its effects. Some of these are discussed in the following chapter, which describes two specific ways in which conditional parenting is put into practice. Even in general terms, though, the results are fairly damning. For example, a group of researchers at the University of Denver has shown that teenagers who feel they have to fulfill certain conditions in order to win their parents' approval may end up not liking themselves. That, in turn, may lead a given adolescent to construct a "false self"—in other words, to pretend to be the kind of person whom his or her parents *will* love. This desperate strategy to gain acceptance is often associated with depression, a sense of hopelessness, and a tendency to lose touch with one's true self. At some point, such teenagers may not even know who they really are because they've had to work so hard to become something they're not.[11]

Over many years, researchers have found that "the more conditional the support [one receives], the lower one's perceptions of overall worth as a person." When children receive affection with strings attached, they tend to accept *themselves* only with strings attached. By contrast, those who feel they're accepted unconditionally—by their parents or, according to other research, even by a teacher—are likely to feel better about themselves,[12] exactly as Carl Rogers predicted.

And that brings us to the ultimate purpose of this book, the central question I invite you to ponder. In the questionnaires that are used to study conditional parenting, a teenager or young adult is typically asked to indicate "strong agreement," "agreement," "neutral feelings," "disagreement," or "strong disagreement" in response to sentences such as "My mother maintained a sense of loving connection with me even during our worst conflicts" or "When my dad disagrees with me, I know that he still loves me."[13] So, how would you like *your* children to answer that sort of question in five or ten or fifteen years—and how do you think they will answer it?

2

GIVING AND
WITHHOLDING LOVE

W hen scientists began to study discipline in the 1950s and '60s,
they tended to classify what parents were doing with their children as being based on either power or love. Power-based discipline included hitting, yelling, and threatening. Love-based discipline included just about everything else. As the research results came in, it quickly became clear that power produced poorer results than love.

Unfortunately, an awful lot of diverse strategies were being lumped together under that second heading. Some of them consisted of reasoning with children and teaching them, offering warmth and understanding. But other techniques were a lot less loving. In fact, some of them amounted to *controlling* children with love, either by withholding it when kids were bad or by showering them with attention and affection when they were good. These, then, are the two faces of conditional parenting: "love withdrawal" (the stick) and "positive reinforcement" (the carrot). In this chapter, I want to explore what both of these techniques look like in practice, the effects they have, and the reasons for those effects. Later, I'll look at the idea of punishment in more detail.

Time Out from Love

Like anything else, love withdrawal can be applied in different ways and with varying levels of intensity. At one end of the continuum, a parent may pull back ever so slightly in response to something the child has done, becoming chillier and less affectionate—perhaps without even being aware of it. At the other end, a parent may announce bluntly, "I don't love you when you act that way" or "When you do things like that, I don't even want to be around you."

Some parents withdraw their love by simply refusing to respond to a child—that is, by making a point of ignoring him. They may not say it out loud, but the message they're sending is pretty clear: "If you do things I don't like, I won't pay any attention to you. I'll pretend you're not even here. If you want me to acknowledge you again, you'd better obey me."

Still other parents separate themselves physically from the child. There are two ways of doing this. The parent can either walk away (which may leave a child sobbing, or crying out in a panic, "Mommy, come back! Come back!") or banish the child to his room or some other place where the parent isn't. This tactic might accurately be called forcible isolation. But that label would make a lot of parents uncomfortable, so a more innocuous term tends to be used instead, one that allows us to avoid facing up to what's really going on. The preferred euphemism, as perhaps you've guessed, is *time-out*.

In reality, this very popular discipline technique is a version of love withdrawal—at least when children are sent away against their will. There's nothing wrong with giving a child the option of going to her room, or to another inviting place, when she's angry or upset. If she has chosen to take some time alone, and if all the particulars (when to leave, where to go, what to do, when to return) are within her control, then it's not experienced as banishment or punishment, and it can often be helpful. That's not what I'm concerned with here. I'm focusing on time-out as the term is usually used, where it's a sentence handed down by the parent: solitary confinement.

One clue to the nature of the technique is provided by the origin of the term. *Time-out* is actually an abbreviation for *time out from positive reinforcement*. The practice was developed almost half a century ago as a way of training laboratory animals. As B. F. Skinner and his followers labored, for example, to teach pigeons to peck at certain keys in response to flashing lights, they tinkered with different schedules by which food was offered as a reward for doing what the experimenters wanted. Sometimes they also tried punishing the birds by withholding food, or even by shutting off all the lights, to see whether that would "extinguish" the key-pecking behavior. This was done with other critters, too. Thus, a colleague of Skinner published an article in 1958 called "Control of Behavior in Chimpanzees and Pigeons by Time-out from Positive Reinforcement."

Within a few years, articles began appearing in these same experimental psychology journals with titles like "Timeout Duration and the Suppression of Deviant Behavior in Children." In that particular study, the children subjected to time-outs were described as "retarded, institutionalized subjects." But soon this intervention was being prescribed indiscriminately, and even discipline specialists who would have been aghast at the idea of treating children like lab animals were enthusiastically advising parents to give their kids a time-out when they did something wrong. Before long it had become "the most commonly recommended discipline procedure in the professional literature for preadolescent children."[1]

We are talking about a technique, then, that began as a way of *controlling animal behavior*. All three of those words may raise troubling questions for us. The last of them, of course, we've already encountered: Should our focus be limited to *behavior*? Time-out, like all punishments and rewards, stays on the surface. It's designed purely to make an organism act (or stop acting) in a particular way.

The middle word, *animal*, reminds us that the behaviorists who invented time-out believed that humans are not all that different from other species. We "emit" more complicated behaviors, including speech, but the principles of learning are thought to be pretty much the same. Those of us who don't share that belief might have second thoughts about subjecting our children to something that was developed for use with birds and rodents.

Finally, we're left with a question that informs this whole book: Does it make sense to raise our kids based on a model of *control?*

Even if its history and theoretical basis don't trouble you, look again at the original label *time-out from positive reinforcement.* Parents aren't usually in the middle of handing out stickers or candy bars when they suddenly decide to stop. So what, exactly, is the positive reinforcement that's being suspended when a child is given a time-out? Sometimes he's doing something fun and is forced to quit. But this isn't always the case—and even when it is, I think there's more to the story. When you send a child away, what's really being switched off or withdrawn is your presence, your attention, *your love.* You may not have thought of it that way. Indeed, you may insist that your love for your child is undiminished by his misbehavior. But, as we've seen, what matters is how things look to the child.

The Results of Love Withdrawal

In a later chapter, I'll say more about alternatives to time-outs. But let's back up and look more carefully at the whole idea of love withdrawal. For many people, the first question would be whether this approach works. Once again, however, that proves to be a more complicated matter than it may seem. We have to ask: "Works to do what?"—and we also have to weigh any temporary change in behavior against what may turn out to be a deeper, longer-lasting negative impact. In other words, we need to look beyond the short-term, and we also need to look at what's going on *underneath* the visible behavior. Remember, the study of college students described in the last chapter found that conditional love can succeed at changing how kids act, but at enormous cost. It turns out that the same is true of love withdrawal in particular.

Consider this account from the parent of a young child we'll call Lee:

> I discovered some time ago that when Lee started to act up, I really didn't have to threaten to take away privileges or even raise my voice. I just quietly announced my intention to leave the room. Sometimes all I had to do was walk *across* the room, away from him, and say I would wait until he was ready to stop yelling or resisting or whatever. Most of the time this was amazingly effective. He would beg, "No, don't!" and would immediately quiet down or do what I asked. At first, the moral I drew from this was that a light touch is sufficient. I could get what I wanted without having to punish. But I couldn't stop thinking about the fear I saw in his eyes. I came to realize that what I was doing *was* punishment as far as Lee was concerned—a symbolic one, maybe, but a pretty damn scary one.

An important study on the effectiveness of love withdrawal basically supports this parent's conclusion: Sometimes it does seem to work, but that doesn't mean we should do it. In the early 1980s, two researchers at the National Institute of Mental Health (NIMH) examined what mothers did with their approximately one-year-old children. It seemed that love withdrawal—deliberately ignoring a child or enforcing a separation—was typically combined with some other strategy. Regardless of which other approach was used, whether it was explaining or smacking, the addition of love withdrawal made it more likely that these very young kids would comply with their mothers' wishes, at least for the moment.

But the researchers were more concerned than reassured by what they saw, and they emphasized that they were not advising parents to use love withdrawal. First, they pointed out that "disciplinary techniques effective for securing immediate compliance are not necessarily effective . . . in the long run." Second, they observed that "children may react to love withdrawal in ways that parents perceive as occasions for further discipline." A vicious circle can be created, with kids crying and protesting, leading to more love withdrawal, leading to more crying and protesting, and so on. Finally, even when this technique did produce results, the researchers seemed uneasy about *why* it worked.[2]

Many years ago, a psychologist named Martin Hoffman challenged the distinction between power-based and love-based discipline by pointing out that love withdrawal, a common example of the latter, actually has a lot in common with more severe forms of punishment. Both communicate to children that if they do something we don't like, we'll make them suffer in order to change their behavior. (The only remaining question is *how* we'll make them suffer: by causing physical pain through hitting, or by causing emotional pain through enforced isolation.) And both are based on getting kids to focus on the consequences of their action *to themselves,* which is, of course, very different from raising children to think about how their actions will affect other people.

Hoffman then proceeded to make an even more surprising suggestion: In some situations, love withdrawal might be even worse than other, apparently harsher, punishments. "Although it poses no immediate physical or material threat to the child," he wrote, love withdrawal "may be more devastating emotionally than power assertion because it poses the ultimate threat of abandonment or separation." Furthermore, "while the parent may know when it will end, the very young child may not since he is totally dependent on the parent and moreover lacks the experience and time perspective needed to recognize the temporary nature of the parent's attitude."[3]

Even children who come to realize that Mom or Dad will eventually start talking to them again (or will soon free them from the timeout) may not entirely recover from the reverberations of this punishment. Love-withdrawal techniques can succeed in making a child's behavior more acceptable to adults, but the engine that drives their success is the deeply felt "anxiety about possible loss of parental love," says Hoffman.[4] This is what gave pause even to those NIMH researchers who found that love withdrawal can produce temporary obedience. Indeed, another group of psychologists observed that this form of discipline tends to "leave the child in a state of emotional discomfort for longer periods" than does a spanking.[5]

There isn't a huge amount of scientific research on love withdrawal, but the little that does exist has turned up disturbingly consistent findings. Children on the receiving end tend to have lower self-esteem. They display signs of poorer emotional health overall and may even be more apt to engage in delinquent acts. If we consider a broader category of "psychological control" on the part of parents (of which love withdrawal is said to be "a defining characteristic"), older children who are treated this way are more likely than their peers to be depressed.[6]

No question about it: A parent has considerable power "to manipulate children through their need for parental affection and approval, and their fears of loss of the parents' emotional support."[7] But this is not like, say, fear of the dark, which most people outgrow. Rather, it's the sort of fear that can be as enduring as it is shattering. Nothing is more important to us when we're young than how our parents feel about us. Uncertainty about that, or terror about being abandoned, can leave its mark even after we're grown.

It makes perfect sense, then, that the most striking long-term effect of love withdrawal is fear. Even as young adults, people who were treated that way by their parents are still likely to be unusually anxious. They may be afraid to show anger. They tend to display a significant fear of failure. And their adult relationships may be warped by a need to avoid attachment—perhaps because they live in dread of being abandoned all over again. (Having experienced love withdrawal as children, adults may have "decided essentially that 'the terms of this bargain are impossible to meet.' That is, they could never expect to earn the approval and support from their parents they needed, therefore [they now try] to structure their lives so as not to depend on protection and emotional comfort from others.")[8]

I don't mean to imply that your child is sure to be screwed up for life just because you sent her to her room once when she was four. At the same time, this list of effects isn't something I thought up in the shower this morning. It's not a matter of speculation or even of anecdotes from therapists. Controlled studies have linked all these fears specifically to the earlier parental use of love withdrawal. Parenting guides almost never mention these data, but their cumulative effect has to be taken seriously.

Indeed, there's one more finding worth mentioning: the effects on kids' *moral* development. Hoffman conducted a study of seventh-graders that found that the use of love withdrawal was associated with a lower-level form of morality. In deciding how to act with other people, these children didn't take specific circumstances into account, nor did they consider the needs of a given individual. Instead, having learned to do exactly what they're told in order to avoid losing their parents' love, they tended just to apply rules in a rigid, one-size-fits-all fashion.[9] If we're serious about helping our children to grow into compassionate and psychologically healthy people, we have to realize how hard that is to do on a diet of love withdrawal—or, as we'll see later, any other sort of punitive consequences.

The Failure of Rewards

Is it unsettling to hear that time-outs and other "milder" forms of punishment may actually not be so benign after all? Well, brace yourself. The flip side of love withdrawal—that is, the other technique associated with conditional love—is none other than positive reinforcement, an approach that's wildly popular among parents, teachers, and others who spend time with children. Even people who warn about the unintended consequences of punitive discipline generally don't think twice about urging us to praise kids for being good.

A bit of background may be appropriate here.[10] In our culture's workplaces, classrooms, and families, there are two basic strategies by which people with more power try to get people with less power to obey. One way is to punish noncompliance. The other is to reward compliance. The reward might be a payment or a privilege, a gold star or a candy bar, a sticker or a Phi Beta Kappa key. But it may also be praise. Thus, to understand the significance of saying "Good job!" to your child, you have to understand the whole carrot-and-stick philosophy of which it's a part.

The first thing to understand is that rewards are remarkably ineffective at improving the quality of people's work or learning. A considerable number of studies have found that children and adults alike are *less* successful at many tasks when they're offered a reward for doing them—or for doing them well. In fact, the first scientists to discover this result were caught off-guard. They expected that some sort of incentive for high achievement would motivate people to do better, but they kept finding that the opposite was true. Studies have repeatedly shown, for instance, that students tend to learn better, all else being equal, when no A's are used to reward them—that is, in classrooms where descriptions of students' performance are used without any letter or number grades attached.

But what if we're more interested in behaviors and values than in achievement? Of course, we'd have to acknowledge that rewards—like punishments—can often succeed in buying temporary obedience. If I offered you a thousand dollars right now to take off your shoes, you'd very likely accept—and then I could triumphantly announce that "rewards work." But, as with punishments, they can never help someone to develop a *commitment* to a task or an action, a reason to keep doing it when there's no longer a payoff.

In fact, one experiment after another has demonstrated that rewards are not only ineffective—they're often counterproductive. For example, researchers have found that children who are rewarded for doing something nice are less likely to think of themselves as nice people. Instead, they tend to attribute their behavior to the reward. Then, when there's no longer a goody to be gained, they're less likely to help than are kids who weren't given a reward in the first place. They're also less likely to help than they themselves used to be. After all, they've learned that the point of coming to someone's aid is just to get a reward.

In short, it almost always backfires to offer children the equivalent of a doggie biscuit for acting the way we want them to. But that's not because we used the wrong kind of biscuits or gave them out on the wrong schedule. Rather, it's because there are problems with the whole idea of trying to change people by rewarding (or punishing) them. It's not always easy for parents to identify what those problems are, which is why I often hear from people who feel vaguely uneasy about rewarding their children but can't quite put their finger on the source of their discomfort.

Here's one way of making sense of what's wrong. Most of us assume that there exists a single thing called "motivation," which people can have a lot of, a little of, or none of. Naturally, we want our kids to possess copious quantities of it, which is to say, we want them to be highly motivated to do their homework, to act responsibly, and so forth.

The trouble, though, is that there are actually different kinds of motivation. Most psychologists distinguish between the *intrinsic* kind and the *extrinsic* kind. Intrinsic motivation basically means you like what you're doing for its own sake, whereas extrinsic motivation means you do something as a means to an end—in order to get a reward or avoid a punishment. It's the difference between reading a book because you want to find out what happens in the next chapter and reading because you've been promised a sticker or a pizza for doing so.

The key point here isn't just that extrinsic motivation is *different* from the intrinsic kind, or even that it's *inferior* to intrinsic, although both statements are true. What I want to emphasize is that extrinsic motivation is likely to *erode* intrinsic motivation. As extrinsic goes up, intrinsic tends to come down. *The more that people are rewarded for doing something, the more likely they are to lose interest in whatever they had to do to get the reward.* Of course, there are always qualifications and exceptions to any one-sentence summary of a psychological finding, but that basic proposition has been proven by literally scores of studies with people of different ages, genders, and cultural backgrounds—and with a variety of different tasks and rewards.[11]

No wonder, then, that kids who are rewarded for being helpful end up being less helpful once the rewards stop coming. And there's plenty of other evidence, too. Give little children an unfamiliar beverage, and those who are offered a reward for drinking it will end up liking it less next week than kids who drank the same stuff without being offered a reward. Or pay children for trying to solve a puzzle, and they'll tend to stop playing with it after the experiment is over—while those who were paid nothing are apt to keep at it on their own time.

One moral from all this is that it really doesn't matter how "motivated" your child is to do something (use the potty, practice the piano, go to school, whatever). Rather, the question you'd want to ask is *how* your child is motivated. To put it another way, it's not the amount of motivation that counts—it's the type. And the type that's created by rewards usually has the effect of reducing the type we want kids to have: a genuine interest that persists long after the rewards are gone.

Not-So-Positive Reinforcement

Now for the really bad news: What's true of tangible rewards (money or food) and symbolic rewards (grades or gold stars) can also be true of verbal rewards. In many cases, the effects of praising kids can be just as dismal as the effects of giving them other sorts of goodies.

For starters, "Good job!" can interfere with how well a job actually gets done. Researchers keep finding that individuals who are praised for doing well at a creative task often stumble at the next task. Why? Partly because the praise creates pressure to "keep up the good work" that gets in the way of doing so. Partly because people's *interest* in what they're doing may have declined (because now the main goal is just to get more praise).[12] Partly because they become less likely to take risks—a prerequisite for creativity—once they start thinking about how to keep those positive comments coming.

Nor does positive reinforcement tend to work any better for outcomes other than achievement. Like other rewards and punishments, the best it can do is temporarily change a child's behavior. For example, kids who were praised for drinking that unfamiliar beverage ended up liking it a lot less as a result—exactly like the kids who received tangible rewards for drinking it. (This particular researcher didn't predict that outcome: She had assumed that praise wouldn't be as destructive as other extrinsic inducements.)

More worrisome was a study in which young children who were often praised by their parents for displays of generosity tended to be slightly *less* generous on an everyday basis than other children were—again, just like kids who received tangible rewards. Every time they heard "Good sharing!" or "I'm so proud of you for helping," they became a little less interested in sharing or helping. Those actions came to be seen not as something valuable in their own right but as something the children had to do to get that reaction again from an adult. In this case, it was generosity that became merely a means to an end. In other cases, it might be painting or swimming or multiplying or anything else for which we offer positive reinforcement.

Praise, like other rewards, usually reflects a preoccupation with behavior—the same legacy of behaviorism that I mentioned earlier. Once we begin to consider the motives that underlie people's actions, it suddenly makes sense that positive reinforcement might misfire. After all, if we want a child to grow into a genuinely compassionate person, then it's not enough to know whether he just did something helpful. We'd want to know *why*.

Take Jack: He shared his toy with a friend in the hopes that his mom would notice and shower him with adulation ("I really like how you're letting Gregory play, too"). But then there's Zack: He shared his toy without knowing, or even caring, whether his mom noticed. He did it for the simple reason that he didn't want his friend to feel bad. Praise for sharing typically ignores these different motives. Worse, it may actually promote the less desirable one by making children more likely to fish for praise in the future.

*   *   *

Up to this point my main argument has been that praise tends to be counterproductive because it's an extrinsic motivator. But now I want to come at this idea from a new angle. The problem isn't just that it's a reward. The problem is that *positive reinforcement exemplifies the idea of conditional parenting.*

Think about it: What's the mirror image of love withdrawal—that is, withholding affection when kids do things we don't like? It would have to be giving them affection when they do things we *do* like: providing it selectively, contingently, often in the explicit hope of reinforcing that behavior. Praise isn't just different from unconditional love; it's the polar opposite. It's a way of saying to children: "You have to jump through my hoops in order for me to express support and delight."

Caring parents are attentive, and they often (though not always) describe something they noticed that the child has done and invite him or her to reflect on its implications. But "Good job!" isn't a description; it's a judgment. And that has unsettling implications for how children are likely to perceive how we feel about them. Instead of "I love you," what praise may communicate is "I love you because you've done well." It's not necessary for us to *say* that in so many words—which, of course, almost no one does. All that's required is that we *do* it—that is, express love and show excitement only under certain conditions. (By the same token, love withdrawal often takes place even though the parent doesn't actually say, "I don't love you because you haven't done well." In both cases, the message comes through loud and clear anyway.)

A few years ago, when my wife and I were trying to hire a babysitter, we met a young woman who crisply summarized her philosophy of child care by saying, "Good behavior gets my attention." She probably meant to contrast this approach with one that focused on reprimanding children for bad behavior. But immediately we knew we didn't want her anywhere near our kids. We didn't ever want them to think that the attention of a caretaker would be doled out in response to how they had acted—in other words, that she would look at them and listen to them only when she decided they had earned it.

I'm grateful to this woman, however, for helping me clarify exactly what I objected to, and why. I also appreciate a seed that was planted by someone else, a woman in the audience at a lecture I gave some time ago. I can no longer recall her name, or even what city I was in. All I remember is that she walked up to me and said that her child's school had just presented her with a bumper sticker that looked like this:

> I'M PROUD OF MY CHILD
> WHO WAS STUDENT OF THE MONTH

She told me that as soon as she got home, she found a pair of scissors, snipped off the bottom half, and pasted on her car the five words that remained—that is, what had been the first line. With a little ingenuity, she not only resisted an invitation to be a conditional parent but turned it into an opportunity to affirm the unconditionality of the pride she felt in her child.

I should emphasize again that there are no absolutes in human behavior. Whether positive reinforcement has a detrimental effect (and, if so, how detrimental) may vary depending on several factors. It matters *how* it's done: the way praise is phrased, the tone of voice that's used, whether it's given in private or in front of others. It matters *to whom* it's done: The child's age and temperament count, as do other variables. And it matters *why* it's done: what kinds of things children are praised for doing and what your purpose is for praising—or, rather, what the child believes your purpose is. There's a difference between congratulating kids for acting in a way that merely makes *your* life easier (for example, eating neatly) and congratulating them for doing something that's genuinely impressive. There's a difference between expressing pleasure in response to mindless obedience (for example, when a child follows one of your rules) and expressing pleasure in response to a really thoughtful question.

It's possible, then, to find ways of minimizing the negative effects of praise. But the much more important point is that even better versions are still less than ideal. (That's why I'll offer *alternatives* to praise in chapter 8 rather than different, maybe slightly less bad ways of praising.) It is surely true, for example, that expressing spontaneous enthusiasm about something children have done is less objectionable than giving them positive reinforcement in order to get them to change their behavior. Only the latter is intended as Skinnerian manipulation. But that doesn't guarantee that the former will be harmless.

In some cases, "Good work coloring inside the lines"—or, for a teenager, "Good work staying in your lane"—may just be a way of communicating information rather than offering a verbal incentive to repeat the behavior. But what's the information that's being communicated? We're not just telling the child what he did; we're telling him we *approve of* what he did. Will he just infer that we're happy for him, that we're joining him in celebrating his accomplishment? That's the best-case scenario. But it's very easy for him to infer from a pattern of selective reinforcement that we approve of him only when he does the things we like. (Look how excited Dad gets when I hit the ball . . . and *only* when I hit the ball.)

This, in turn, often morphs into conditional *self*-approval. The chain might proceed as follows: (1) "I like the way you've done such-and-such" can sound to the child very much like (2) "I like *you* because you've done such-and-such"—and that, in turn, may imply (3) "I *don't* like you when you don't do such-and-such." The last step is for the child to feel (4) "I'm not likable when I don't do such-and-such." If it proves to be an example of conditional parenting, therefore, praise can be dangerous regardless of the motives of the praise-giver, and even when there's no deliberate attempt to be controlling. This is particularly true if our positive comments and other expressions of love are mostly reserved for those occasions when the child does something that pleases us.

You may have encountered some people who seem to share the concerns about praise offered here, but it's possible that all they're really objecting to is how *often* we praise kids, or how kids don't have to do much these days to elicit a "Good job!" There's some truth to this observation, to be sure. I've actually heard parents at a playground chirp, "Good swinging" to a toddler. (For God's sake, it's gravity!) But I have real concerns about this objection. On one level, it simply misses the point: Positive reinforcement isn't objectionable just because it's offered too frequently or too easily. The issues are much deeper than that.

On another level, this criticism has the potential to make things worse. Someone who announces that it's pointless to give kids a pat on the head for every little thing they do will typically add that we ought to be more selective, more discriminating about praising—which means that kids should have to do more to earn our approval. And of course that means that our parenting would become even more conditional than it already is. These critics are probably correct to observe that when kids are praised constantly, it turns into background noise and they barely even hear it anymore. To which we might reply: Good! It's when praise is timed and phrased for maximum impact that we really need to worry. That's when (at least from the child's point of view) the unconditionality of our love is most in doubt.

Back in the 1970s, a researcher in Florida named Mary Budd Rowe was investigating classroom teaching styles when she noticed something interesting. Children who were frequently praised by their teachers seemed more tentative in their responses. They were more likely than other kids to answer in a questioning tone of voice ("Um, photosynthesis?"). They were less likely to share their ideas with other students or to stick with a task once they started it. And they were apt to back off from something they had proposed as soon as the teacher disagreed with them.[13]

This study confirmed a truth that we can observe in our own homes: Children's sense of their competence, and perhaps of their worth, may come to rise or fall as a result of our reaction. They look to us, figuratively and sometimes literally, to see whether we approve of what they've done. (It's a little like toddlers who take their cue from us when they fall down, searching our faces to see whether they've hurt themselves. If we seem distraught—"Oh, my God! Honey, are you all right?"—they're more likely to burst into tears.)

As a result of praise, children become less able or willing to take pride in their own accomplishments—or to decide what *is* an accomplishment. In extreme cases, they can turn into "praise junkies" who, even as adults, continue to rely on other people for validation, feeling thrilled or crestfallen depending on whether a spouse, a supervisor, or someone else in whom they have vested power tells them they've done a good job.

All young children have a deep need for their parents' approval. That's why praise often "works" in the short run to get them to do what we want. But we have a responsibility to avoid exploiting their dependence for our own convenience—which is exactly what we're doing when we give them a big smile and say things like "I really like how fast you got ready for school this morning!" Kids may come to feel manipulated by this "sugar-coated control,"[14] even if they can't quite explain why. But whether or not they catch on and rebel, there's something decidedly distasteful about the practice. It's not all that different from waiting until your child is thirsty and then giving her water only after she does something to make your life a little easier.

Worse, positive reinforcement often creates a vicious circle that's reminiscent of what we find with love withdrawal: The more we praise, the more our children need to be praised. They seem insecure, they long for another pat on the head; we give it to them, and their longing only increases. Carol Dweck, a psychologist at Columbia University, has done some preliminary research that seems to make sense of what's going on here. When we offer comments that "imply contingent regard (and thus presumably foster feelings of contingent worth . . .)," young children start displaying signs of helplessness. Positive reinforcement is a form of conditional love, and Dweck argues that what we're accepting only conditionally isn't just a particular characteristic or behavior. Rather, the child comes to see her "whole self" as good only when she pleases the parent. That's a powerful way of *undermining* self-esteem. The more we say "Good job!" the worse the child comes to feel about himself, and the more praise he needs.[15]

Naturally, this should make us skeptical about any claim that praise is fine because kids seem to want it. If you need to earn money and the only job available is one involving repetitive, mind-numbing labor, you may accept it as a last resort. But that's not an endorsement of this kind of work. It just means we take what we can get. What kids really need is love without strings attached. But if all that's offered—the only alternative to criticism or neglect—is approval based on what they've done, they'll lap that up and then, perhaps vaguely unsatisfied, come back for more. Sadly, some parents who received too little unconditional love when they were children end up misdiagnosing the problem and assume that it was praise they lacked. Then they "Good job!" their own children to death, ensuring that another generation fails to get what's really needed.

Many parents have told me that these ideas are hard to hear, especially for the first time. It's bad enough for someone to suggest that you may be doing something wrong with your kids, but it's even worse to be told that the very thing you prided yourself for doing right—such as praising your children so they'll feel good about themselves—may actually do more harm than good.

Some people, I've found, respond by asking, "What's the alternative?" That's a perfectly reasonable question, as long as we're exploring alternatives to the whole idea of conditional parenting (as I'll do later) rather than just looking for superficial changes in what we say to kids—a new, improved version of praise.

Some people become uncomfortable and make little nervous jokes: "Heh-heh. I guess I can't tell you I liked your book, right, because that would be praising you. Heh-heh-heh."[16] That's understandable. It takes a while to accept a new idea, particularly one that invites us to reconsider much of what we've been doing, and what we've been assuming. We have to get used to it, try it out, and during the transition period our discomfort may express itself in a variety of ways.

Some people wonder whether the implication is that they're lousy parents because they have long relied on love withdrawal and positive reinforcement (even if they never used those labels). In most cases, though, the reality is just that no one has ever invited them to think about things this way before, or presented the evidence to challenge all that uncritical advice we constantly hear to praise children more or give them time-outs.

Some people, however, don't ask for suggestions, or try to be funny, or worry. Instead, they brush off these criticisms, pointing out (with some justification) that in the larger scheme of things, we could do a lot worse to our kids than express enthusiasm about what they've done. Indeed, a lot worse *is* done to children every day. But that's not a proper basis for comparison—at least, not for anyone who wants to be the best parent he or she can be. The point is that we can do better.

The Self-Esteem Controversy

Love withdrawal and positive reinforcement can produce a number of disturbing outcomes, from a feeling of helplessness to an unwillingness to help others, and (once children are grown) from a fear of abandonment to a resentment of their parents. But one result that threads its way through the summaries of research findings in this chapter and the preceding one has to do with the way people subjected to conditional parenting come to regard themselves.

The usual term for this is, of course, *self-esteem*, which has been something of a buzzword over the last few decades. Before wrapping up this chapter, I want to spend a few pages parsing this concept because it's quite relevant to the idea of conditional parenting. A number of people in the fields of psychology and education, and especially those who are associated with what has been called the self-help movement, seem to believe that high self-esteem is good, low is bad, and that by raising someone's level of self-esteem we automatically bring about a range of beneficial effects: academic achievement, constructive life choices, and so on. On the other hand, self-esteem has become a lightning rod for social conservatives, a shorthand for everything they see as misguided about our society and particularly our schools.

My own view is that there are real problems with both positions. I conducted a fairly extensive review of the research a few years back[17] and discovered, somewhat to my surprise, that higher self-esteem isn't always accompanied by better outcomes and that even when it is, this doesn't mean it *caused* those better outcomes.

But that doesn't leave me in the camp of the "anti-self-esteemers," who are contemptuous of the whole concept. Some of them take this view because they believe that if children are basically happy with themselves, they'll have no motivation to achieve anything. If their attention is focused on the value of who they are, rather than on what they do, then they probably won't do very much. You have to feel dissatisfied in order to learn or produce. No pain, no gain.

This proposition rests on several faulty premises, which I'll spell out in chapter 5. For the moment, though, I want to call attention to the fact that, while many of these critics claim that higher self-esteem doesn't produce any benefits, the core of their argument is really that it's just a bad thing, regardless of its effects. For them, the nastiest possible epithet is *feel-good,* suggesting that they believe there is something fundamentally suspect about being pleased with oneself. Lurking just below the surface of their polemics is the fear that children may end up being content without having earned the right to feel that way. Here we have left the world of evidence and entered (through the back door) the realm of moralistic first principles. It is a place of puritanical fervor, where people should not be permitted to eat except by the sweat of their brows and children must not think well of themselves until they can point to some tangible accomplishment.

In other words, what the conservatives are attacking is really *unconditional* self-esteem. Yet researchers are coming to realize that it's precisely this dimension that is critical to predicting the quality of people's lives. If we're interested in someone's mental health, the relevant question may not be how much self-esteem she has. Rather, it's how much her self-esteem *varies* depending on what's going on in her life—for example, how successful she is or what other people think of her. The real problem may not be self-esteem that's too low ("I don't feel very good about myself"), but self-esteem that's too contingent ("I feel good about myself only when . . .").[18]

Edward Deci and Richard Ryan, two research psychologists who have underscored the importance of this distinction, acknowledge that even people with something close to "true"—or unconditional—self-esteem "would probably feel pleased or excited when they succeed and disappointed when they fail. But their feelings of worth as people would not fluctuate as a function of those accomplishments, so they would not feel aggrandized and superior when they succeed or depressed and worthless when they fail."[19]

That extreme fluctuation is only the beginning of the consequences of basing one's sense of worth on living up to a set of expectations, either other people's or one's own. A brand-new study finds that contingent self-esteem is related to "a greater likelihood of drinking as a means of gaining social approval or avoiding social rejection" among college students. Other research links it to anxiety, hostility, and defensiveness. Such people may lash out when their self-esteem is threatened, which can happen regularly. Or they may become depressed and take refuge in self-destructive behaviors. If they feel good about themselves only when they think they *look* good, they become susceptible to eating disorders.[20]

By contrast, unconditional self-esteem, the very sort that's most likely to be ridiculed in some quarters, turns out to be the best goal to shoot for.[21] People who, as a rule, don't think their value hinges on their performance are more likely to see failure as just a temporary setback, a problem to be solved. They also seem less likely to be anxious or depressed.[22] And one more thing: They're less likely to be concerned about the whole issue of self-esteem! Spending time evaluating how good you are, or deliberately trying to feel better about yourself, not only doesn't tend to work very well, but may be a bad sign. It's a marker for other problems—specifically, an indication that your self-worth is vulnerable and contingent. "Thus, a paradox of self-esteem:

If you need it, you don't have it, and if you have it, you don't need it."[23]

So, what leads people to develop this unhappy condition of contingent self-esteem? Under what circumstances do they come to think of themselves as good only *if* . . . ? One likely cause is competition: placing someone in a situation where one person can succeed only if others fail, and where glory is reserved only for the winner. This is an excellent way to undermine people's faith in themselves and to teach that one is worthwhile only if one triumphs.[24] There's also reason to think that contingent self-esteem can result from a style of parenting in which children are overcontrolled, as I'll explain in the following chapter.

Most of all, though, contingent self-esteem seems to result from being esteemed contingently by others. And this brings us back to where we started: When children feel they're loved by their parents only under certain conditions—a feeling typically evoked by the use of love-withdrawal techniques and positive reinforcement—it's very hard for them to accept themselves. And everything goes downhill from there.

3

TOO MUCH CONTROL

One recent afternoon, my wife walked in the door with our children, fresh from a trip to the park. She was shaking her head and sputtering: "I can't *believe* the way some of those parents talk to their kids—so degrading and hostile. Why do they even bother to *have* kids?" Having reacted the same way myself more than once, I decided to begin writing down some of what we heard and saw around town. Within a few days, I had recorded these incidents, among many others:

- A toddler was harshly reprimanded for throwing a stuffed bear in the children's area of the public library, even though no one else was in the vicinity.

- A child who had been asking for a cookie in the supermarket noticed that another little boy was eating one. When he pointed this out to his mother, she told him, "Well, that's probably because *he* uses the potty."

- A little boy gave a loud whoop of delight while jumping off a playground swing, and his mother hissed, "Stop that foolishness right now! No more swings for you today. Once more and you go on time-out."

- At the water table in the children's museum, a mother tried to prevent her young son from doing various things by falsely claiming that signs posted in the area specifically prohibited whatever he was up to—for example, "That sign says not to splash." When he asked why, she replied, "It just does."

I gave up my note-taking project before long. Apart from the sheer number of these incidents, they were fairly similar to one another, and recording them quickly came to seem redundant, not to mention depressing. Over and over, we witnessed parents on the playground abruptly announcing it was time to go, sometimes even grabbing the child by the arm. (If she cried, this was usually attributed to her being "tired.") We watched parents doing an unwitting imitation of an army sergeant intimidating his troops, nose to nose, finger stabbing the air only inches from the child's face, hollering. And how often at restaurants had we seen parents fussing at their kids—correcting their manners, reprimanding them about their posture, commenting on what (and how much) they were eating, and generally making dinnertime something from which the children couldn't wait to escape. (No wonder so many kids aren't hungry during family meals, but develop an appetite a short time later.)

Let me assure you that I was a lot more judgmental before I had children of my own. Until you've pushed your own stroller, you don't really understand how people this tiny can manage to push your buttons and sap your patience. (Of course, neither are you able to appreciate the transcendent moments of delight they can provide.) That's something I try hard to keep in mind when I wince at another parent's behavior. And I remind myself that I'm ignorant about the history of each family I've observed for a few minutes—what the parent might have been through that morning and what the child did just before I happened on the scene.

Still. Despite all the allowances we care to make, and all the qualifications we might want to offer, there's a general truth here: For every example of a child who is permitted to run wild in a public place, there are hundreds of examples of children being restricted unnecessarily, yelled at, threatened, or bullied by their parents; children whose protests are routinely ignored and whose questions are dismissed out of hand; children who have become accustomed to hearing an automatic "No!" in response to their requests, and a "Because I said so!" if they ask for a reason.

Don't take my word for it. Pretend you're an anthropologist and really watch what's happening the next time you're at a playground or a shopping mall or a birthday party. You won't see anything you haven't seen before, but you may begin to notice details to which you hadn't really paid attention. Certain generalizations about what you're witnessing may suggest themselves. But beware: It's not always pleasant to become more sensitized to what's around you. Watch too carefully and pretty soon a day at the park is no day at the park. As one California mother wrote to me:

> Have you been to the grocery store lately? It has become more painful than it's ever been! [Watching] parents use bribes, humiliation, punishment, rewards, and generally abusive tactics is almost unbearable. What's happened to my lovely mental block? . . . Every "If you don't settle down, we're never coming to the store again!" and "If you stop screaming, we'll go for ice cream, sweetie!" threatens to suffocate me. How, I wonder, did I manage to tune it out before?

*   *   *

Think again about the various techniques of conditional parenting described in the last two chapters. One reason they're so harmful has to do with the child's experience of feeling controlled. And it works the other way around, too: When we use punishments and rewards and other strategies to manipulate children's behavior, they may come to feel they're loved only when they conform to our demands. Conditional parenting can be the consequence of control even if it wasn't the intention, and, conversely, control can help to explain the destructive effects of conditional parenting.

But excessive control is a problem in its own right, which is why it merits its own chapter. And it's not limited to any specific form of discipline, to a time-out or a star chart, a spanking or a "Good job," a privilege dangled or a privilege snatched away. Replacing one method with another won't have much effect if we fail to grapple with this basic fact: *The dominant problem with parenting in our society isn't permissiveness, but the fear of permissiveness.* We're so worried about spoiling kids that we often end up overcontrolling them.

Granted, some kids *are* spoiled—and some kids are neglected. But the issue that's much less commonly discussed is the epidemic of micromanaging children, acting as though they were wholly owned subsidiaries of us. Thus, one critical question, to which I'll return later, is how we can offer guidance and set limits (both of which are necessary) without overdoing the control. First, though, we have to be clear about the extent to which we may indeed be overdoing it, and why that's a temptation we need to resist.

The way many kids are treated suggests a lack of respect for their needs and preferences—in fact, a lack of respect for children, period. A lot of parents act as though they believe that kids don't *deserve* respect in the way adults do. Many years ago, the psychologist Haim Ginott invited us to consider the way we might react if our child accidentally left behind some item that belonged to him or her—and then to contrast that with the way we might react if a chronically forgetful friend of ours did the same thing. Few of us would think of berating another adult in the tone that is routinely used with kids: "What is the *matter* with you? How many times do I have to remind you to look around for all your things before you leave? Do you think I have nothing better to do than . . ." and so on. With an adult, we'd be more likely to say, simply, "Here's your umbrella."[1]

Some parents interfere by force of habit, barking out "Stop running!" even when there's little risk of injury to person or property. Some act as though they're trying to rub a child's face in his own powerlessness and show him who's boss. ("Because I'm the mommy, that's why!" "My house, my rules!") Some try to control children with physical force, while others prefer guilt ("After all I've done for you! You're breaking my heart. . . ."). Some parents nag kids continuously, emitting a steady hum of reminders and criticisms. Others give no evidence of objecting to what their children are doing until, seemingly out of nowhere, they explode; an invisible tripwire has been crossed—which may have more to do with the adult's mood than with the child's behavior—and suddenly the parent becomes furious and frighteningly coercive.

Obviously, not all parents do all these things, and some never do any of them. Studies have shown that child-rearing beliefs and behaviors tend to vary on the basis of culture, class, race, and how much pressure the parents themselves are experiencing, among other factors. (See the Appendix for more on these topics.) Researchers also assure us that most parents don't use a single discipline style across the board; they tend to respond differently to different kinds of misbehavior.[2]

But perhaps the more interesting question is how parents come to decide what constitutes "misbehavior" in the first place. Some regularly apply that concept to what you or I would regard as innocuous actions—and then crack down on their children.[3] This may be part of what is sometimes called an "authoritarian" style of raising kids. Such parents are more strict and demanding than they are accepting and encouraging. They rarely offer explanations or justifications for the rules they impose. They not only expect absolute obedience, and use punishment freely to obtain it, but also believe it's more important for children to comply with authority than to think for themselves or express their opinions. They insist that kids need to be carefully monitored, and when a rule is broken—which just confirms their dark suspicions about what children are really like—authoritarian parents tend to assume the child deliberately chose to break it, irrespective of his or her age, and now must be held accountable.

Disturbingly, these same themes of "subservience to the demands of the parents and . . . an early suppression of impulses not acceptable to them" show up in a classic post–World War II research project that was designed to explore the psychological underpinnings of fascism and, in particular, the childhoods of individuals who grow up hating whole groups of people and seem to be infatuated with power.[4]

Of course, this represents the outer edges of the control spectrum. It's natural, upon hearing about such extreme cases, to say, "Well, obviously that doesn't describe me. I'm not an authoritarian, nor would I scream at my child on the playground for having a good time." But almost everyone gives in to the impulse to overcontrol, at least on occasion. Some do so as a result of their conviction that children must learn to do what they're told (and, after all, adults know better than kids, don't they?). Some people have controlling personalities and developed the habit of imposing their will on their children at the very beginning.[5] Others just become desperate now and then, particularly in response to a child's act of defiance. And many parents are truly concerned about their children's well-being but have never considered the possibility that what they've been doing constitutes excessive and counterproductive control.

It's easy for most of us to observe Bad Parenting on Parade, to watch people who are much more controlling than we are, and to take comfort from saying, "At least I'd never do that." But the real challenge is to reflect on the things we *have* been known to do and ask whether they're really in our children's best interest.

Which Kids Do What They're Told?

Let's put aside for the moment the ambitious goals we have for our children and just focus on what leads them to comply with our requests. If all we cared about was getting them to do something, or to stop doing something, right now, while we're standing there, then we'd have to admit that it sometimes works to use our power to coerce that behavior—for example, by threatening, punishing, or loudly demanding.[6] But only sometimes. On balance, the kids who do what they're told are likely to be those whose parents *don't* rely on power and instead have developed a warm and secure relationship with them. They have parents who treat them with respect, minimize the use of control, and make a point of offering reasons and explanations for what they ask.

The researchers in one classic study began by distinguishing between the sort of parent who is sensitive, accepting, and cooperative, and the sort who assumes "she has a perfect right to do with [her child] what she wishes, imposing her will on his, shaping him to her standards, and interrupting him arbitrarily without regard for his needs, wishes, or activity-in-progress." Lo and behold, it was the mothers in the first category—those who were less controlling—whose very young children were likely to do what they were told.[7]

In a second study, the two-year-olds who were most likely to comply with a specific request turned out to be those whose parents "were very clear about what they wanted, but in addition to listening to their children's objections, they also accommodated them in ways that conveyed respect for the children's autonomy and individuality."[8]

A third study raised the stakes a bit by focusing on preschoolers who had been identified as unusually defiant. Some of their mothers were asked to play with them as they usually did, while others were trained to "engage in any activity that the child might choose and to allow the child to control the nature and rules of the interaction." They were asked to refrain from commanding, criticizing, or praising. (Notice that praising was included alongside other forms of manipulation.) After the play sessions, the mothers, at the request of the experimenters, issued a series of commands to their children having to do with putting away each of the toys. The result: Children who had been subject to less control—that is, those who had been given more say about how to play— were more likely to follow their mothers' instructions.[9]

Striking as these experimental results are, the problems with traditional, control-based discipline become even clearer once we look at what kids do *after the adult leaves the room.* One researcher wondered not only which toddlers would be likely to comply with a request to do something (clean up), but also which ones would comply with a request *not* to do something (namely, play with certain toys) once they were left alone. Both questions had the same answer: The kids who toed the line were those whose mothers were generally supportive and warm, and who tended to avoid forceful control.[10]

The evidence goes on and on. One pair of psychologists looked at what promotes children's wholehearted, "committed" compliance, as opposed to the more reluctant "situational" kind. Another pair wanted to know what leads a child to follow the directions of an adult who is not her mother or father.[11] In both cases, the results were better when children were raised by parents who were respectful and responsive rather than by those who emphasized control.

One reason that a heavy-handed, do-what-I-say approach tends not to work very well is that, in the final analysis, we really *can't* control our kids—at least, not in the ways that matter. It's very difficult to make a child eat this food rather than that one, or pee here rather than there, and it's simply impossible to force a child to go to sleep, or stop crying, or listen, or respect us. These are the issues that are most trying to parents precisely because it's here that we run up against the inherent limits of what one human being can compel another human being to do. Particularly with infants, and then again with adolescents, the goal of control ultimately proves to be an illusion.[12] Sadly, though, that doesn't stop us from trying newer, cleverer, or more forceful strategies to get kids to comply. And when these techniques fail, that's often taken as evidence that what's needed is . . . more of the same.

Opposite Extremes

There's something paradoxical about the fact that it's those parents who are most concerned about controlling their children who may end up having the least control over them. But that's not the end of the story. Far more significant is the fact that this power-based approach isn't just ineffective—it's also terribly damaging, even when it appears to work. As the late Thomas Gordon, who created Parent Effectiveness Training, once remarked to me, "Autocratic environments make people sick."

Of course, people don't all get sick in the same way. Psychotherapists have long realized that a single underlying cause can lead to patterns of results that are very different from one another. For example, some people who have doubts about their own worth are constantly putting themselves down and acting insecure. But other people with the same doubts come across as arrogant and self-congratulatory: They seem to be trying to compensate for low self-esteem with grandiosity. Thus, two apparently opposite personalities may share a common root.

So it is when parents insist on absolute control. Some of these children become *excessively compliant,* and others become *excessively defiant.* Let's consider each of these reactions in turn.

Many parents dream of having kids who always do what they're told, but as I pointed out in the Introduction, it's actually not a good sign when children are cowed into obedience. We make fun of what used to be called "yes-men" in the office, those deferential employees who never disagree with the boss, so what makes us think that "yes-children" would be ideal?

In 1948, the journal *Child Development* published one of the first research studies on this subject, which found that preschool-age children of controlling parents tended to be "quiet, well-behaved, non-resistant." However, they also didn't interact much with their peers and seemed lacking in curiosity and originality. "Authoritarian control . . . obtains conformity but at the expense of personal freedom," the researcher concluded.[13]

More than four decades later, in 1991, the same journal featured a study of some 4,100 adolescents. The idea, again, was to see how well these kids were doing, psychologically and socially, and then compare the results to how they were being raised. It turned out that those who had authoritarian parents often scored high on "measures of obedience and conformity to the standards of adults." But, the researchers added, "these youngsters appear to have paid a price where self-confidence is concerned—both in terms of self-reliance and in terms of their perceptions of their own social and academic abilities. The overall pattern suggests a group of young people who have been over-powered into obedience."[14]

Excessive compliance, then, is one result of excessive control. But the same kind of parenting pushes some children to the other extreme, where they rebel against anything and everything. Their will, their judgment, their need to have some say over their own lives have all been squelched, and the only way they can recover a sense of auton-omy is to become excessively defiant.

When we make children feel powerless, forcing them to submit to our will, this often generates intense anger, and just because that anger can't be expressed at the moment doesn't mean it disappears. What happens to it depends on the child's personality and the specifics of the situation. Sometimes the result is more battles with the parent. As author Nancy Samalin comments, even "when we 'win,' we lose. When we make children obey by force, threats, or punishment, we make them feel helpless. They can't stand feeling helpless, so they pro-voke another confrontation to prove they still have some power."[15] And where do they learn how to use that power? From us. Not only does authoritarian parenting make them mad; it also teaches them how to direct that anger against another person.[16]

Such children may grow up with a constant need to thumb their noses at authority figures. Sometimes they bring all that hostility with them to school or the playground. (Studies suggest that children raised by controlling parents, even children as young as three years old, are especially likely to be disruptive and aggressive with their peers, the result being that these peers may not want to have anything to do with them.[17] Obviously, such enforced isolation doesn't bode well for their development.)

And sometimes, if a child is afraid of defying you to your face, he'll figure out a way to do it behind your back. Lay-down-the-law parent-ing may produce kids who seem to be so well behaved as to be the envy of the neighbors. Often, however, they've just learned to be sneakier about their misbehavior, which sometimes turns out to be appallingly mean-spirited. They seem to be perfect, but they're actually leading a "double life," as one therapist put it: "Because our parents insisted on exercising control over our lives, we created one life that they knew about, and one that remained a secret from them."[18] Such children may be at risk for various psychological problems down the line. Also, they may be terrified of, and permanently alienated from, the people who treat them this way. As with conditional love, therefore, tight control can sometimes yield results in the short run, but at the cost of fatally damaging our relationships with our children over time.

One mother offered an intriguing bit of testimony in a message she contributed to an online discussion group. She described a Christmas spent with her husband's relatives, who were raised—and who now raise their own children—with firm discipline. During the vacation, they told stories about the various escapades of their youth. "Those well-behaved, regularly disciplined, polite children were impetuous hooligans every time their parents' backs were turned," she reported. "They did stuff I never could have invented." On her side of the family, by contrast, "there has never been a [behavior] chart, an incentive, a schedule of punishments, a grounding, a spanking, or a removal of 'privileges.' " Nor, she swears, has there been any serious misbehavior.

I don't mean to say that defiance is always something to worry about. Some amount of nay-saying is quite common and perfectly healthy, especially around age two or three, and then again during the early teen years. Rather, what I'm describing here is an exaggerated, reactive kind of defiance, which lasts longer and runs deeper. Such children are living proof that a style of parenting aimed mostly at eliciting obedience often fails even on its own terms, in addition to creating a raft of other problems.

What's the alternative to being either excessively compliant *or* excessively defiant? What do such children look like? In response to requests from their parents—and, later, from other people—they'll choose to say yes sometimes and no at other times, without feeling compelled either to comply or to defy. They often do what they're asked, especially when they're convinced it's reasonable or very important to the person who's asking. These are likely to be the children of parents who have built up a reservoir of trust by treating them with respect, explaining the reasons for their requests, and avoiding unrealistic expectations of obedience. Such parents have made their peace with the fact that their kids will assert themselves by being defiant now and then, and they don't overreact when that happens.

Overeating, Underenjoying, and Other Costs of Control

In chapter 2, I described the effects of contingent self-esteem, citing the work of University of Rochester psychologists Richard Ryan and Edward Deci. (Deci also participated in that study of college students that found various unhappy consequences of conditional parenting.) These two researchers, along with their associates and former students, have spent the last few decades collecting evidence that bad things tend to happen when people of various ages feel controlled, whether the control is imposed through punishments, rewards, conditional love, straightforward coercion, or other means.

In looking at parenting, they've found that the more children feel restricted and controlled, the greater the chance of "outright resistance to what socializers intend to foster"—and the more unstable the children's identity, or sense of self, will tend to be.[19] Go back to that study of college students. Why was it so damaging to hear "I love you only when you . . ." from their parents? Because that message made them feel controlled from the inside. They grew up feeling they had to behave—or succeed—in particular ways in order to please their parents, and ultimately in order to feel good about themselves. The key phrase in that sentence is *had to:* They didn't feel free, psychologically speaking, to do otherwise.

Internalizing a drive to "be good," or work hard, or do whatever else it takes to please Mom or Dad is not good news if the result doesn't feel like a real decision. And, according to that study, it didn't. Those students who thought their parents loved them only conditionally were much more likely than their peers to say that the way they acted was often due more to a "strong internal pressure" than to "a real sense of choice." They also indicated that their happiness after succeeding at something was usually short-lived, their opinion of themselves fluctuated a lot, and they often felt guilty or ashamed.[20]

Deci and Ryan believe that children are born not only with certain basic needs, including a need to have some say over their own lives, but also with the ability to make decisions in a way that meets their needs; they're equipped with "a gyroscope of natural self-regulation." When we control kids excessively—for example, by offering them rewards and praise for doing what we want—they start to become dependent on external sources of control. The gyroscope begins to wobble and they lose their ability to regulate themselves.[21]

FOOD

Food consumption offers a very literal example of this. It's true that kids don't always choose the healthiest things to eat. (That's why we need to teach them what is and isn't good for their bodies, and provide them with restricted choices such that whichever item they pick will be acceptable.) On the other hand, even without our intervention, young children will usually consume the number of calories their bodies need over time. Sometimes they'll go for days eating so little that we become concerned, and then they suddenly put away huge portions. If they eat something fattening, they'll tend to eat less, or something less caloric, afterward. In terms of how much they eat, then, children seem to have a remarkable capacity for self-regulation.

Unless, that is, we try to run their bodies for them. Two nutritionists in Illinois conducted a fascinating experiment a few years ago. They observed 77 children between the ages of two and four, and also learned how much their parents attempted to control their eating habits. They discovered that those parents who insisted their children eat only during mealtimes (rather than when they were hungry), or who encouraged them to clean their plates (even when they obviously weren't hungry), or who used food (especially desserts) as a reward wound up with children who lost the ability to regulate their caloric intake. Some of the parents appeared to have their own issues with food, which they were in the process of passing on to their kids. But whatever the reason for their excessive control, it was beginning to take its toll even before some of these children were out of diapers. The children had "few opportunities to learn to control their own food intake" and came to stop trusting their bodies' cues about when they were hungry. One result: Many of them were already starting to get fat.[22]

MORALS

This finding about food is interesting, even alarming, in its own right, but it's just one illustration of a wider danger. External regulation can interfere with the development of internal regulation not only with regard to eating but also with regard to ethics. A heavy-handed parenting style does nothing to promote, and actually may undermine, children's moral development. Those who are pressured to do as they're told are unlikely to think through ethical dilemmas for themselves. This can quickly create a vicious circle: The less chance they have to make decisions about the right way to act, the more likely they are to act in ways that will cause their parents to cite their irresponsibility as a reason for continuing to deny them the right to choose.

One much-cited review of the research on child development reported that, while children of authoritarian parents don't stand out, one way or the other, "on contrived measures of resistance to temptation," more meaningful evidence suggests that "they do show lesser evidence of 'conscience' and are more likely to have an external, rather than internal, moral orientation in discussing what is the 'right' behavior in situations of moral conflict."[23]

INTEREST

Yet another consequence of too much control: When kids feel forced to do things—or are too tightly regulated in the *way* they do things—they're likely to become less interested in what they're doing and less likely to stick with something challenging. In an intriguing experiment, parents were invited to sit on the floor next to their very young children—not even two years old—who were playing with toys. Some of the parents immediately took over the task or barked out instructions ("Put the block in. No, not there. *There!*") Others were content to let their kids explore, providing encouragement and offering help only when it was needed. Later, the babies were given something else to play with, this time without their parents present. It turned out that, once they were on their own, those who had controlling parents were apt to give up more easily rather than trying to figure out how the new toy worked.

About a decade later, another study found very similar results with six- and seven-year-old children: Those whose parents had played with them in a controlling manner (telling them what to do, criticizing, or praising) seemed to lose interest in what they were doing. They spent less time playing with the toys when they were alone, and they also said they found the toys less fun than did kids whose parents had been less controlling.[24]

SKILLS

The first of those studies showing a diminution of kids' interest was conducted back in the mid-1980s by Wendy Grolnick, a former student of Deci and Ryan's, and her associates. (The second study was conducted by Deci himself, among others.) Almost two decades later, Grolnick discovered that controlling parents don't merely make kids less *interested* in what they're doing: They may also lead kids to be less *proficient* at what they're doing. This time, she looked at how third-graders and their parents worked together on a couple of projects that resembled homework (one involving the use of maps and the other involving the rhyme schemes of poems), after which each child was left alone and asked to do similar tasks. Those whose parents had been more controlling didn't do as well on their own.[25]

Interestingly, the parents who were most controlling (at least on the poetry assignment) were those who themselves felt controlled—by hearing from the experimenter that their children would soon be tested on the skills involved in these tasks.[26] The same thing happens with teachers: Lean on them to "raise standards," and they turn into drill sergeants. The ironic result is that their students end up achieving at lower levels than their counterparts in classrooms where there's less top-down emphasis on "accountability."[27]

In her very useful and concise book *The Psychology of Parental Control*, Grolnick summarizes a great deal of other research showing that "controlling parenting has been associated with lower levels of intrinsic motivation, less internalization of values and morals, poorer self-regulation," and poorer feelings about oneself—to say nothing of "unwanted side effects for the parent-child relationship." She adds, "These issues relate not only to children's development and well-being but also to their success as happy, functioning adults during the course of their lives." Her review of the data strongly suggests that, while children have different needs at different ages, the effects of too much control are damaging no matter how old they are. And while parenting styles clearly vary across race, class, and culture, too much control seems to have negative effects across the board.[28]

Of course, terms like *excessive* and *too much* raise the question of whether there's an ideal amount of control. My response is that the attempt to figure out what's good for kids is a qualitative inquiry more than a quantitative one. Depending on how we define *control*, it may make more sense to look for alternatives to it than just to offer less of it. Children need *structure* in their lives, for example—and some need more than others—but that's not the same as saying they just need a moderate amount of control.[29] How can we tell the difference? There are certainly some gray areas here, but as a rule, reasonable structures are imposed only when necessary, in a flexible manner, without undue restrictiveness, and, when possible, with the participation of the child.

The result feels quite different from using coercion or pressure to impose your will, which is what's usually thought of as control.

As parents, we need to be involved in and aware of the details of our children's lives. Nothing in this book should be interpreted as an argument for sitting back and letting children raise themselves. We might say it's our job to be "in control," in the sense of creating a healthy and safe environment, offering guidance, and setting limits— but it's not our job to be "controlling," in the sense of demanding absolute obedience or relying on pressure or continuous regulation. In fact, although it may sound paradoxical, we need to be in control of helping them to gain control over their own lives. The goal is empowerment rather than conformity, and the methods are respectful rather than coercive.

There may be times when some control, in the usual sense, is unavoidable, and here the trick is indeed to avoid overdoing it. But we need to think in terms of an approach to parenting that's fundamentally different from control, rather than just trying to find a happy medium between "too controlling" and "not controlling enough." In chapter 9, I'll offer some suggestions for how we can do that.

4

PUNITIVE DAMAGES

Punishment . . . control . . . authoritarian parenting . . . love withdrawal . . . conditional affection—all of these concepts overlap. It's the first one, however, that's most familiar to us and easiest to understand. To punish kids, very simply, is to make something unpleasant happen to them—or prevent them from experiencing something pleasant—usually with the goal of changing their future behavior. The punisher makes them suffer, in other words, to teach them a lesson.[1]

Fundamental questions about the wisdom of this approach may suggest themselves even before we look at the results of scientific investigations. For example, it may occur to us to ask: How likely is it that intentionally making children unhappy will prove beneficial in the long run? And: If punishment is so effective, how come I have to keep doing it to my child over and over?

The available research does nothing to allay such doubts. The results of a classic parenting study, published in 1957, seemed to catch even the authors by surprise. After reviewing all the data from their investigation of kindergartners and their mothers, they reported that "the unhappy effects of punishment have run like a dismal thread through our findings." Punishment proved to be counterproductive regardless of whether the parents were using it to stop aggression, excessive dependence, bedwetting, or something else. The researchers consistently found that punishment was "ineffectual over the long term as a technique for eliminating the kind of behavior toward which it is directed."[2] Newer and better-designed studies have only served to strengthen this conclusion, finding, for example, that parents who "punish[ed] rule-breaking behavior in their children at home often had children who demonstrated higher levels of rule-breaking when away from home."[3]

By now there is an especially impressive collection of research demonstrating the destructive effects of corporal punishment in particular—that is, the practice of spanking, slapping, or otherwise causing physical pain as a form of discipline. The data overwhelmingly show that corporal punishment makes children more aggressive and leads to a variety of other damaging consequences. (It's not even clear that it succeeds at getting temporary compliance.)[4] Hitting children clearly "teaches them a lesson"—and the lesson is that you can get your way with people who are weaker than you are by hurting them.

I believe the research supports a zero-tolerance policy for spanking, given that it's unnecessary, unproductive, and potentially very harmful. But this, too, may be a case where data are not absolutely necessary. Fundamental values may be enough to justify our opposition. As sickening as it is that some men hit their wives or girlfriends, it's arguably even worse for adults to hit children—in any manner and for any reason.

Still, just as the problems with control are not limited to punishment, so the problems with punishment are not limited to the physical kind. The late sociologist Joan McCord put it well:

> If parents and teachers were to substitute non-physical punishments for physical ones, they might avoid teaching children to hit, punch, and kick; yet, they would nevertheless perpetuate the idea that giving pain is a legitimate way to exercise power. . . . The consequences could be no less undermining of compassion and social interests.[5]

The problem, in other words, rests with the idea of forcing children to undergo something unpleasant. The unpleasantness can consist of physical assault, deprivation of affection or attention, humiliation, isolation, or anything else.

This is worth emphasizing, first of all, because even some writers who firmly oppose corporal punishment seem to take on faith that other sorts of punishment are harmless or even necessary. (Three shining exceptions, who have written eloquently on the problems with the very idea of punishment, are Thomas Gordon, Haim Ginott, and William Glasser.)

A number of consultants, meanwhile, have responded to the understandable reluctance of many parents to use punitive tactics by repackaging them as "consequences." In some cases, the change is purely semantic, the implication being that a friendlier name will make the same practices less offensive. But sometimes we're told that if the punishments are less severe, or "logically" related to the misbehavior, or clearly spelled out in advance, then they're okay to use—and, indeed, shouldn't be considered punishments at all.

I don't buy it. More important, I don't think kids buy it. While it's certainly true that a bad thing can be made worse by adding such elements as unpredictability or lack of clarity—or by really overdoing it or being excessively nasty—these aren't the main reasons that punishment has the effects it does.

Announcing how we plan to punish children ("Remember, if you do *x*, then I'll do *y* to you") may salve *our* conscience because we gave them fair warning, but all we've really done is threaten them. We've told them in advance exactly how we'll make them suffer if they fail to obey. This communicates a message of distrust ("I don't think you'll do the right thing without the fear of punishment"), leads kids to think of themselves as complying for extrinsic reasons, and emphasizes their powerlessness. All the destructive effects predicted by logic, experience, and research are likely to follow regardless of these minor modifications—and regardless of whether we call punishment by a different name.[6]

Sometimes parents are advised to use a time-out instead of spanking their kids—as though these were the only two options available. The reality, as we've seen, is that both of these tactics are punitive. They differ only with respect to whether children will be made to suffer by physical or emotional means. If we were forced to choose one over the other, then, sure, time-outs are preferable to spankings. For that matter, spanking kids is preferable to shooting them, but that's not much of an argument for spanking.

Another version of what might be called Punishment Lite is known as "natural consequences," which invites parents to discipline by inaction—that is, by refusing to help. If a child is late for dinner, we're supposed to let her go hungry. If she leaves her raincoat at school, we're supposed to let her get wet the following day. This is said to teach her to be more punctual, or less forgetful, or whatever. But the far more powerful lesson that she's likely to take away is that we could have helped—but didn't. As two authors note in their discussion of the practice, "When you stand by and let bad things happen, your child experiences the twin disappointments that something went wrong and you did not seem to care enough about her to lift a finger to help prevent the mishap. The 'natural consequences' approach is really a form of punishment."[7]

One of the most striking features of punishment—any punishment—is the way it creates a vicious circle for all concerned, very much like what we find with love withdrawal and positive reinforcement. No matter how many times we've watched as the child being punished lashes out in anger or pain, no matter how many times a punitive intervention fails to bring about any improvement (and, more likely, actually makes things worse), we may assume that the only possible response is to punish again—perhaps even upping the ante. Interestingly, research finds the worst effects aren't due to the parent's initial intervention but rather to the use of punishment *after* the child fails to comply with the first request. It's the reactive use of punishment, the choice to employ it once we've already locked horns with the child, that proves most worrisome. Therefore, it's most important to refrain from punishing precisely when we're most angry or frustrated.[8]

The more important vicious circle, however, takes place not at the time we confront a child, but *over* time—that is, as events play out over many years. Repeatedly punishing a young child may help to turn him into a defiant adolescent; yet we're advised to continue, and even intensify, the punishing: Ground the disobedient teenager, cut off his allowance, use our power to *make* him act responsibly. *The more this strategy fails, the more we assume the problem is with the child, rather than with the strategy itself.* And if we do stop to reconsider what we're doing, we assume we've just been implementing it ineffectively— as opposed to realizing the trouble is with the whole idea of making children suffer to teach them a lesson. Ginott was absolutely right: "Misbehavior and punishment are not opposites that cancel each other; on the contrary, they breed and reinforce each other."[9]

Why Punishment Fails

That punishing kids doesn't work is very difficult to deny in light of all the available evidence. *Why* it doesn't work is harder to say with certainty. Nevertheless, we can hazard some guesses.

- *It makes people mad.* Like other forms of control, the use of punitive consequences often enrages whoever is on the receiving end, and the experience is doubly painful because he or she is powerless to do anything about it. What history teaches us about nations echoes what psychology teaches us about individuals: Given a chance, those who feel like victims may eventually become victimizers.

- *It models the use of power.* The example that corporal punishment sets for children is violence—that is, the use of force to solve problems. In fact, though, all punishment teaches something similar. Children may or may not learn the lesson we had in mind when we punished them ("Don't do *x* again"). But they'll surely learn that when the most important people in their lives, their role models, have a problem, they try to solve it by using power to make the other person unhappy so he or she will be forced to capitulate. Punishment not only makes a child angry; it "simultaneously provides him with a model for expressing that hostility outwardly," notes one researcher.[10] In other words, it teaches that might makes right.

- *It eventually loses its effectiveness.* As kids grow older, it becomes harder and harder to find things to do to them that will be sufficiently unpleasant. (By the same token, it becomes increasingly difficult to find rewards that are sufficiently appealing.) At some point, your threats begin to sound hollow and your kids just shrug off "You're grounded!" or "No allowance for you this week!" This doesn't prove that kids are tough or obstinate, nor does it mean that you need help devising more diabolical ways to make them suffer. Rather, what it suggests is that trying to help kids become good people by punishing them for doing bad things may have been a foolish strategy from the beginning.

  Think about it this way: When young children wonder why they should be nice or resist certain temptations, parents have a choice. They can draw upon the respect and trust they've cultivated by loving their kids unconditionally, using reason and persuasion to explain how doing this thing rather than that thing is likely to affect other people. Or they can just appeal to naked power: "If you don't cut that out, you'll be punished."

  The problem with the latter approach is that once your power begins to ebb—and it will—you've got nothing left. As Thomas Gordon pointed out, "The inevitable result of consistently employing power to control [your] kids when they are young is that [you] never learn how to *influence*." The more you rely on punishment, therefore, "the less real influence you'll have on their lives."[11]

- *It erodes our relationships with our kids.* When we punish, we make it very hard for our children to regard us as caring allies, which is vital for healthy development. Instead, we become (in their eyes) enforcers to be avoided. Very young children begin to wrap their minds around the fact that their parents, those huge, all-powerful people on whom they are totally dependent, occasionally make them miserable *on purpose*: Those giants who hold me and rock me and feed me and kiss away my tears sometimes go out of their way to take away things I like, or make me feel unworthy, or hit me on the backside (even though they keep telling me *I'm* always supposed to "use my words"). They tell me they're acting this way because of something or other that I did, but all I know is now I'm not sure I can trust them or feel completely safe with them. I'd be pretty stupid to admit to them that I'm angry, or that I did something bad, because I've learned that I might be given a time-out or talked to in a voice that has all the love drained out of it or even smacked. I'd better keep my distance.

• *It distracts kids from the important issues.* Suppose a child is told that, because he just punched his brother, he has to go to his room and miss his favorite TV program. Let's peek in on him, sitting on his bed. What do you imagine is going through his mind? If your guess is that he's been reflecting on his actions, perhaps saying to himself thoughtfully, "Y'know, now I see that hurting people is wrong"—then, by all means, keep sending your kids to their rooms whenever they misbehave.

If, however, like anyone who has ever spent time with a real child (or has ever been one, for that matter), you find that scenario laughably improbable, then why would you ever impose this—or any other—punishment? The idea that time-outs are an acceptable form of discipline because they give kids time to think things over is based on an absurdly unrealistic premise. More generally, punishment doesn't lead children to focus on what they've done, much less on why they did it or what they should have done instead. Rather, it leads them to think about how mean their parents are and maybe how they're going to get their revenge (on the kid who got them into trouble).

Above all, they're likely to focus on the punishment itself: how unfair it is and how to avoid it next time. Punishing kids— with the threat that you'll do so again if they displease you in the future—is an excellent way to hone their skills at escaping detection. Tell a child: "I don't want to catch you doing that again," and the child will think, "Okay. Next time you won't catch me." It also sets up a strong incentive to lie. (By contrast, children who aren't punished are less afraid of owning up to what they've done.) Yet punitive parents, faced with the predictable dishonesty that accompanies traditional discipline—"I didn't do it! It was already broken!"—are likely to respond to this not by questioning their use of punishment, but by punishing the child again, this time for lying.

- *It makes kids more self-centered.* The word *consequences* is tossed around a lot, not only as a euphemism for punishment but also as a justification for it—as in "Kids need to learn that there are consequences for their actions." But consequences to whom? The answer given by all punishment is: to yourself. A child's attention is firmly directed to how she personally will be affected by breaking a rule or defying an adult—that is, what consequence she will face if she's caught.

  When we punish, in other words, we lead children to ask, "What do they (the grown-ups with the power) want me to do, and what will happen to me if I don't do it?" Notice that this is a mirror image of the question evoked in a home or classroom in which children are promised a reward for being good: "What do they want me to do, and what will I get for doing it?" Both questions are entirely about self-interest. And both are completely different from what we'd like kids to ask themselves—for example, "What kind of person do I want to be?"

  No wonder a pair of researchers, after discovering that punishing children interferes with their moral development, made sense of that finding by pointing out that punishments "direct the child to the consequences of his behavior for the actor, that is, for the child himself."[12] The more we rely on punitive consequences, including time-out—or rewards, including praise—the less likely children are to consider how their actions affect other people. (They may, however, become more likely to perform a cost-benefit analysis—that is, to weigh the risks of being caught and punished against the pleasures of doing whatever it is they're not supposed to do.)

These responses—calculating the risks, figuring out how not to get caught, lying to protect oneself—make sense from the child's perspective. They're perfectly rational. What they're not is moral, and that's because punishment—*all* punishment, by its very nature—impedes moral thinking. Thus, when defenders of traditional discipline insist that kids are going to face consequences for their behavior when they're out in the "real world," the reasonable response would be to ask what sort of adult out there in the real world is dissuaded from unethical behavior only when he himself will pay the price (if he's caught). Our answer would have to be: the sort of adult most of us hope our children won't become.

*   *   *

The argument I've been making is largely a practical one. By any meaningful criteria, punishment simply doesn't work very well, and it's not realistic to expect that more punishment (or a different kind) will turn things around. But how are we to respond to parents who contend that explaining, reasoning, empathizing, and so on can't have more than a limited impact, so we need to "put some teeth into" what we're telling kids and "get their attention" by imposing a consequence, too?

To begin with, notice that this claim is based on the assumption that without the addition of some coercive enforcement mechanism, children will ignore the most important people in their world. That's a hard case to make. Sure, kids sometimes ignore specific things we tell them, demonstrating a remarkable case of selective hearing when we call them to dinner or ask them to clean up, but that doesn't mean they're oblivious to our words and actions. On the contrary, even the words of the gentlest parent—or perhaps I should say *especially* of the gentlest parent—carry enormous clout just because of who's saying them.

Still, could someone argue that threats and punishments command children's attention in a different way? Yes, but the way they do so is terribly counterproductive. The very features of punishment that make it impossible to ignore also virtually ensure that no good can come out of it. What's getting the kids' attention here is pain, along with the fact that someone on whom they're dependent has caused that pain. This is hardly likely to produce the effect that most of us are looking for.

Some parents rationalize the use of punishment by insisting that they really, truly love their kids. No doubt this is true. But it creates a deeply confusing situation for children. It's hard for them to sort out why someone who clearly cares for them also makes them suffer from time to time. It creates the warped idea, which children may carry with them throughout their lives, that causing people pain is part of what it means to love them. Or else it may simply teach that love is necessarily conditional, that it lasts only as long as people do exactly what you want.

Another rationalization is that punishment isn't destructive as long as it's imposed for a good reason and as long as that reason is explained to the child. The truth is that *explanation doesn't minimize the bad effects of punishment so much as punishment minimizes the good effects of explanation.*[13] Suppose you explain things to your child and try to help her focus on how her actions have made someone else feel. You say: "Annie, when you grabbed the Legos away from Jeffrey, you made him sad because now he can't play with them." But what if you're also in the habit of punishing her for certain offenses? The benefits of your explanation may well be wiped out. If Annie knows from experience that you might send her to the time-out chair or do something else unpleasant to her, she's not thinking about Jeffrey. She's just worried about what this will mean for her. The more anxious she's learned to become about the possibility of punishment, the less chance that meaningful moral learning will take place.

If you combine everything in this chapter with the discussion in chapter 2, then a larger pattern begins to emerge. What I've described as a "doing to" approach, which encompasses conditional parenting, actually exists on a continuum—something like this:

| harsh corporal punishment | milder spankings | other punishments | tangible rewards | verbal rewards |

I don't mean to say that hitting your child and saying "Good job!" are morally equivalent. But they are conceptually connected. My concern is with *all* of these techniques as well as with the assumptions that link them. In my experience, parents are less likely to explore the "working with" alternative as long as they think it's enough just to pick one of the "doing to" options on the right side of this diagram. That's why I've spent so much time emphasizing how important it is to reject the whole model.

In effect, I've also been challenging a view that might be called "the more, the merrier." This is the tendency to dismiss arguments that any specific parenting practice is bad news and ought to be replaced by another. "Why not do both?" some people ask. "No reason to throw anything out of your toolbox. Use everything that works."

To begin with, we should respond once again: "Works to do what—and at what cost?" But the real problem is that different strategies sometimes work at cross-purposes. One may wipe out the positive effects of the other. Thus, the effect of punishment is such that it can undermine the benefits of good parenting if the two approaches are combined.[14]

You may recall the bit of folk wisdom, confirmed by generations of farmers and grocers, warning that a rotten apple placed in a barrel full of good apples can spoil them all. It would be pushing things to postulate a kind of psychological ethylene released by traditional discipline, analogous to the gas given off by bad fruit. But it does seem that the quest for optimal results may require us to abandon certain practices rather than simply piling other, better practices on top of them. We have to eliminate the bad stuff, like punishment and rewards, in order for the good stuff to work.[15]

5

PUSHED TO SUCCEED

Although it's not widely known, the word *stress,* when used to describe someone's emotional state, is actually a metaphor. Originally, the term was limited to the scientific study of metals and other materials. It referred to the "strain or deformation" (I'm quoting from my dictionary) that results from excessive force. A steel bar is capable of tolerating only so much stress before it snaps.

So, what is it that, figuratively speaking, creates a comparable force on children? And what happens to them when they "snap"?

Once a child's age is recorded in two digits, the stakes are raised in the discipline game. Adolescents can get into more trouble, and when they (understandably) rebel against being controlled, parents are often tempted to resort to even tighter regulation and more severe forms of punishment. But older children may experience stress for another reason, too. Increasingly they get the message that they're expected to be not only compliant but successful, not only to be good but to do well.

For the last couple of decades, books by mental health professionals and other authors have been warning us that children are being hurried and pressured and overscheduled. A study published in 2002 found disturbingly high rates of drinking (especially among boys) and depression (especially among girls) among suburban eleven- and twelve-year-olds. The researchers pointedly traced those symptoms back to the fact that these kids were already being led to concentrate on getting into top-ranked colleges.

Furthermore, seventh-graders who reported that their parents placed a lot of emphasis on academic achievement were likely to show signs of distress and "maladaptive perfectionism." Those problems were far less common among their classmates whose parents were more concerned about their children's *well-being* than about their *achievement*.[1] Notice that these two goals not only are different, but sometimes pull in opposite directions. And, as the psychoanalyst Erich Fromm once lamented, "Few parents have the courage and independence to care more for their children's happiness than for their success."[2]

In extreme cases, the "press for success" can reach a fever pitch, such that the child's present is essentially mortgaged to the future. Activities that might bring meaning or enjoyment are sacrificed in a ceaseless effort to prepare for Harvard (I've come to refer to this process as "Preparation H"). The bottom line is never far from the minds of such parents, who weigh every decision about what their children do in school, or even after school, against the yardstick of how it might contribute to future glories. They are not raising children so much as living résumés, and by the time high school arrives, the kids have learned to sign up for activities strictly to impress college admissions committees, ignoring (or, eventually, losing sight of) what they personally find interesting in the here-and-now. They have acquired the habit of asking teachers, "Do we need to know this?"—rather than, say, "What does this mean?"—as they grimly set about the business of trying to ratchet up their GPA or squeeze out another few points on the SAT.

Such achievement pressures are found in lots of families where the kids are perfectly well behaved and never give their parents or teachers any trouble. In particular, highly successful parents (by which I mean parents who are financially successful, not necessarily people who are successful *as* parents) may impose intense and often unrealistic demands on their offspring. That investigation of eleven- and twelve-year-olds carried the provocative title "Privileged but Pressured? A Study of Affluent Youth," and one of its authors had previously discovered that relatively wealthy teenagers have higher rates of substance abuse and anxiety than do their counterparts in the inner city.[3]

That's a point well worth mentioning to the parents of suburban teenagers (and soon-to-be-teenagers). At the same time, some of the details cited by books that warn about the costs of pushing kids to excel may be a bit less relevant outside of counties with names like Fairfield and Westchester and Marin. Not all children have after-school schedules that would exhaust a CEO—or, if they do, it may say more about their need to hold down a job as soon as they're old enough. Some families are more worried about paying off their car loans than figuring out the best route for maneuvering a luxury tank from music lessons to gymnastics. And if there are parents who basically serve as full-time consultants for their children's "careers," let's not forget that some people across town can only imagine what it must be like to have the disposable income (and disposable time) to err in that direction.

In short, the nature of the pressures experienced by children tends to vary by neighborhood. But that doesn't mean that only rich kids feel pushed. Struggling working-class parents may be determined to give their children opportunities that they themselves never had, and even more determined to make sure their children take full advantage of those opportunities. The sort of stress this produces isn't exactly the same as what's felt by the kid whose parents insist on hiring a tutor just on principle. But it's stress just the same.

The effects, moreover, are particularly damaging if kids (of any income level or ethnic background) are being pressured not just to do well but to do better than their peers. Such children come to regard everyone around them as potential obstacles to their own success. The predictable results include alienation and aggression, envy (of winners) and contempt (for losers). And their self-esteem often suffers along with their relationships. After all, when your sense of competence depends on triumphing over others, you will, at best, feel reassured and confirmed only sometimes. By definition, not everyone can win.

Back in the 1980s, a pair of psychologists studied more than eight hundred high school students and discovered that those who had become competitive were "unique by virtue of their greater dependence on evaluation- and performance-based assessments of personal worth." Translation: The way they viewed themselves hinged on how well they did at certain tasks and on what other people thought of them.[4] Competition makes self-esteem conditional and precarious, and it has that effect on winners and losers alike. What's more, the effect isn't limited to "excessive" competition. Rather, it appears that anytime children are set against one another such that one can succeed only by making others fail, there is a psychological price to be paid.

All of this offers a new lens, so to speak, through which to view warnings that we're doing too much for our children, indulging them, becoming overly involved in their lives. The real question, I would argue, isn't how much we're doing but *what* we're doing. Sure, it makes sense to ease up if we've gotten carried away with making kids accomplish more—or, worse yet, with trying to position them as superior to their peers. But that doesn't mean we should be doing less parenting. It means we should be doing better parenting—for example, being more supportive and less controlling. (I'll say more about how to do so in chapters 7 through 10.)

Rather than just asking whether we're doing too much for our kids, it may be more useful (though potentially more unsettling) to ask *for whom* we're doing it. At first it may seem that parents who push are guilty only of placing their children's happiness ahead of their own, as a recent book about "hyperparenting" put it. But look again: In some cases, what's really going on is a phenomenon known as BIRG (Basking in Reflected Glory). The term usually refers to the pride and exultation of sports fans when their team wins, but it also seems an apt description of parents who derive a vicarious sense of vindication from the success of their kids. These are the folks who manage to let you know, within a few minutes of meeting them, that their child is in the gifted program, or made the all-state tennis team, or got into Stanford—early acceptance, no less. (I used to parody this posture by announcing to my friends that I was terribly worried because my daughter still moved her lips while she was reading even though she was already two years old.)

Obviously, there's nothing wrong with being proud of our kids. But when the bragging seems excessive—when it's too intense, or too frequent, or starts up too quickly—it's possible that the parent's identity is a little too wrapped up in the child's accomplishments. This is particularly true when the boasts sound, well, more triumphant than loving. They have a competitive ring to them, the not-so-subtle point being that the child in question isn't just smart but smarter than every other kid. (It's the same with those ubiquitous bumper stickers: MY CHILD IS AN HONORS STUDENT AT THE SO-AND-SO SCHOOL—with the understood postscript AND YOURS ISN'T.)[5]

Listening to these parents, you begin to suspect that the accomplishments haven't exactly happened on their own, but have been coaxed out of the child by a mom or dad who is hovering too close, pushing too hard, and maybe loving not too much but too conditionally. You can't help wondering whether their kids believe they'd still be loved even if they stopped being so impressive. The unconscious equation "My kid's a success, therefore I am, too"—or maybe even "My kid's a success, and I'm the reason"—is directly tied to tactics such as the selective use of positive reinforcement, where children figure out that they have to make good in order to get hugs and smiles, and that their parents aren't proud of them for who they are, only for what they do.

Back when I was growing up, some parents tried to start their children in kindergarten a year early, or arrange for them to skip a grade later on, so they would be that much further ahead on the road to . . . wherever it was they were racing. These days, the same sort of parents make a point of *waiting* a year before having their kids start school so that they'll be older—and therefore, presumably, more adept—than their classmates. (This practice is known as *redshirting*—another term borrowed from competitive sports.) The 180-degree shift in strategy is almost comical, but the real question in either case is whether the decision is really being made on the basis of what's best for the child.[6] Again, we need to ask not just whether the parent is too involved, but what form the involvement takes and what's motivating it.

At School

When you're truly focused on what's in your kids' best interests—and willing to question the conventional wisdom—you may end up over-turning some very popular assumptions about the nature of success. Take grades. Even many thoughtful and respectful parents have accepted on faith that it's a good sign when kids get good grades. They're therefore delighted to see their children doing so. Even before taking a hard look at the methods that some parents use to make children work toward that goal, however, I want to sound a note of caution about the whole idea of grades.

My concerns are based on the fact that there are different kinds of motivation, which aren't equally desirable (see pp. 33–34). There's a huge difference between a student whose objective is to get a good grade and a student whose objective is to solve a problem or understand a story. What's more, the research suggests that when kids are encouraged to focus on getting better marks in school, three things tend to happen: They lose interest in the learning itself, they try to avoid tasks that are challenging, and they're less likely to think deeply and critically.[7] Let's explore each of these.

1. Just as children who are rewarded for their generosity usually end up being less generous, so students who get A's—or, more to the point, students whose main goal is to get A's—are apt to become less interested in what they're learning. This doesn't

happen with every child; some seem to have a natural immunity to the destructive effects of grades. But the risk is very high for most children. As far as I know, every single study that has looked at this question has found that students who are told that an assignment will be graded are less likely to enjoy what they're doing—and to want to come back to it on their own time—as compared with students who do the exact same assignment but without any mention of grades. Even a terrific story, or an exciting science project, quickly becomes less appealing when it's construed as something you have to get through to snag the A or 100 or gold star. The more a child is thinking about grades, the more likely it is that his or her natural curiosity about the world will start to evaporate.

2. Grades lead students to pick the easiest possible assignment when they're given a choice. Impress upon them that what they're doing "counts" toward a grade, and their response will likely be to avoid taking any unnecessary risks. It doesn't take kids long to figure out that doing easier tasks is the surest route to better results. They'll choose a shorter book, or an essay on a more familiar topic, in order to minimize the chance of doing poorly. This doesn't mean they're "unmotivated" or that they're being lazy. It means they're being rational. They're responding to adults who, by telling them the goal is to get a good grade, are sending the message that *success matters more than learning*. One study found that parents who valued achievement above other goals were more likely to want their children to choose projects "that would involve a minimum of struggle and likely result in success" rather than those "where they'll learn a lot of new things but also make a lot of mistakes."[8] By contrast, when parents make it clear that learning (and excitement about learning) is more important than the quality of the product, kids are more inclined to stretch themselves, to tackle something interesting and new, even if they're not sure how well they'll end up doing.

3. A quest for good grades often leads students to think in a more shallow and superficial way. They may skim books for what they'll "need to know," doing just what's required and no more. They may devise tricks for acing the exam. They may even cheat. Kids who are good at playing the game will pass the test, get the A, and please the parents. But do they end up remembering what they were taught? Do they come up with new and inventive ways of solving problems? Do they ask thoughtful questions about what the teacher said, or think critically about what was in the book? Do they make connections between diverse ideas and look at a topic from different angles? Sometimes, perhaps, they do, but the research says these things are less likely to happen if the point is not so much to understand as to produce a glowing report card. The title of one scholarly article about rewards in general is a good description of grades in particular: "Enemies of Exploration."

In sum: The more we want our children to (1) be lifelong learners, genuinely excited about words and numbers and ideas, (2) avoid sticking with what's easy and safe, and (3) become sophisticated thinkers, the more we should do everything possible to help them forget about grades. Better yet, we'd want to encourage teachers and principals to minimize (or even eliminate) the use of grades. As someone who works with educators all over the country, I can tell you that many of the schools that are truly committed to high-quality learning—and to ensuring that students don't lose their natural *love* of learning—make a point of avoiding letter and number grades altogether. They find more informative and less destructive methods, such as written summaries or personal conversations, for letting parents know how well their children are doing and where they might need help. And, no, these students don't have any trouble getting into college as a result of the absence of grades.

Such schools are still in the minority, of course. Most continue to rely on traditional report cards, and it's understandable that parents would feel reassured by good ones and worried about bad ones. We're swept along with the tide. We want our kids to get good grades because that seems to be the best indicator of school success, and also because few of us have ever been told about the destructive effects of grades—or the alternatives to them. What's more, *we* were rated and graded when we were in school. But that just makes it more important to understand the potential harms of a practice we've come to take for granted, and to realize that the important question isn't what grade our kids get, but whether they've come to see grades as more important than learning.

Grades by themselves are problematic. But when we really push our kids to get better grades—in effect, taking a flawed goal and marrying it to a flawed method—the damage is doubled.

The evidence is pretty clear that too much control *in general* can have a negative impact, not only on children's mental health but also on how well they do in school. Kids are less likely to succeed on a range of measures of classroom achievement if their parents don't give them much opportunity to make decisions or to feel a sense of self-determination.[9] It's also clear that too much parental control *specifically related to school assignments* is potentially damaging. That conclusion emerged from the study showing that kids end up learning less well when their parents use a controlling style while doing homework with them (p. 60).

But now let's add that control *specifically related to grades* is also bad. Some parents promise children anything from candy to cash to cars when they bring home a good report card. (Since grades themselves are usually designed to function as extrinsic motivators, this amounts to offering a reward for a reward.) Some parents use punitive control, threatening their children with various unpleasant things if the news from school isn't good. Two different studies have proved that these tactics at best don't help and at worst exacerbate the problem. Specifically, children who were offered incentives for good grades or given consequences for bad grades tended to become less interested in learning and, as a result, less likely to do well in school later on, apparently as a direct result of these parental interventions. In fact, the more that achievement was the parent's chief concern, the lower was the child's achievement.[10]

This paradox, of course, is strikingly similar to the way that heavy-handed discipline techniques can make children less likely to do what they're told. In both situations, we're witnessing the way that control tends to backfire. In the case of grades, the research is just confirming something that many of us have seen. You push kids hard—say, to do their homework—and often they'll try to salvage their autonomy either through outright rebellion or through a kind of passive resistance: They forget, they whine, they put off studying and find other things to do. The more you lecture them about the importance of good grades, or rely on carrots and sticks to make it worth their while to get them, the more they resent being controlled and the lower their grades fall.

What's troubling about this is not that kids may end up with lower grades. After all, I've been arguing that grades aren't terribly mean-ingful. Rather, what ought to concern us is the possibility that kids may fight back against the pressure to do better in school by investing less effort, with the result that they actually *learn* less. Never mind dis-appointing report cards: If we push children too hard, they may wind up doing less (or poorer quality) thinking.

Of course, there's a chance that coercion will carry the day, that when we tighten the screws, some kids may hit the books and bring up their grades exactly as we intended. We might even succeed in get-ting them into the college of our—excuse me, their—choice. But again, exactly as with discipline, there's usually a steep price to be paid for such victories. What has our intervention done to the way kids feel about themselves, and about us? What does the stress do to their emo-tional health? And what about their *interest* in reading and thinking? If grades by themselves can make learning seem like a chore, just imag-ine how that effect is multiplied by the addition of parental pressure to improve those grades.

"I don't hear parents discussing how to help children love reading," one New York teacher observes. "I hear them discussing how they got these children to read at as young an age as possible."[11] And those backward priorities have effects that are both predictable and persistent. For example, a friend of mine who counsels students in Florida once told me about a high school client of his who was on the honor roll and had amazing board scores. It remained only to knock out a dazzling essay on his college applications that would clinch the sale. "Why don't we start with some books that had an impact on you," suggested the counselor. "Tell me about something you've read for pleasure—not for an assignment." A painful silence followed. There were no books to be listed; the very concept of reading for pleasure was unfamiliar to this stellar student. I have told this story during lectures to parents and educators, only to see heads nodding all over the auditorium. In many places, such students are the rule rather than the exception. Why would they want to read something that wasn't required? No grade? No test? No point.

Ironically, some parents are pleased when they no longer have to stand behind their kids, goading, exhorting, pushing them to try harder. At some point the children internalize these pressures and, so to speak, take the whip into their own hands. They feel something is wrong with them when they don't succeed. By now, the motivation to study and achieve is *internal*, but it surely isn't *intrinsic*. They do it on their own, but it doesn't feel freely chosen—and it doesn't feel joyful. That kind of internalization is something we ought to fear and strive to prevent. After all, the curiosity that bubbles up out of young children doesn't disappear naturally, like baby teeth. Rather, it's smothered by specific things that happen—things that don't have to happen—in families and schools.

So: Grades are bad, and using controlling techniques to make kids focus on bringing up their grades is worse. Worst of all, though, is when those controlling techniques add up to conditional parenting.

Some parents don't offer money for straight A's; instead, they pay off their kids with affection and approval. In effect, they're using their love as a lever to get their kids to succeed—to the point that their children may come to feel as though their parents' positive feelings for them rise and fall with their grade point average.

The situation is particularly ominous when love seems to be "contingent upon meeting very high and often unrealistic standards," as one researcher put it. When children feel they must keep doing impressive things so their parents will be proud of them, their acceptance of themselves may become equally conditional. "Some of these kids live in constant fear of letting their parents down," observes Lilian Katz, an expert on early-childhood education. In fact, a new study finds that children whose parents use love-withdrawal techniques are especially likely to harbor an unhealthy fear of failure. (Interestingly, the study also suggests that the parents' decision to use these techniques may be related to their own fear of failure.)[12]

Apart from being psychologically destructive, this pattern can be literally counterproductive, undermining (once again) exactly what the parents had hoped to promote. For example, some children engage in what's known as "self-handicapping": They cease to make an effort in order to create an excuse for not succeeding. This lets them preserve the idea that they're smart. They're able to tell themselves that if they *had* studied, they might have done incredibly well. The more vulnerable their sense of self-worth, the more tempting the urge is to protect it by just giving up. To put this another way, by handicapping their performance they increase the chances of failing, but they do so to avoid having to think of themselves as failures—and therefore as being unworthy of love.

At "Play"

In some families, success is more about athletics than about academics. But the pressure to achieve that success—along with the costs—

isn't all that different. Wendy Grolnick, whose research on parental control I've already described, has been struck not only by the results of her scientific studies but also by what she sees around town. She tells a story, for example, of chatting with a boy's mother at a swim meet one day and noticing the woman's use of the plural, as in "We decided we would swim this year," even though she clearly wasn't talking about getting in the water herself. Her son climbed out of the pool right about then and walked over to her, obviously upset, saying that he had had enough of competition. The mother made a visible effort to maintain her composure, glanced around to see if anyone was listening, and informed him he was going to continue swimming whether he liked it or not. When the boy protested, she said, "If you don't swim today, it's over. You are not going to do this to me again." The boy began to sob miserably.[13]

Anyone who has spent time at ballparks, soccer fields, or hockey rinks has similar stories to tell of appalling parental behavior. Dads and moms who scream at referees, at coaches, at opposing teams, even at their own children are everywhere, it seems; the problem has become endemic. But more telling, perhaps, are the parents who use a lighter touch, those who make a point of announcing that winning doesn't really matter that much. They recoil from the behavior of that abusive parent down the block, but they nevertheless manage to make clear to their children that participation in competitive sports is expected. And so is success.

Following some of my lectures, I've had parents seek me out to emphasize that "we only ask of our Zach that he do his best." My first reaction is that having to do your best at a game is a far cry from simply having fun. My second reaction is that it's often perfectly clear to Zach that something else is going on underneath these soothing assurances. I want to ask: "When Zach comes home and says he did his best, do you react the same way as when he comes home with a trophy? If not, then he's probably figured out that your attention and excitement depend at least partly on his achievement—or, more precisely, on his defeating other kids." It doesn't matter whether we're talking about a trophy or an A, about scoring the winning goal or making the honor roll. The point is that kids in such families feel they must succeed in order to be loved.

In extreme cases, we find parents who need their children to triumph so that they themselves can feel successful. But even people who aren't like that, even those who pride themselves on not getting carried away, may want to rethink their everyday behavior and weigh what they're doing against what they want for their children in the long run. Are our goals likely to be achieved if we push our kids to succeed? If they're doing it mostly for us? If it's not really fun but they're afraid to say so?

Many years ago, I was a guest on a well-known afternoon talk show. Sitting alongside me was a seven-year-old boy named Kyle whose parents were devoting most of their time, as well as an inconceivable amount of money, to the project of making him into a tennis star. His mother insisted that it was entirely the boy's decision to play—even though she herself was a tennis star and his intensive lessons had started when he was two. (Later, she slipped and said something about why she and her husband had "put him" in tennis as opposed to another sport.) We learned that he practiced between two and five hours a day, and we watched a tape of him energetically returning serves and scampering around the court. Then, in the final moments of the program, as the closing credits were crawling up the screen, someone in the audience asked Kyle how he felt when he lost. He lowered his head and, in a small voice, replied, "Ashamed."

This quiet, one-word reply comes back to me as I think about the consequences of pushing children. Few parents go to the lengths that Kyle's did, thank goodness, but the shame he felt in losing, in letting down the people who were expecting, if not demanding, results from him, will be familiar to plenty of children in our own neighborhoods.

Perhaps part of the problem is with tennis itself and other sports. Just as there are better ways to communicate about children's school performance than giving letter grades, so I believe there are better ways for kids to have fun (and get exercise and acquire physical skills) than by playing games in which one person can succeed only by making someone else fail.[14] However, even parents who aren't inclined to consider those alternatives might want to ask whether their children regard sports as something closer to work than to play—and, if so, why.

The Little Engine That Must

In the early 1980s, as I began what turned out to be a multiyear investigation of the effects of competition, I had a few hunches about what I might discover. I guessed the data would show that competing wasn't good for our psychological health or for our relationships. I was right. But I also expected to find evidence confirming what I'd always heard was true—that competition "motivates" many people to do their best. Therefore, the *absence* of competition might be associated with lower levels of achievement at work and at school. The trade-off, then, would be that we'd have to give up some excellence in order to have healthier, happier people.

Boy, was I wrong. The research overwhelmingly showed that competition holds people back from working or learning at their best. For a variety of reasons, optimal performance at most tasks not only doesn't require people to try to beat one another—it requires that they be freed from such an arrangement. There is no trade-off. Cooperation makes more sense than competition if we care mostly about bottom-line results, just as it does if our prime concern is how people feel about themselves and those around them.

I mention this now because the same sort of trade-off is sometimes believed to exist with respect to unconditional parenting. The argument goes like this: When we know that we'll receive approval only when we work hard or produce results, then we'll be inclined to do just that. By contrast, as one group of psychologists asked rhetorically, "If people were unconditionally loved in all domains of life, would they still be as driven to succeed?"[15]

It's an important question, and I want to respond to it in four ways. First, even if this line of thinking did make sense, it probably would apply only to adults. Children need to be loved unconditionally. Again, assuming that it's a good thing for *anyone* to feel accepted only when he or she is successful, it would seem important to start out in life with a secure foundation that comes from having been accepted without any strings attached.

Second, it's worth asking what, exactly, is supposed to be the basis for deciding whether or not to value someone. "Working hard" and "producing results" are actually two very different things. If we demand results, then what do we do about people who give it their all but, for various reasons—many of them outside their control—don't end up reaching their goal? If, instead, our approval is based on hard work, the problem is that this can't always be measured. One person may have tried harder even though another worked for a longer time. It ends up seeming pretty silly to try to fine-tune love or acceptance to match something as intangible as effort.

Third, even if conditional approval did produce results, we find ourselves once again having to consider all the hidden costs—that is, the broader, deeper, and longer-lasting effects of a strategy that, at first glance, seems to work. Even if there were a trade-off, the downside of conditional acceptance almost certainly outweighs the upside of getting more things done. That downside is disturbingly clear from the research described in chapters 1 and 2. For example, even if those college students really did study harder in a desperate effort to win their parents' affection (pp. 21–22 and 57–58), few of us would say it's worth the price of having them come to resent their parents and to feel guilty and unhappy and unfree. If people were unconditionally loved, would they still be as driven to succeed? Anyone who understands what it means to be driven would reply, "Let's hope not!"

But just because people aren't driven doesn't mean they're not successful. This, then, is my fourth and final response: As with competition, it turns out there really isn't a trade-off at all because conditional acceptance usually *doesn't* work, even to reach the limited goal of higher achievement. At best, its effectiveness is limited to some people, at some tasks, on some occasions.

Those who believe otherwise have made a number of mistaken assumptions. For starters, they've assumed that people who are raised to believe they're basically competent have no reason to accomplish anything. I once heard someone defend that belief by declaring that "human nature is to do as little as necessary." This prejudice is refuted not just by a few studies but by the entire branch of psychology dealing with motivation.[16] Normally, it's hard to *stop* happy, satisfied people from trying to learn more about themselves and the world, or from trying to do a job of which they can feel proud. The desire to do as little as possible is an aberration, a sign that something is wrong. It may suggest that someone feels threatened and therefore has fallen back on a strategy of damage control, or that rewards and punishments have caused that individual to lose interest in what he's doing, or that he perceives a specific task—perhaps correctly—as pointless and dull.

Suppose, for example, a child does "as little as necessary" in school. This, as we've seen, might prove to be an example of self-handicapping. (She's been made to feel stupid, so she stops making any effort in order to convince herself that she would have succeeded if she *had* tried.) Or it might be the fallout from extrinsic motivators: She's chasing a good grade and realizes she's more likely to get one by sticking with things she already knows. Or it might be because, instead of learning meaningful things, she's required to complete yet another boring worksheet or to read yet another chapter of a dreary textbook. Undoubtedly we could come up with other explanations for why she's doing as little as she can get away with, and every one of those explanations would raise questions about what's going on in her classroom or her family. There's simply no justification for assuming her response is an inevitable result of "human nature."

As I've already pointed out, children who are unconditionally loved are more likely to accept *themselves* unconditionally. But that would worry us only if we confused positive self-regard with arrogant self-

satisfaction. Someone who has a core of faith in himself and an underlying conviction that he's a good person doesn't thereby become more
likely to sit around and do nothing. There's not a shred of evidence
that unconditional self-esteem promotes laziness, or that to have high
standards you must feel lousy about yourself for failing to meet them.
To the contrary, people who know they're loved irrespective of their
accomplishments often end up accomplishing quite a lot. Being
accepted without conditions helps them to develop a healthy confidence in themselves, a sense that it's safe to take risks and try new
things. From deep contentment comes the courage to achieve.

This speaks directly to another, closely related set of assumptions
made by people who defend the idea of conditional acceptance. They
seem to think that the anxious energy of perpetual self-doubt is
required to get things done, that the fear of failing motivates people
to improve. Again, it is difficult to imagine a point of view more at
variance with everything we know about motivation and learning. We
may *want* children to rebound from failure, but that doesn't mean they
will. The more likely result, all things being equal, is that they'll expect
to do poorly on similar tasks in the future. This expectation can set a
self-fulfilling prophecy into motion: They feel incompetent and even
helpless, and that leads them to act in ways that prove them right.
Also, they come to prefer easier tasks, and to be less interested in whatever they're doing.[17] Even those exceptional kids who really do buckle
down and try harder when they fail may be doing so out of an anxious, compulsive pressure to feel better about themselves rather than
because they enjoy learning. Thus, even if they manage to understand
what they're reading today, they may not *want* to read tomorrow.

It's a very simple and very obvious truth once you think about it:
Being afraid of failing isn't at all the same thing as embracing success.
In fact, the former gets in the way of the latter. We've already seen considerable evidence that conditional parenting and conditional self-esteem
are unhealthy. Now we have to add that they're also unproductive. They
lead to "emotion-focused coping and repair of the self, rather than
problem-focused coping," as two researchers pointed out. In other

words, you're so busy trying to deal with the implications of failing that you don't have the time and energy to do what it takes to succeed.

Even apart from this practical problem, these researchers went on to remark, the idea that we should raise children to feel good about themselves only when they've earned that right by being successful seems to imply that "some children's low self-esteem is warranted and that children who do not achieve in socially desirable ways, such as getting good grades . . . or being good at sports, rightly believe that they are not worthy human beings."[18]

Like other toxic messages that children hear, this one sometimes comes from their teachers, coaches, and peers, to say nothing of the mass media and the larger culture in which they live. But there is no getting around the fact that the pressure to do well—or, worse, to out-perform others—typically begins at home. In any case, it falls to us as their parents to counteract those pressures, to challenge those messages of conditional acceptance, and to make sure our kids feel loved no matter what.

6

WHAT HOLDS US BACK?

Everything up to this point leads us to one overwhelming question: Why do we do it? If conditional and control-based parenting are really as bad as I say they are—and, more important, if they're as bad as scientific research and real-world experience show they are—then why are they so popular? Or, to put it differently, what holds so many of us back from being better parents?

Perhaps you're eager at this point to hear more about the alternatives. But specific suggestions for doing this thing or saying that thing to our kids are unlikely to take root and have a real impact if we haven't addressed the reasons that we've been tempted to do things differently for so long. To redo what we do, we have to rethink what we think. And that means we have to figure out the sources of a parenting style that's traditional and conditional. If we skip that step, we'll just come up with reasons to dismiss any new ideas, or, even if we do try them, we may find ourselves reverting to what feels comfortably familiar as soon as we hit a bump in the road.

The reasons we parent as we do might be said to fall roughly into four categories: what we see and hear, what we believe, what we feel, and, as a result of all of those, what we fear. These labels aren't terribly precise, and the explanations themselves overlap. Still, we can begin to make sense of current parenting styles by first investigating the influences on our behaviors that are right on the surface. Then we can proceed to look at some relevant beliefs and cultural norms that underlie those influences. Finally, we can turn our attention to how our needs and fears—shaped largely by how *we* were raised—influence the way we interact with our own children.

What We See and Hear

Are there any parents who haven't been a little startled at some point to hear themselves saying to their kids exactly the same thing—sometimes in exactly the same tone of voice—that their parents used to say to them? I call this "How did my mother get in my larynx?" It's the most obvious explanation for why we treat our children as we do: We learned how you're supposed to raise kids from watching how someone raised us. We may have picked up specific rules (no running in the house; no dessert until you've finished your dinner) and even specific expressions ("How many times do I have to tell you . . . ?" "Fine, but don't come crying to me when you . . ."). More important, we probably picked up a general understanding of what the parent's role is— that is, how a mom or dad is supposed to act around the kids.

The less aware we are of that learning process, the more likely we are to reproduce parenting patterns without bothering to ask whether they make sense. It takes some effort, some sharp thinking, even some courage to step back and decide which values and rituals ought to find a place in our new families and which ones are pointless or even pernicious. Otherwise, we just end up following a script that we had no part in writing. We become like the wall-building neighbor in Robert Frost's poem who "moves in darkness" because "he will not go behind his father's saying." In short, we should be able to answer the question "Why do you do that with your child?" by offering a reason rather than having to shrug and mutter, "Well, that's the way *I* was raised."

Making it even more difficult for many parents to choose a different path is that *their* parents (and in-laws) may still be influencing them, offering explicit judgments and suggestions about how children ought to be treated. Friends, too, and even strangers are often eager to volunteer their advice, as are newspaper columnists, talk-show hosts, and authors of discipline books. So are pediatricians, whose biases and hunches about psychological issues are taken seriously just because of their medical credentials. I recently received an e-mail message from a pediatrician (and mother) who told me that, after reading about the destructive effects of reward-and-punishment discipline, she found herself

> frustrated that none of this had been in my [medical] training. We were taught the standard behaviorist stuff, time-out, etc.— and even though I knew deep down that it didn't seem right somehow, I couldn't put my finger on why. I had parents of children that I saw from infancy coming back with their five-year-olds, saying "it just doesn't work." For a while I thought we just had to use a different method of behavior modification. [But as I began to read more], I couldn't believe we had fallen for such an awful way of raising children.

If all the advice we received from doctors, neighbors, and family members reflected a wide variety of opinions, these bits of wisdom would likely conflict with one another and perhaps cancel each other out. We'd be left relatively unaffected (unless, of course, we were more affected by our relatives). But what we hear from diverse sources really isn't all that diverse. There are exceptions here and there, but generally the advice we get tends to push in one direction. And it's precisely the direction I'm suggesting we need to question.

New parents frequently report, for example, that the grandparents are likely to warn them—falsely, according to all the available research—that babies will be spoiled if they're picked up as soon as they cry. And if a child is allowed to participate in making decisions about matters that concern her, parents may be sternly informed that "this kid has you wrapped around her finger."

Friends and neighbors, depending on their personalities, may be overt or subtle in the way they express it, but they, too, are likely to think that you need to get tough with your child when he's out of line; they're likely to believe that your problems would be solved by more discipline and "limit-setting." In public places you can even feel the judgment radiating from strangers—typically for being too lenient, rarely for being too controlling. And even if all those other people kept their opinions to themselves, the way we see them raising their own children is a powerful influence, especially when we witness the same basic style day after day in place after place. The sheer pervasiveness of the traditional approach may lead us to assume that so many parents can't be wrong.

Nor do most authors of discipline books help to correct this imbalance, as I pointed out earlier. Thus, when we look to the experts for advice, we're likely to have our assumptions reaffirmed. If they—and the people we know—challenged us instead, if they asked whether we're sure that what we're doing reflects unconditional love for our children, if they reminded us that punishments and rewards are unproductive and unnecessary, then we might well think twice about what we're doing. As things stand, we're offered little reason to think even once.

To point to what we see and hear as an explanation for why many of us continue to interact with our children in less than desirable ways is plausible as far as it goes, but it just sets the question back a step. "Okay," you reply, "so we're influenced by all those other people. But why do they treat *their* kids the way they do? What drives so many parents to choose—and recommend—this approach?"

Intrinsic features of the worst kind of discipline may supply part of the answer. Even very thoughtful people can get hooked into doing things that don't make sense. First of all, bad discipline is easy. Very little is asked of us when we respond to children's misbehavior by doing something unpleasant to them. "Doing to" strategies are mostly mindless. "Working with" strategies, on the other hand, ask a lot more of us. And, of course, if we're not even familiar with the latter, we may persist with the former just because we don't know what else to do.

Second, bad discipline can be "effective." By this I mean that there are plenty of situations in which bribes or threats or other coercive interventions can make a child obey an adult for the time being. "You can forget about going to that party on Saturday if you don't shut off that video game right now!" may well succeed in getting the game turned off. Meanwhile, the cumulative negative impact of all the times we've resorted to such a strategy isn't always immediately obvious. Therefore we don't see a downside that would make us hesitate about doing it again.

What We Believe

The immediate consequences, or surface appeal, of traditional approaches to raising children can explain a lot, as can the influence of the people around us. But I think we also have to consider some widely shared beliefs and values that make people more receptive to those approaches.

HOW WE REGARD CHILDREN

Are we really a child-friendly society? Naturally, each of us loves his or her own offspring, but it's often startling to see how many parents are downright disdainful of other people's kids. When we add the folks who aren't parents at all, it becomes even clearer that our culture isn't especially supportive of children in general, nor is there a surfeit of fondness for particular children unless they're cute and well behaved. If there's any collective affection, it's conditional at best. Indeed, surveys of American adults consistently find what one newspaper report called "a stunning level of antagonism not just toward teen-agers but toward young children as well." Substantial majorities of our fellow citizens say they disapprove of kids of all ages, calling them rude, lazy, irresponsible, and lacking in basic values.[1]

Politicians and businesspeople make a show of demanding "world-class" schools, but that usually refers to high test scores and the preparation of suitably skilled employees rather than to meeting the needs of the children who attend these schools. It's true, as two social scientists point out, that "some parents—those who have enough income—spend lavishly on their children, generating the notion that we are a child-centered society"—an impression that may be reinforced by how children are conspicuously targeted by advertisers and entertainment conglomerates. However, these authors continue,

> public spending for children is often meager and always surrounded by contention, and it embodies the peculiar conception that children are not valuable as persons in their own right but only for the adults they will grow up to be. . . . The saccharine myth [that] . . . children are [America's] most precious natural resources has in practice been falsified by our hostility to other people's children and our unwillingness to support them.[2]

During any (recent) given year, more than 1.3 million children are homeless in the United States. Between 22 and 26 percent of young children are classified as poor, which is far higher than the rates in other industrialized societies.[3] Americans continue to tolerate the real suffering that lies behind these statistics, and this speaks to our attitude toward children as surely as does the number of people who grouse about "these kids today."

Here's the point: If children in general aren't held in great esteem, it becomes easier for parents, even basically good parents, to treat their own kids disrespectfully. And to the extent that we ourselves harbor a dim view of children, we may be less likely, as I suggested in chapter 1, to offer unconditional love to any child, even our own, since we fear they'll just take advantage and try to get away with as much as they can. If you don't trust them, you go out of your way to control them. It's not a coincidence that authoritarian parents, who demand absolute obedience, also tend to attribute unflattering characteristics to children—and sometimes to people in general. A study of more than three hundred parents found that those who held a negative view of human nature were likely to be very controlling with their kids.[4]

HOW WE THINK CHILDREN ARE TREATED

I argued earlier that children are far less likely to be allowed to run wild than to be restricted unnecessarily, yelled at, threatened, or bullied by their parents. This, however, is not the conventional view. It's more common to ignore the epidemic of punitive parenting and focus instead on the occasional example of permissiveness—sometimes even to the point of pronouncing an entire generation spoiled. It's revealing, and even somewhat amusing, that similar alarms probably have been raised about *every* generation throughout recorded history.

But this distorted portrait has serious consequences. To create the impression that kids today are out of control is to lay the groundwork for advice about how we need to stop indulging them, return to more traditional discipline, and so on. Parents who accept that description (of kids who are insufficiently controlled) are more receptive to this *pre*scription (for more control).

Exactly the same is true of the complaint that kids have it too easy these days because we go overboard in trying to shelter them from the hard knocks of life. This claim is typically supported by entertaining anecdotes rather than by anything resembling evidence. It seems to flourish less because it's true than because it's useful for justifying an old-fashioned form of parenting that isn't particularly supportive or nourishing. Furthermore, this way of framing the problem invites us to blame parents or kids rather than investigating the deeper causes of problems we all face.[5]

The fact that some kids are ignored, left to their own devices, and deprived of meaningful interaction with adults doesn't constitute proof that we live in a child-centered or indulgent culture, nor does it mean that kids experience too little frustration in their lives. Actually, children are plenty frustrated, in large part because their points of view aren't taken seriously. Parents who seem oblivious to how their children are annoying strangers and getting into mischief are often equally oblivious to their children's needs. That's an argument not for more discipline, but for grown-ups to spend more time with kids, to give them more guidance, and to treat them with more respect.

COMPETITION

It's been said that competition is our state religion. At work and at play, at school, and even at home, other goals and values are frequently eclipsed by the constant imperative to be Number One. It's no surprise, then, to find so many parents pushing their children to outshine their peers—and using the techniques of conditional parenting to try to make that happen.

Moreover, the relationships we have with our children may come to be seen in zero-sum terms. Numerous discipline books offer guidance on how to win our battles with them, how to outmaneuver them and get them to comply with our demands, thereby allowing us to emerge triumphant. The real question, of course, is whether we really want to see our kids as opponents to be beaten. If we wonder why parent-child relationships are so often adversarial, we have to understand this as one more symptom of a hypercompetitive society. The moms and dads who are most likely to try to control their children, and who do the most damage to them, are those who need to win.

CAPABILITIES OF CHILDREN

Treating children harshly seems to imply that we don't appreciate all that they can do, that we don't see them as people with their own distinctive points of view. But in another, more important sense, those who rely on traditional discipline have a tendency to *over*estimate what children can manage on their own. Such parents don't understand—or else they just ignore—how kids below a certain age simply can't be expected to eat neatly or keep quiet in a public place. Young children don't yet possess the skills that would make it sensible to hold them accountable for their behavior in the same way that we hold an adult or even an older child accountable.

Research confirms that parents who "attribute greater competence and responsibility to misbehaving children" are more likely to get upset with them, to condemn and punish them. They become frustrated by what they see as inappropriate behavior, and they respond, in effect, by cracking down on little kids for being little kids. It can be heartbreaking to watch. By contrast, parents who understand children's developmental limitations tend to prefer "calm explanation and reasoning" in response to the same actions.[6] They know their job is to teach—and, to some extent, just to be patient.

Parents who berate their children and rely on coercive measures, then, may be doing so partly because they hold unrealistically high expectations with respect to behavior. Similarly unrealistic expectations sometimes show up in the realm of intellectual proficiency. Pushing a five-year-old to spell correctly usually suggests a failure to understand the predictable way that children gradually come to master language, and it has the effect of turning writing into an unpleasant experience for them. In general, many parents who pride themselves on holding "high standards" for their kids may in fact expect too much of them—and may then make things worse by resorting to various tactics of control when their expectations aren't met.

CONFORMITY

The more that people in a culture want children to conform to traditional rules and authority (as opposed to thinking for themselves), the more likely, according to research, that they will use corporal punishment. The United States has often been described as a place where people value self-reliance and self-directedness, even to a fault. But here, too, some individuals and subcultures continue to prize conformity. The more this is true in a given family, the more those parents will restrict their children and employ strict discipline to rein them in.[7]

JUSTICE AS RETRIBUTION

Lots of people believe that when any individual, even a small child, does something bad, then something bad should be done to that individual in return. "The idea of making an offender suffer for his crime can be traced to the 'blood vengeance' practices of primitive societies."[8] It's also related to an economic model of human interaction that makes us think everything, including love, must be earned (pp. 17–19). Never mind whether punishment works, whether it teaches any desirable lessons or has any constructive effects on children's values or behaviors. Many parents continue to use it because they see punishment as a moral imperative. Indeed, you have to swim against the tide in our culture if you choose to respond to children's misbehavior in any way other than by imposing an unpleasant consequence.

RELIGION

There's no one-to-one correspondence between religious convictions and parenting philosophy. People of various faiths, and people who are not religious at all, can be found treating children in every conceivable way. Still, there's no denying that an authoritarian approach has deep roots in certain religious belief systems. Says one expert, "Breaking the child's will has been the central task given parents by successive generations of preachers, whose biblically based rationales for discipline have reflected the belief that self-will is evil and sinful."[9] This ideology, ultimately connected to a dark view of human nature, has been prescribed from before the time the Pilgrims landed right through the current writings of James Dobson and other fundamentalists. Sometimes the word *love* is used to justify a grim process of forcing the child to capitulate.[10]

Further, while many religious people equate the idea of unconditionality with aspects of their faith, a case could be made, drawing on the holy books of Christianity and Judaism, that the deities in these religions offer the ultimate in *conditional* love. Both the Old and New Testaments repeatedly promise extravagant rewards for those who are properly reverent, and horrific punishments for those who aren't. God loves you if and only if you love Him—and, in some cases, if you meet various other criteria. Do what you're told; you'll become rich and get to watch your enemies die. Stray from the faith; you'll suffer a range of consequences, which the Bible describes in almost sadistic detail.[11] And for some believers, of course, even more significant blessings or curses await us after death. It's not a stretch, then, to see the relevance of certain religious traditions to both conditional and control-based parenting.

EITHER/OR THINKING

If I had to identify a single belief system that most prominently drives the use of questionable parenting strategies, it would be the tendency to assume there are only two ways to raise children. You can do this or you can do that, and since one option is obviously unappealing, you're left with the other (which invariably involves some kind of control).

The most popular false dichotomy runs as follows: "We need to take a hard line with kids and stop letting them do anything they feel like." In effect, traditional discipline is contrasted with permissiveness. Either I punish my child or else I let her "get away with" whatever she did. Either I take a hard line or I draw no line at all. When kids do something inappropriate, most of us feel a need to take *some* action rather than doing nothing. Therefore, if our repertoire is limited to punishment, that's what we end up doing by default.

Paradoxically, neglecting and punishing aren't even really opposites. Both share the feature of offering absolutely no productive, respectful adult guidance of the sort that kids need. No wonder we find that some parents are punitive *and* neglectful, by turns. Once one of these choices proves disastrous, they swing to the other. As one mother confessed, "I'm permissive with my kids until I can't stand them; then I get so authoritarian that I can't stand myself."[12] In other families, meanwhile, each parent plays one of the two roles. One is the disciplinarian and the other is permissive—as though two flawed strategies somehow add up to a productive approach.

If we were forced to choose between them, it's not even clear from the available evidence that punishment is better than neglect.[13] But we *don't* have to choose, because there are other possibilities. The fact that freezing cold temperatures are uncomfortable doesn't mean we have to put up with boiling heat. And that point also applies, incidentally, to another artificial choice: "Instead of punishing (or criticizing) kids when they're bad, try rewarding (or praising) them when they're good." The problem is that rewards and punishments are really just two sides of the same coin . . . and that coin doesn't buy very much. Fortunately, there are alternatives to either version of carrot-and-stick manipulation.

In theory, it would be better to choose from among three alternatives rather than only two, but here, too, we must be careful. A number of writers on discipline and other issues try to make their views seem more palatable by positioning themselves as the reasonable "middle ground" between two extremes. Call it the Goldilocks Gambit: Some approaches are too this, some approaches are too that, but my approach is just right. The "this" position is usually some sort of extremely punitive, power-based parenting, while the "that" position is a variant of loosey-goosey, anything-goes neglect.

In the abstract, most of us would agree that something in between those extremes would be better—and on some issues, I indeed recommend a "third way." But we should never be talked into accepting someone's suggestions just because they're placed between caricatured alternatives. Moreover, some writers may be starting with a question based on a dubious premise, such as "How much should we control our children?" Pick one: (a) constantly and excessively, (b) not at all, or (c) the ideal amount, as explained in the author's copyrighted five-point program. Rather than picking the obvious choice, we may want to challenge the way the issue has been framed and consider alternatives to the whole idea of control.

In fact, the "reasonable middle ground" option may not be all that reasonable when evaluated on its merits. One example in the discipline field is Diana Baumrind's schema, which has been adopted by lots of researchers as well as practitioners. She describes parenting as being "authoritarian" on one side, "permissive" on the other, or "authoritative" (read: just right) in the middle. In reality, her favored approach, supposedly a blend of firmness and caring, is actually quite traditional and control-oriented—even if less so than option 1. In fact, a close reading of Baumrind's research raises questions about the recommendations she offers, particularly her endorsement of "firm control."[14]

The larger point is that we may be tempted to accept a certain approach just because of how the discussion about parenting has been framed, and specifically because we believe that rejecting one or two other approaches requires us to embrace a given alternative. To recognize that there are many possible ways of raising children, and to question the validity of various other ideologies, is to free us to explore new directions that may end up making a lot more sense than the conventional wisdom.

What We Feel

Our parents taught us how to parent, showing by example how to talk with and be with children. But what we experienced in our families of origin has an impact on us, and therefore on what kinds of mothers and fathers we become, that transcends any specific child-rearing strategies that we may end up recycling. Bringing up kids isn't just a skill one acquires, like cooking or carpentry; the psychological forces involved make these issues much more complicated. And many of those forces may operate without our even being aware of them.

Frankly, I hesitate to delve into these matters because many such discussions, replete with earnest references to one's "inner child" and such, set my teeth on edge. But I can't see any way around it. It's pointless to talk about what holds you back from being a better parent without reflecting on how the way you were raised shapes your internal architecture. It affects not only what you do with your kids, but what you don't do. It has an impact on how you divide responsibilities with your co-parent, and whether you treat boys and girls differently. It helps to determine whether your everyday behavior conveys a basic respect or disrespect for children. It's related to what makes you angry or sad and how you express those feelings.

Granted, fancy psychological explanations aren't always necessary to account for the bad choices we make as parents. Sometimes we lose our patience just because children require so much of it: They can be loud, messy, and self-centered. As I noted at the beginning of this book, raising kids isn't for wimps, and some kids are tougher to raise than others. Still, the fact that this particular child is a real handful simply isn't sufficient to explain why his parents use love-withdrawal techniques or other instruments of control. In fact, a fair amount of research suggests that people's basic parenting styles "are already in place before [they] gain direct experience with their own offspring." These styles are deeply rooted in experiences they had long ago.[15]

A man left a message on my website recently that read, in part, "I watch, as if a spectator at a train wreck, as my friends use the same parental behaviors that wounded them when they were little. It is not a pretty sight." Nor, I would add, is it a simple matter to determine why this happens. The folks he's talking about presumably didn't sit down and consciously decide to make their own kids as unhappy as they were. Something else must account for this repetition. Something else must account for the odd, illogical, even tragic fact that even many people who are highly critical of their parents nevertheless end up creating a family eerily similar to the one from which they escaped. (Or the one from which they *thought* they had escaped.)

One explanation was offered by Alice Miller: "Many people continue to pass on the cruel deeds and attitudes to which they were subjected as children, so that they can continue to idealize their parents."[16] Her premise is that we have a powerful, unconscious need to believe that everything our parents did to us was really for our own good and was done out of love. It's too threatening for many of us even to entertain the possibility that they weren't entirely well-meaning—or competent. So, in order to erase any doubts, we do the same things to our own children that our parents did to us.

Another way of making sense of this issue was suggested by John

Bowlby, the British psychiatrist who inspired the field known as attachment theory. He argued that if you haven't experienced empathic parenting, it's hard for you to become such a parent yourself. The same might be said of unconditional love: If you didn't get it, you don't have it to give. People who were accepted only conditionally as children may come to accept others (including their own kids) in the same way. Indeed, we have evidence that this is true (p. 22). Such parents learn to think of love as a scarce commodity that must be rationed. They assume that children need to be strictly controlled, just as they were.

As a rule, when your basic emotional needs haven't been met, those needs don't just vanish when you're older. Instead, you may continue to try to satisfy them, often in indirect and even convoluted ways. That effort sometimes requires an exhausting, near-constant focus on yourself in order to prove that you really are smart or attractive or lovable. What's more, the people who need you to focus on *them,* notably your children, may find you emotionally unavailable. You're too busy trying to get what you lack. And, as two Canadian researchers have shown, parents who are thinking mostly about their own needs and goals tend to be less accepting of their children—and more likely to act in punitive and controlling ways with them—than are parents who are concerned with the needs of their kids or of the family as a whole. Those who habitually put their own needs first are also more likely to believe that their children's misbehaviors are deliberate and rooted in their nature or personality, rather than emerging from a particular situation.[17]

Kids may be put in a position where they feel their job is to keep their parents happy, to reassure them, to make them feel capable. Sometimes children are subtly encouraged to provide what the parent fails to get from her partner (or even from herself), and perhaps to provide adultlike companionship. The child may be steered into becoming a friend, or even a parent, to the parent. All of this can take place without anyone's realizing what's going on. But whether or not the child manages to figure out how to become what the parent wants, the child's development may be warped because the adult's needs have taken center stage.

What We Fear

When we add up all the feelings and beliefs and behaviors that affect us—influences that are both personal and cultural, conscious and unconscious—we may discover that they affect our parenting partly by making us afraid. Some people's fears are more overwhelming and less rational than others', but all of them can help to explain why children are treated in the ways I've been describing.

FEAR OF PARENTAL INADEQUACY

Frankly, I'd be worried about a new parent who wasn't apprehensive about what lay ahead. My wife and I well remember when the adrenaline (and pitocin) rush gave way to something approaching panic: standing outside the hospital after the HMO decided we had been there long enough, cradling a car seat with a newborn snoozing in it, looking like the proverbial deer caught in the headlights, and thinking, "There must be some mistake here. We don't know how to take care of one of these." (It would have been even worse had we realized that we weren't bringing home just a baby but also a future three-year-old and eight-year-old and fourteen-year-old.)

No one sets out to be a bad parent. We all love our children and want more than anything to keep them safe and happy. But sometimes we also feel helpless and confused, frustrated when things don't go as planned, and secretly (or not so secretly) doubtful about being able to do what we should. The fear of being clueless can lead in several possible directions, all of them problematic. Such a parent may be a sucker for advice that is reassuring but bad. ("I don't know what I'm doing, so I'll just take my cue from my mother-in-law, who seems very sure of herself when she announces that babies should be left alone to 'cry it out'"; or "I'll just go along with this expert, who encourages me to give my kid a gold star every time he does what I tell him.")

The fear of incompetence[18] leads some parents to give in to all of their children's demands, which, of course, is very different from meeting their needs and working with them to solve problems. Other parents, meanwhile, overcompensate for their doubts by pretending to be absolutely certain, completely in charge. After a while, the role of the crisply controlling, always authoritative Parent-with-a-capital-P becomes so comfortable that they forget it's just a role, much less why they came to adopt it. Such parents may impose rigid rules for children that aren't open to question or qualification, as though they are trying to convince everyone, including themselves, that they really do know what they're doing.

FEAR OF POWERLESSNESS

Each of us was once completely vulnerable and dependent on someone else. On an unconscious level, some people fear that once the thin veneer of adulthood is shattered, time will rush backward and they will revert to being powerless. They deal with that fear by pretending they're *in*vulnerable as adults. Because it's terrifying to be out of control, they need to believe they're always in control.

Alas, that can easily turn into a need to have control over others, to come out on top and feel triumphant, to regard disagreements even with their children as battles that they must win. They fear that to yield an inch, to change their minds, to admit they're wrong, to fail to put their foot down, will be to lose everything.

This is particularly true of people who were raised in traditional families where the parent's word was law. That experience causes children "to learn that no one is ready to respond to their needs and wishes in conflict situations," as two researchers put it. The feeling of powerlessness that this engenders never really goes away, with the result that, years later, they may try to attain some degree of control by controlling their own children.[19] Thus, paradoxical though it may seem, the parents who "see themselves as lacking power are most likely to make use of coercive control tactics."[20]

Some people's lives are organized around a need to look or act powerful in order to stave off the terror of being at someone else's mercy. Their interest in controlling others isn't limited to children; they feel obligated to demonstrate that they're superior to other adults, too. But it's easier, and more socially acceptable, to do it with kids. Norman Kunc, who conducts workshops on inclusive education and noncoercive practices, points out that "what we call 'behavior problems' are often situations of legitimate conflict; we just get to call them behavior problems because we have more power" than children do. (You're not allowed to say that your spouse has a behavior problem.)[21]

We have studies showing that abusive parents are especially likely "to see themselves as victims of the malevolent intentions of children." But which came first: the behavior or the belief? Perhaps by seeing ourselves as the victims, or by talking about how "manipulative" a child is, "we are trying to justify our negative reaction by looking for equally negative motives in the child."[22]

Even parents who are by no means abusive may be driven by a need for control and a fear of losing it. It's unsettling for most of us to find that someone has sneaked in during the night and replaced our helpless infant with a toddler who has a will of her own. What had been an adorable baby now has the nerve to pursue her own agenda and oppose some of our demands. Will we resist the temptation to try to figure out ways of outsmarting her? Will we be able to shift from doing *to* a baby to working *with* a child? It's a test that not all of us pass. (We're tested again about a decade later, give or take, when the child's need for autonomy surges anew—and it's even more difficult to get compliance from someone who is older, cleverer, and less dependent on us.)

Our fears often lead us to dig in our heels, which is a big mistake. One evening my three-year-old son resists—mostly by inaction and selective hearing—my repeated requests to finish his game and get undressed. As the minutes tick by, I give him the choice of taking off his shirt or having me do it. He doesn't respond, so I take it off and carry him upstairs. He cries loudly, miserably, inconsolably, wailing that he wanted to do it himself. I remind him (gently and rather reasonably, I think) that he had the opportunity to do so and didn't take advantage of it. But he's crying and he's three, and I'm talking to myself.

Now he wants to go back downstairs and have me put his shirt on again so he can take it off himself. No, I tell him, it's too late. I'm looking ahead, thinking about the clothes still to be removed and the waiting bath that's losing its warmth. But he's not ready to look ahead or move forward. We're at an impasse—until I realize that I'm being as irrational as he is. My insistence on doing things my way is not only making both of us unhappy but wasting time. So we do it his way: We go downstairs, we put on the shirt, he takes off the shirt, we go upstairs, he gets in the bath. But as a result of my resistance to giving up control, it takes an hour or two before his smile returns and our relationship is repaired.

FEAR OF BEING JUDGED

Some parents live in terror of what other people—not only their friends and relatives, but the nameless and omnipresent judge known as "they"—will think of their children, and thus of their own parenting skills. This fear is particularly debilitating when it's accompanied by the other two fears just mentioned. But even relatively secure parents are sometimes made uncomfortable by the possibility that someone somewhere might be thinking, "Boy, that mother doesn't know *what* she's doing. I mean, just look at her kids!"

Consider how much of what we do with our children is driven by worries about how we'll be perceived by other adults. A grown-up hands something to our baby and we pipe up, "Can you say thank you?"—ostensibly addressing the baby, even though he obviously can't say thank you and may be too young even to learn from our example. What we're really doing is speaking through the child to the adult, making it clear that *we* know the polite response as well as the right way to bring up kids.

As I've said, people in our culture are far more likely to fault parents for controlling too little rather than too much—and to approve of children because they're "well behaved" rather than because they're, say, curious. So when you combine the parent's anxiety about being judged with the likely direction of that judgment, you end up with this unsurprising fact: We're most likely to resort to coercive tactics, and to become preoccupied with the need to control our children, when we're out in public.[23] As is true of many other fears, this can set up a self-fulfilling prophecy, so that cracking down on kids for fear of what other people will think may produce more of exactly the kind of behavior that we don't want anyone to see.

FEAR FOR OUR CHILDREN'S SAFETY

All caring parents worry about their kids, particularly when the newspapers are full of hair-raising stories of bad things happening to good people. Until I became a parent, I didn't realize how hard it can be to know when those concerns are appropriate and when they're exaggerated—and when our responses cross the line that divides reasonable precautions from stifling overprotection.

Still, it's pretty clear that some parents rationalize an inappropriate degree of control over their children on the grounds that terrible things will happen otherwise. I'm not talking about keeping an eye out for a child, being aware of what's going on in his life, and setting age-appropriate limits. Obviously, those things make sense. I'm talking about the kind of control described in chapter 3, where the parent gives the child too few opportunities to make decisions about what he's doing, in the name of protecting him. (Worse yet is when children are overcontrolled because we fear for the safety of *things*—that is, possessions.) This can quickly take a toll on a child's self-confidence as well as on her relationship with us.

FEAR OF BABYING

It's more than being sick of changing diapers that leads some parents to try to speed up toilet training, just as it's more than a desire to introduce children to the wonders of the written word that leads them to drill preschoolers on learning their letters. I've watched people push toddlers to start toddling, criticize them for crawling, insist that they can walk up the stairs by themselves now. I've seen forks placed in very young hands, accompanied by the command to "eat like a big boy."

The assumption that sooner is always better may come from a fear of later. That fear, in turn, can reflect the belief that children shouldn't be "babied." It's time to wean them, time to potty-train them, time to get them walking and talking and doing more things on their own. Parents worry when their children act in ways that they think are too young. But why? A friend of mine likes to take the long view, asking rhetorically, "Do you really think she'll still be crawling (or wearing pull-ups) in junior high school? What's the rush?" (And speaking of junior high school, when was the last time you heard the parent of a young adolescent pushing *that* child to grow up faster—to use more makeup, attend more unsupervised parties, become more sexually active, or hurry up and get a driver's license already?)

The people most likely to have made their peace with going slow are the parents of children with developmental disabilities. They've had to face down their worst fears and work through them. But the trick is for parents of all children to relax and let them proceed at their own pace. It's one thing to be too exhausted to carry a four-year-old; it's something else to refuse to carry him for fear that kids of that age just *shouldn't* be carried—and, more generally, that kids always ought to do whatever they're capable of doing.

These days, my nine-year-old daughter gets a kick out of watching TV shows intended for much younger children. At first this made me uneasy. Eventually I realized several things. First, she gets more than enough intellectual stimulation during the day and deserves to enjoy some unchallenging entertainment. (If adults can relax with stupid sitcoms or paperback thrillers, why can't a fourth-grader slum with preschool programs?) Second, when I watched some of these shows with her, I realized that she was actually using her sophisticated skills to predict plot developments, criticize inconsistencies, consider alternative courses of action for the characters, and figure out the technical tricks that create various illusions.[24] Third, and most important, watching a TV program (or reading a book) that's "below her level" doesn't make her dumber. The real peril consists of pushing her to grow up faster.

The fear of babying is first cousin to the fear that our children will be left behind. This helps to explain the popularity of noxious, fear-stoking books with titles like *What Your Two-Day-Old Should Know*. Whenever I see parents eyeing the other kids in a room to gauge who's already doing what, I'm reminded of siblings who, upon being served dessert, immediately glance at the other one's portion to make sure it isn't bigger. The compulsion to compare reflects a fear, uniquely cultivated in our competition-crazy society, that other people's children are ahead of one's own. People who act as though childhood is a race invariably visit a variety of unproductive pressures on their children.

FEAR OF PERMISSIVENESS

Just as the concern that one's children will be outperformed by their peers is associated with an unhealthy press for success, so the fear of permissiveness can promote unhealthy overcontrol. As I've already observed, it's not permissiveness itself, but the fear of permissiveness, that causes the most serious problems in our culture. That fear is often stoked by discipline books, as Thomas Gordon once pointed out: "First, they mistakenly hold up permissiveness as the evil culprit; then they scare parents into believing that the only thing they can do to overcome it is to exercise strong parental authority—that is, be strict, lay down rules and vigorously enforce them, set firm limits, use physical punishment, and demand obedience."[25]

The empirical link between assumptions and fears, on the one hand, and child-rearing practices, on the other, has been well established. For example, mothers who believe that babies can be spoiled by too much affection do indeed tend to provide less supportive environments.[26] But with older children, too, we can scarcely tally up the damage caused by parents who impose autocratic dictates, or offer only conditional acceptance, because they're terrified that anything else amounts to being too permissive. Freeing people from this fear is an important step toward helping them become the loving parents they're capable of being.

In my experience, what distinguishes truly great parents is their willingness to confront troubling questions about what they've been doing and what was done to them. When a suggestion is made that there may be a better way to handle a conflict with their children, they resist the temptation to respond defensively, "Well, that's what my parents did with me, and obviously I turned out okay." To get better at the craft of raising children, we need to be open to seeing what's unpleasant in order to evaluate what our parents did right and where we might be able to improve on their approach. Those of us who were lucky enough to be treated with respect will, of course, want to do the same with our own children. The rest of us must resolve *not* to treat our children the way we were treated, but rather the way we wish we had been treated.

In listing assumptions such as those regarding retribution and religion, competition and conformity, my point isn't to refute those beliefs but to shine a spotlight on them so we can consider whether they influence our child-rearing practices. And my objective is necessarily even more limited when it comes to the deeply personal stuff. Notwithstanding what you may have heard from some other authors, the prospects for meaningful transformation from reading a book are not good. I can only hope that Freud was right in thinking that insight might be the first step toward change. Real understanding, the kind that involves the gut as well as the head, may not be sufficient for doing things differently with one's children, but it probably is necessary.

The upshot is this. We're unlikely to meet our long-term goals for our kids unless we're ready to ask the following question: *Is it possible that what I just did with them had more to do with my needs, my fears, and my own upbringing than with what's really in their best interests?* The answer may well be a reassuring no—and, one hopes, there will be more no's than yeses to that question as we go along. But we have to be willing to keep asking it. Once we can look at the possible reasons for acting the way we do—which, of course, aren't limited to those listed in this chapter—we can move on to specific ideas for how to become better parents.

7

PRINCIPLES OF
UNCONDITIONAL PARENTING

I might as well warn you now: What follows will not be a step-by-
step recipe for How to Raise Good Kids. First of all, I would have
to be a nearly perfect parent myself, which I'm not, before I presumed
to offer other people a definitive, fail-safe guide to raising *their* children. Second, I have my doubts about the wisdom of such an
approach in any case. Very specific suggestions ("When your child
says *x*, you should stand at location *y* and use *z* tone of voice to utter
the following sentence . . .") are disrespectful to parents and kids
alike. Raising children is not like assembling a home theater system
or preparing a casserole, such that you need only follow an expert's
instructions to the letter. No one-size-fits-all formula can possibly
work for every family, nor can it anticipate an infinite number of situations. Indeed, books that claim to offer such formulas, while
eagerly sought by moms and dads desperate for a miracle cure, usually do more harm than good.

What I will do, in this chapter and those that follow, is lay out some
broad principles, some ways of thinking about how to create alternatives to traditional parenting. These are derived from research, from
a synthesis of the work of other thoughtful advisors, from my own

experience, and from my observations of other families. You'll have to decide whether each idea seems reasonable and, if so, how it may apply to raising your own children.

The recommendations I'll be offering are, frankly, more challenging than those proposed in a lot of other books. It's harder to make sure children feel loved unconditionally than it is just to love them. It's harder to respond to them in all their complexity than it is to focus just on their behaviors. It's harder to try to solve problems with them, to give them reasons for doing the right thing (let alone to help them formulate their own reasons), than it is to control them with carrots and sticks. "Working with" asks more of us than does "doing to."

Oddly, "working with" ideas are often held to a much higher standard. One researcher, noting that young children typically misbehave even after having been told to stop, observes that parents then conclude that talking to children doesn't work. But punishment, including corporal punishment, usually isn't effective either, he points out. In fact, half the toddlers in one study misbehaved again within about two hours—and four-fifths of them misbehaved again before the day was over—regardless of how their parents responded the first time. "The difference . . . is that, when spanking does not work, parents do not question its effectiveness."[1] (Indeed, it's common in that case to assume the child requires *more* traditional discipline.)

No specific intervention, neither mine nor anyone else's, is guaranteed to be effective. But trying to impose our will on a child is almost certain to be *in*effective at producing anything beyond resentful temporary obedience. (Often, as we saw in chapter 3, it doesn't even produce that.) What I'll be describing has a much better chance of success, with far fewer risks to a child's healthy development or to our relationship with that child.

The shift away from older methods, however, has to be accompanied by a shift in goal. Specifically, our main question shouldn't be "How do I get my child to do what I say?" but *"What does my child need—and how can I meet those needs?"* In my experience, you can predict much of what happens in families just from knowing which of those questions is more important to the parents. You don't even have to know the answers they've found—that is, which tactics are used to get compliance (in the first case), or what the child is thought to need (in the second). The questions are what count.

To focus on children's needs, and to work with them to make sure their needs are met, constitutes a commitment to *taking children seriously*. It means treating them as people whose feelings and desires and questions matter. A child's preferences can't always be accommodated, but they can always be considered and they need never be dismissed out of hand. It's important to see a child as someone with a unique point of view, with very real fears and concerns (often quite different from our own), and with a distinctive way of reasoning (which is not merely "cute").

When I find myself reacting with horror to certain discipline experts and the casually callous advice they offer, it's typically because they don't seem to honor—or, in some cases, even to *like*—kids. I apply the same standard when I watch other parents. I'm not so concerned with whether they make all the same choices or use the same strategies that I do, but with whether their actions and words and tone of voice make it clear that they take their kids seriously.

The following three chapters will offer suggestions for doing so in three specific ways: expressing unconditional love, giving children more chances to make decisions, and imagining how things look from the child's point of view. First, though, I want to propose a baker's dozen guiding principles. Each of these has practical implications that may be more surprising and challenging than its capsule description would imply.

Here they are all together:

1. Be reflective.
2. Reconsider your requests.
3. Keep your eye on your long-term goals.
4. Put the relationship first.
5. Change how you see, not just how you act.

6. R-E-S-P-E-C-T.
7. Be authentic.
8. Talk less, ask more.
9. Keep their ages in mind.
10. Attribute to children the best possible motive consistent with the facts.
11. Don't stick your no's in unnecessarily.
12. Don't be rigid.
13. Don't be in a hurry.

1. BE REFLECTIVE.

In a moment of frustration, my wife once put her finger on a dilemma that many parents face. She said, "I don't know how to make the kids do what I say without doing things I find unappealing." There's no easy solution to this problem, but there's one response that we definitely ought to avoid, and that is to rationalize whatever we're doing so that it no longer seems unappealing to us. Poof! No more dilemma. Similarly, some parents manage to convince themselves that whatever rules they've established, even those with no compelling justification, are somehow in their children's best interests.

The best parents are introspective and willing to give themselves a hard time. I'm not suggesting that you become consumed with guilt and feelings of inadequacy; there is such a thing as being too self-critical (or critical in an unproductive way). But most of us would benefit by spending more time reviewing what we've done with our children in order to be better parents tomorrow than we are today.

Try to figure out what may be driving your parenting style. The more transparent you are to yourself—the better you come to understand how your own needs and experiences affect the way you act with your children (such as what drives you crazy and why)—the more likely it is that you'll improve. For example, the qualities that particularly irritate some people about their children turn out to be unwelcome reminders of their own least appealing features. As Piet Hein, the Danish poet and scientist, put it: "The errors hardest to condone/ In other people are one's own."

In short: Be honest with yourself about your motives. Don't stop being troubled by things you do that really are troubling. And be alert for signs that the way you interact with your children may have drifted toward a controlling style without your even being aware of it.

2. RECONSIDER YOUR REQUESTS.

Here's a very unsettling possibility: Perhaps when your child doesn't do what you're demanding, the problem isn't with the child but with what it is you're demanding. It's remarkable how few books written for parents even raise this possibility. The vast majority of them take whatever their readers want their kids to do as the point of departure, and then offer techniques for getting compliance. In most cases, these techniques involve "positive reinforcement" or "consequences"—that is, bribes or threats. In some cases, they involve more thoughtful and respectful ways of interacting with children. But almost never are parents encouraged to reconsider their requests.

One recent book, for example, stresses the importance of becoming more responsive and more skillful at win-win negotiation. I found the specific ideas useful and the general approach refreshingly humane. But in offering advice to parents who had asked how to get their kids to make their beds or eat their vegetables, the author seems not to have considered the possibility that these objectives might be problematic. If we're giving children reasonably healthy meals, is it ever necessary to force them to eat something? And why does the only place in the world that is truly a child's own have to be maintained according to the parent's standards? Even relatively progressive books tend to focus on *how,* rather than *whether,* to get the child to do what the parent wants.

In some cases, the trouble is that parental demands are out of step with what can reasonably be expected of children at a certain age. (More about this in a moment.) But even when a child can do something, it's still worth asking whether he should. Some parents want to know how to get their kids to practice the piano. The more pressing question, however, is: If the whole process is excruciating for the child, why are you forcing him to take lessons? Is it for him, or for you? Might he end up disliking music as a result? And so it goes for many other issues.

Of course, there are some things we expect children to do that clearly *are* reasonable, even if we may disagree about which items belong in that category. My central point, though, is that, before searching for some method to get kids to do what we tell them, we should first take the time to rethink the value or necessity of our requests.

3. KEEP YOUR EYE ON YOUR LONG-TERM GOALS.

I began this book by inviting you to think about what you want for your children over the long haul, and to consider the possibility that certain parenting strategies may actually impede the realization of your goals. Now that we've examined some of those strategies more closely, it may make sense to weigh them against each of the objectives you've identified.

Suppose, for example, you want your child to grow into someone who is (a) ethical, (b) able to sustain healthy relationships, (c) intellectually curious, and (d) fundamentally content with him- or herself. The task, then, would be to ask whether each of these goals is more or less likely to be achieved as a result of using love-withdrawal techniques such as time-out, or selectively reinforcing the behaviors you like, or saying (even if not in so many words) "Because I'm the parent, that's why!" In fact, anything you do with your children on a regular basis should be evaluated in light of your ultimate goals.

Such reflection doesn't always have to be done quite so systematically. In a more general sense, we ought to keep in mind what we're really looking for. It's too easy to get trapped in the minutiae of everyday life, all the squabbles and frustrations that upstage the important questions. The good news is that when parents do manage to keep their broader objectives in view—indeed, when they focus on anything more ambitious than just getting their kids to obey right this instant— they tend to use better parenting skills and they get better results.[2] At the very least, we need to keep a sense of perspective. Whether your child spills the chocolate milk today, or loses her temper, or forgets to do her homework doesn't matter nearly as much as the things you do that either help or don't help her to become a decent, responsible, compassionate person.

4. PUT THE RELATIONSHIP FIRST.

Speaking of paramount goals, there's no overstating the importance of the relationship we create with our children. My friend Danny recently summarized what he's learned from years of fatherhood: "Being right isn't necessarily what matters." In fact, it matters very little if your children stiffen when you walk into the room.

In a purely practical sense, misbehavior is easier to address—and problems are easier to solve—when children feel safe enough with us to explain the reasons they did something wrong. Kids are more likely to come to us when they're in trouble, to look to us for advice, and to *want* to spend time with us when they can choose whether to do so. Furthermore, when they know they can trust us, they're more likely to do what we ask if we tell them it's really important.

Of course, a solid and loving relationship isn't justified primarily because it's useful; it's an end in itself. That's why we need to ask whether it's worth jeopardizing that relationship in order to get a baby to sleep through the night, or a toddler to start using the potty, or a child to mind his manners. There will be times when, in order to do the right thing, we have to put our foot down and cause our kids to become frustrated with us. But before we resort to controlling interventions, before we make a child unhappy, and certainly before we do anything that could be construed as placing conditions on our love, we should make absolutely sure it's worth the possible strain on the relationship.[3]

5. CHANGE HOW YOU SEE, NOT JUST HOW YOU ACT.

Unconditional parents don't just behave differently, such as by avoiding the use of punishment. They *see* things differently. When a child does something inappropriate, conditional parents are likely to perceive this as an infraction, and infractions naturally seem to call for "consequences." Unconditional parents are apt to see the same act as a problem to be solved, an opportunity for teaching rather than for making the child suffer. Again, it's not just the choice of a "working with" as opposed to a "doing to" response; it's that these responses emerge from how one makes sense of what happened. Moreover, to see children's behavior as a "teachable moment" invites us to include them in the process of solving the problem, which is more likely to be effective.

6. R-E-S-P-E-C-T.

Part of what I mean by taking children seriously is treating them with respect. My value judgment is that all people deserve this. My hypothesis is that kids are more likely to respect others (including you) if they themselves feel respected. Even parents who obviously love their children don't always act as though they respect them. Some sound snide or sarcastic. They write off their kids' requests, dismiss their feelings of anger, or trivialize their fears. They interrupt their kids in a way they wouldn't dream of doing with another adult, yet they become incensed when their kids interrupt them. And they may also talk *about* their children in a belittling way: "Oh, she's just being a prima donna." "Just ignore him when he gets like that."

To treat children respectfully means making an effort to avoid doing these things, but it also means realizing that children are more knowledgeable about some matters than we are—and I don't just mean that they know which dinosaurs were meat-eaters. Thomas Gordon said it well: "Children sometimes know better than parents when they are sleepy or hungry; know better the qualities of their friends, their own aspirations and goals, how their various teachers treat them;

know better the urges and needs within their bodies, whom they love and whom they don't, what they value and what they don't."[4] In any case, we can't always assume that because we're more mature we necessarily have more insight into our children than they have into themselves.

Thus, it's disrespectful for a parent to tell a child what she is and isn't experiencing—for example, to respond to an angry declaration that she hates her brother by exclaiming, "Why would you say that? Of course you don't!" Apart from failing to help the situation, such responses may well be read as a kind of conditional acceptance. The child may come to believe that her feelings aren't important, that there's something wrong with her for having them, and that she can only be loved if she gets upset about the things Mommy thinks it's okay to get upset about.

7. BE AUTHENTIC.

Some people are accused of trying to be a friend to their children rather than a parent. I agree that this confusion can be unseemly and unhelpful. But while we have to be more than pals, we mustn't stop being people with them. We shouldn't hide behind the role of Father or Mother, to the point that our humanity (or our human connection with them) disappears.

I don't mean that we should disclose all the intimate details of our lives to our children. Some things we don't tell them until they're old enough, and some things we'll never tell them. But there's a dimension of genuineness that's missing in the way some parents act with their kids, and that absence can be keenly felt even if the children can't quite identify what's lacking in, or not quite right about, the relationship.

Real people have needs of their own, things they enjoy doing, things they hate. Kids should know that. Real people sometimes become flustered or distracted or tired. They're not always sure what to do. Sometimes they say things without thinking and later regret them. We shouldn't pretend to be more competent than we are. And when we screw up, we should admit it: "You know, sweetie, I've been thinking about what I said last night, and I think I might have been wrong." My advice is to make a point of apologizing to your child about something at least twice a month. Why twice a month? I don't know. It sounds about right to me. (Almost all the specific advice in parenting books is similarly arbitrary. At least I admit it.)

There are two reasons to apologize. First, it sets a powerful example. I noted earlier that it makes no sense to *force* children to say they're sorry when they're not. A far more effective way to introduce them to the idea of apologizing is to *show* them how it's done. Second, apologizing takes you off your perfect parent pedestal and reminds them that you're fallible. In fact, it shows them that it's possible to acknowledge (to ourselves and to others) that we make mistakes, and that things are sometimes our fault, without losing face or feeling hopelessly inadequate.

The reasons that apologizing is so important are also the reasons that most parents don't do it. After all, it can feel reassuring to stand on that pedestal, that position of ultimate and unquestionable authority. To say you're sorry is to make yourself vulnerable, which isn't easy for many of us—in part because of the extreme vulnerability we experienced as children.

What's more, many parents fear that reaching out to develop genuine, warm relationships with their kids may compromise their capacity to control them. Much of conditional parenting can be traced back to the fact that when those two objectives clash, control tends to be favored over connection. You can see this even in the subtle ways parents distance themselves from their kids, such as by talking about themselves in the third person ("Mommy has to leave now") long after the child is able to understand how pronouns work.

Children will still look up to us even if we're candid about our limitations, even if we speak to them from our hearts, and even if they can see that, for all the privileges and wisdom that adulthood confers, we're still just people struggling to make our way in the world, to do the right thing, to balance people's needs, to keep learning—just as they are. In fact, the more real we are with them, the more likely it is that they'll feel real respect for us.

8. TALK LESS, ASK MORE.

Dictating to kids (even in a nice way) is far less productive than eliciting ideas and objections and feelings from them. If talking to our children about what they've done wrong fails to bring about the results we were hoping for, it isn't because some stronger form of discipline is required. It may be because we did most of the talking. Maybe we were so busy trying to get them to see our point of view that we didn't really hear theirs. To be a great parent is more a function of listening than of explaining.

A father in Ontario wrote to tell me about the day his four-year-old daughter brought home a bag of snacks from school.

She dumped them on the living room floor and made a big mess, and I asked her to put them back in the bag and set them on the table. She refused. My initial reaction was that this was a challenge to my authority. She had "disobeyed" me, and therefore punishment was in order. Otherwise, she wouldn't listen to me in the future. [Instead, though,] I asked her, "Why don't you want to put them away?" She replied, "Because I want to eat them." The problem solved itself after this. All I had to say was, "You can still eat them after you put them in the bag—all I want is the living room clean." She immediately put them in the bag and set them on the table.

As a rule, our first priority is to figure out the source of the problem, to recognize what children need. For example, two- and three-year-olds often act out because they're undergoing a bumpy transition from babyhood into personhood. They're wrestling with the attractions of freedom and independence, the power of being able to do new things, while simultaneously trying to cope with unwelcome limitations on the exercise of their will. They want more autonomy than they're given—and sometimes more than they can handle. They're also scared about standing apart from (and in opposition to) their parents. The last thing they need during such tumult is a parent who is focused just on setting limits and keeping control.

Sometimes the reasons for troublesome actions are a function of a specific child or situation. When kids are too young to explain—or, in some cases, even to understand—those reasons, we have to piece together the clues that might help us make sense of what's going on. When my son, Asa, became cranky and clingy during his third year, we realized that it was probably related to the departure of the babysitter who had helped to take care of him since he was born. Not only was he likely grieving for her, but he was also wondering, on some level, whether this meant that Mommy or Daddy, too, might just up and disappear one day. Telling him to stop fussing would be fruitless and frustrating.

When children *are* old enough to tell us why they're unhappy or angry, the question then becomes whether they feel safe enough to do so. Our job is to create that sense of safety, to listen without judgment, to make sure they know they won't get into trouble for telling us what they've done or be condemned for what they feel. I don't say this because I'm a relativist who believes that all things people do are equally valid and can't be judged. I say this because I'm a pragmatist who realizes that you have to know the source of a problem in order to solve it, and also that people who are afraid of being judged are less likely to speak openly and therefore less likely to give you the information necessary to understand the source of the problem. That's why taking this credo seriously—"talk less, ask more"—is good advice for becoming not only a better parent but also a better spouse, friend, manager, or teacher.

On the other hand, not all types of asking are equally productive. Rhetorical questions, which aren't really intended to elicit a thoughtful response, are pointless at best: "Why can't you look at people when they're talking to you?" Even worse are questions where there is one right answer, and the point is not for the child to reflect but merely to guess what response you're looking for: "What do you think you could say to your sister since you just bumped into her?"

After offering a short list of similar "questions that get us nowhere fast," the author Barbara Coloroso suggests that, before asking something, you might "question why you are asking it." Laying bare our motives can offer guidance about whether it's worth asking.[5] Hint: It's when we're not entirely sure what the child will say, and when we're open to more than one response, that a question is most likely to be beneficial.

On occasion, we would do well to avoid talking *or* asking. In many situations, we get into trouble as parents because we feel obliged to say something, even though the best advice would be to keep quiet. Sometimes when a child is very sad, suggests child psychologist Alicia Lieberman, "only staying near wordlessly does honor to the child's experience. Hugging and holding (if the child allows) can convey feeling much better than words. In fact, to use language in these conditions is necessarily to misuse it. There will be time for words later."[6]

Obviously, there is no recipe for when to speak up and when to hold back. Sometimes we deal with children's unhappiness or rage or inappropriate behavior by talking too much, occasionally by talking too little, and most often by talking in a way that isn't particularly helpful. Overall, though, the prescription to talk less and ask more can be a useful guide, particularly if we apply it in a way that helps us to become more responsive and supportive.

9. KEEP THEIR AGES IN MIND.

Any piece of advice, in this book or anywhere else, may have to be applied differently with children of different ages; the strategies we use with children have to change as they grow. For example, when a baby starts to cry because you removed an inappropriate item she was playing with, it's fine to distract her with a new game or toy. But distraction is ineffective and even insulting when applied to an older child, just as it would be if *you* complained about something that was bothering you only to have your spouse try to change the subject.

Controlling parents, as I've mentioned, are likely to hold children to unrealistically high expectations, partly because they don't understand just how unrealistic those expectations are.[7] They might, for example, punish a toddler for failing to do what he said he would do, or demand that a preschooler sit quietly through a long family dinner. The reality is that very young children simply can't grasp the obligation entailed by making a promise; to hold them responsible for doing so is, to use the phrase preferred by early-childhood experts, "developmentally inappropriate." It's similarly unrealistic to expect children to stay still for long periods of time. It's normal for them to fidget, to be loud, to forget to turn off a battery-operated toy, and to become unnerved by what seem to us to be tiny changes in their environment. We have to keep our expectations keyed to what they're capable of doing.

10. "ATTRIBUTE TO CHILDREN THE BEST POSSIBLE MOTIVE CONSISTENT WITH THE FACTS."

This sentence, from author and educator Nel Noddings,[8] is one of the wisest pieces of advice I've ever come across. It springs from two facts. One: We usually don't know for sure why a child acted the way he did. Two: Our beliefs about those reasons can create a self-fulfilling prophecy. If we assume that an inappropriate action was motivated by a child's sinister desire to cause trouble or to see how much he can get away with—or if we attribute such behaviors to his being a natural troublemaker—he may become exactly what we fear. Children construct a theory about their own motives based in part on our assumptions about their motives, and then they act accordingly: "You think I'm just plain bad and need to be controlled all the time? Fine. Watch me act as though you're right."

Sometimes in my workshops I invite participants to recall an incident from their own childhoods in which they did something wrong— or were accused of doing something wrong. I ask them to try to remember as many details as possible about this event: what was said or done to them by an adult and what happened as a result. I'm always struck by how vivid people's memories are, as if these things had happened weeks ago rather than decades ago. This exercise often serves as a reminder of what punishment feels like from the child's point of view, how much harm it does and how little good. But I've also been struck by how frequently the stories people tell are about how a teacher or parent didn't have all the facts and leaped to the assumption that they had done something bad even when this wasn't true. It's a good lesson to remember, if only because we don't want our kids to grow up and tell stories about *us* in workshops one day.

Even when parents don't say out loud that the child must have acted as he did because he's stupid or destructive or bad, it matters if they believe this is true. It's not just the attributions we utter that matter, but the ones we make in our heads. Though we may never speak an unkind word about our children, assumptions about their motives invariably affect the way we treat them. The more negative those assumptions, the more inclined we'll be to control them unnecessarily.

The good news is that we can create an "auspicious circle" in place of the vicious one. If we don't have any concrete evidence to the contrary, why not assume there may be an innocuous explanation for what just happened? Maybe what looked like a deliberate act of aggression was actually accidental. Maybe what appeared to be an act of thievery wasn't that at all. We can help kids to develop good values by treating them as though they were already motivated by those values. They thereby come to believe what's best about themselves and live up to our trust in them.

The most obvious case in which it makes sense to attribute the best possible motive has to do with immaturity. Mischief often can be explained by a simple lack of skills or guidance, an innocent desire to explore, an inability to foresee what happens when you take that thing and do this to it. When parents holler angry rhetorical questions at their children—"Why in the world would you do that? Are you dense?"—I imagine the child replying, "No, I'm not dense! I'm *three!*" Similarly, even though you may grow tired of picking the spoon off the floor for the umpteenth time, it's important to realize that a one-year-old keeps pushing it off the high chair just because kids of that age get a kick out of dropping things—not because she's "testing limits," and certainly not because she's trying to make Mommy miserable. Just because a child's action may have a negative effect on you doesn't mean that was the child's intention.

So how can we set an auspicious circle into motion instead? Consider a five-year-old boy who picked up a large rock and appeared ready to throw it. "A teacher standing nearby said casually, 'Lend me the rock,' and demonstrated, by touching the rock to the child's head, how the rock could hit a classmate's head. The teacher then returned the rock to the child, saying, 'Carry it carefully.'" After relating this anecdote, which took place in a Japanese school, Catherine Lewis, a specialist in early-childhood education, remarks that she was surprised by the fact that the teacher "neither asked the child to put down the rock nor implied that the child intended to throw it." Instead, the teacher

> implied that the problem was one of information—that the boy hadn't thought carefully about how the rock might hurt others. The teacher's action also implied that the boy was capable of self-control; after all, the teacher gave the rock back to the boy. In contrast, if the teacher had taken away the rock or imposed punishment, the boy might have inferred that he was untrustworthy or incapable of self-control; and he might well have focused on punishment as the reason not to throw rocks, rather than on the danger of injuring others.

Lewis acknowledges that "if the boy were an alienated 12-year-old who indeed intended to hurt a classmate, and the teacher returned the rock to him, he might simply figure the adult was a fool."[9] Similarly, it would be silly or disingenuous to suggest to a child who has viciously kicked someone that he probably didn't mean any harm.[10] That's why Noddings's motto is to attribute to children the best possible motive *consistent with the facts*. But there are plenty of times when the facts are unknown to us, and our inclination should be to give the child the benefit of the doubt.

Again, this advice is especially important with young children, whose apparent misbehavior really is likely to be due mostly to their age (in which case our positive assumptions are probably accurate) and whose sense of themselves is still in formation (so our assumptions, positive or negative, affect them more). However, even with older children, our first reaction shouldn't be to blame: "Well, you must have done something to make him mad." Rather, we need to sympathize and try to understand why our children acted as they did.

11. DON'T STICK YOUR NO'S IN UNNECESSARILY.

The belief that parents today don't say no to their children often enough is a subset of the more general claim that permissiveness is running rampant, that kids are spoiled because adults fail to control them enough. I've already discussed this assumption, but it may make sense to address the specific issue of putting one's foot down.

The reality is that most parents are constantly saying no. According to descriptive studies, young children in particular are prevented from doing something they want, or made to do something they'd rather not, literally every few minutes.[11] (If you don't believe this, try keeping track of what happens in your house over the course of a day.) Of course, no responsible parent can avoid all such interventions. But it's worth asking whether we do them to excess.

When safety is at risk, for example, we have to intervene, no matter how much frustration it may cause. But even here things aren't always clear-cut. Consistent with the imperative to keep their ages in mind, it's important to realize that children become better able to anticipate and avoid dangers as they get older. (Of course, they're more likely to develop these skills if they're given the support they need and treated with trust and respect.) This means that many parental restrictions become increasingly less necessary and more confining. And then, of course, there's the question of *how* we intervene when we feel we must do so: gently or rudely? Empathically or disrespectfully? With or without an explanation?

Even when children are young, it's often debatable whether what they wanted to do really was dangerous. Sometimes we invoke the idea of safety to justify saying no for other reasons. We may tell kids to stop doing things that are actually pretty harmless, or we may say no automatically when they propose something out of the ordinary. We sometimes refuse to allow a child to do something just because it's inconvenient for us. Your preschooler wants to begin a huge crafts project, which you know will create a mess too large for him to clean up. Are you justified in saying no? Your six-year-old wants you to take part in another extended role-playing game in which each of you pretends to be an animal. You have nothing urgent to do at that moment, but you're tired of these games and would prefer that she entertain herself. Your ten-year-old asks you to bring him a snack while he's watching TV. Is that a reasonable request, one that allows you to set an example of how we do nice things for one another, or should you insist that he come get it himself? And while we're at it, is it okay for your child to choose to sleep on the floor? To sit backward on her chair during dinner?

These aren't cases of meeting kids' needs. They're wants, and therefore it's impossible to stipulate the correct parental response in advance. Still, my recommendation is to say yes whenever possible. That should be the default response, such that you need a good reason *not* to go along with what's being proposed, or to step in and forbid something. Of course, this begs the question of what constitutes a good reason, but it's a sensible way to frame the issue, particularly if we've gotten into the habit of refusing most requests. (I'll say more later about negotiating solutions together as an alternative to simply granting or denying permission.)

When I say that we should make sure we're not saying no too often or unnecessarily, I don't mean that *our* convenience, our wants, don't count, too. They do. But they shouldn't count for so much that we're gratuitously restricting our children, prohibiting them from trying

things out. When you come right down to it, the whole process of raising a kid is pretty damned inconvenient, particularly if you want to do
it well. If you're unwilling to give up any of your free time, if you want
your house to stay quiet and clean, you might consider raising tropi-
cal fish instead.

Some parents argue that deprivation is desirable for its own sake:
"Children have to get used to frustration; they might as well learn that
they're not going to be able to do everything they want to in life."
Sometimes this seems to be a way for these parents to rationalize saying no, which is their preference for other reasons. But anyone who
takes this claim seriously need only observe how often children end
up experiencing frustration even in a family where the parents try to
say yes as often as they can. There are more than enough opportunities for learning to deal with limits, for confronting the fact that it's
impossible to get everything one wants. Kids don't need parents to add
to those occasions by saying no when they could have said yes.
Besides, what best prepares children to deal with the challenges of the
"real world" is to experience success and joy. People don't get better
at coping with unhappiness because they were deliberately made
unhappy when they were young.

Apart from wanting to let our children feel competent, enjoy
exploring their world, and try out new possibilities (even when they
don't work out as planned), there's also a practical reason to limit our
no's. It's very difficult to enforce an endless series of prohibitions. This
creates a dilemma: On the one hand, we may feel compelled to back
off and just let them have their way in the end. The result is that we
won't be taken seriously when we really do have to draw a line. On
the other hand, we may refuse to reconsider and therefore spend an
awful lot of our time in a state of conflict, which is highly unpleasant
for all concerned. My advice: Pick your battles.

Of course, the issue isn't only the number of times we say yes or
no. Either response can be unwise in certain circumstances. Just as one
can acquire the habit of denying most requests that a child makes, it's
equally easy to end up giving in to every demand: "Oh, go ahead and

take the damn cookie, then."[12] Sometimes we acquiesce out of laziness; it's easier to let the kid have what he wants, especially if we feel helpless, confused, and frustrated about how to handle our children's demands, which can sometimes seem relentless.

What matters most is the reason for our decisions, and the extent to which we're willing to provide guidance, to support children's choices, to be there with them—all of which is a lot more challenging than just saying yes *or* no. What I'm talking about might be called mindful child-rearing, which is the opposite of being on autoparent. It requires enormous reserves of attention and patience. In some cases, it asks us to question the way we ourselves were raised.

Clearly, we can't attend carefully to every request and think through the implications of every possible response—particularly when we're feeling overloaded. But even if we can't do it all the time, we should strive to do it as much as possible. In sum: Don't say no if you don't absolutely have to. And try to think about the reason for everything you say.

12. DON'T BE RIGID.

A foolish consistency is the hallmark of ineffective parenting (as Ralph Waldo Emerson almost said). Waive the rules on special occasions; forget about their bedtime now and then; suspend the prohibition on eating in the living room under certain circumstances. Make it clear to your kids that what you're doing is, in fact, an exception, something they shouldn't expect all the time, but don't let a fear of creating a precedent prevent you from being flexible and spontaneous.

The same considerations apply to how you respond to misbehavior. Any given action has to be understood in a context, as a function of specific situations and causes. Allowances should be made for a child's having an off day, or for the possibility that *you're* feeling less tolerant this evening. Moreover, keep in mind that the children who are most likely to complain about inflexibility—and to sound like lawyers as they desperately cite mitigating circumstances—are the kids whose parents use punishment. Conversely, it's amazing how much less stressed and defensive everyone is, and how there's less pressure to insist on a uniform definition of justice ("Whenever this happens, the response must be that"), when we think in terms of problems to be solved rather than infractions to be punished. The absence of punishment also frees up parents to respond differently to each of their children without stirring up angry charges of favoritism. Equitable treatment for siblings doesn't always mean equal treatment, and it's a heck of a lot easier to be flexible when no one's focused on which penalty will be imposed.

I agree with many observers that children generally do better when there's some degree of predictability in their lives. But it's easy to overdo this—or, more precisely, to overlook the fact that children also have other needs that may override this one. There's little value in having an environment that's predictably unpleasant, such as a family in which kids can count on being overcontrolled, or treated without much respect, or loved only conditionally. The point isn't just whether children know what to expect; it's whether what they've come to expect makes sense.

Lastly, apart from differences between situations, or between children, there's the matter of differences between parents. It's true that when Mom and Dad have very different thresholds for junk food, or for staying out late, children quickly figure out whom to ask or even how to play one against the other. But again, it's possible to overdo or misapply the consistency that's so commonly called for in parenting guides. We may refer to it as "keeping a united front," but, as Alice Miller pointed out, it can feel to the child as though two giants are united against *him*.[13] Furthermore, it's healthy for children to see that adults sometimes disagree, which helps to underscore that we're human. It also allows us to show them how people can resolve their disagreements respectfully—or, in some cases, how we can just learn to tolerate differences. These important life lessons are lost when both parents feel compelled to take the same position on every issue in front of the kids, not to mention the inherent dishonesty of doing so.

13. DON'T BE IN A HURRY.

I used to offer this advice to parents of young children mostly as a joke. Obviously, we can't always control our schedules, even if it would be nice to have more time. But I've become more serious about this issue and the importance of doing all we can, as often as we can, to avoid situations where we feel compelled to use coercion. Parents become more controlling when time is short, just as they do when they're in public. The combination of the two conditions is a killer.

When you have some quiet time, sit down (with your co-parent, if you have one) to determine where it might be possible to change your schedule in order to reduce the likelihood of having to rush your child. What if we woke up fifteen minutes earlier? What if we went grocery shopping on Saturday? What if we changed the bath time? It's often easier than you think to avoid urgency, the goal being to allow children to feel unhurried so they can enjoy being children.

Another benefit: Rearranging your schedule gives you the luxury of waiting out a child who is being defiant or resistant, rather than pulling out the threats or otherwise imposing your will. If she's refusing to do something that you've decided must be done, you can say, "Sorry, sweetie, but you have to put your coat on. It's very cold out and we're going to be walking for a while. But if you'd rather wait for a minute, that's fine. Tell me when you're ready." (I find myself using that last sentence quite often.) If you back off and give kids some time, they usually come around. Realize, however, that even though you're allowing kids to decide when to comply, you're still imposing your will on them, and therefore this technique should not be used indiscriminately. Consistent with the second principle in this chapter, you should insist on compliance only after thinking seriously about whether a given request really is non-negotiable, and why.

Even on those occasions when we are in a bit of a hurry, it's important not to be minute-wise and hour-foolish. Trying to rush a small child is a fool's errand. Therefore, it often makes sense to spend a little time now to save more time later. My two-year-old son fell asleep on the way to the supermarket one afternoon. If I had plopped him in the cart and rushed through the aisles, he would have been miserable (and children's misery really does love company). Instead, I roused him gently, and then, even though I didn't have much time to spare, I sat quietly with him inside the store for a few minutes, pointing out things I knew he'd be interested in, the idea being to help him wake up gradually. We managed to get through the shopping fairly quickly and without any fuss.

There's a more general point lurking beneath this whole discussion: Rather than trying to change your child's behavior, it usually makes more sense to alter the environment. What's true of time is true of space. A locked gate that keeps a toddler in your yard is a lot more sensible than an attempt to rely on fear or even persuasion to keep her from wandering into the street. In general, do what you can to head off problems. If you anticipate that your child will have trouble sitting still (say, at a restaurant), then take along books, toys, or other diversions rather than placing the burden on her to behave herself.

Finally, I can't resist pointing out that the phrase "don't be in a hurry" has another meaning. It might be thought of as a reminder to slow down and savor your time with your kids. When our first child was born, we quickly vowed to sling a poopy diaper at the next person who earnestly informed us that "they grow up so fast." Yeah, yeah, yeah, we said.

But it's true.

8

LOVE WITHOUT
STRINGS ATTACHED

Unconditional acceptance may be desirable, but is it possible? Before responding to this critical question, let's be clear about what we're asking. The issue here is not whether people can accept *themselves* without conditions—that is, whether anyone has truly unconditional self-esteem. (See pp. 226–27n21.) Rather, what we want to know is whether it's realistic to think that we can accept and love our children for who they are, with no strings attached.

Here I think the answer is clearly yes. Lots of parents feel that way. But is it possible, on a day-to-day basis, to act with our children in such a way that they never doubt our love? Keep in mind that we have to frustrate them by saying no sometimes. Occasionally we may become impatient or even angry with them. And children often have trouble distinguishing people's underlying feelings from their passing moods. So can we ensure that they'll always feel unconditionally loved?

Probably not. But our objective should be to come as close as possible to that ideal. After all, perfect happiness may also be an unreachable goal; it is, as one writer put it, an imaginary condition that's usually attributed to children by adults, and to adults by children. But that doesn't (and shouldn't) stop people from trying to be happier than they are.[1] The same is true of kindness, wisdom, and other qualities that are imperfectly realized.

The fact that so many parents seem to accept their children only conditionally doesn't make that practice any less damaging or any more acceptable. And remember, we're not talking about spoiling kids or taking a hands-off approach to raising them. Unconditional parents play an active role in the lives of their children, protecting them and helping them learn right from wrong. In short, the question isn't whether we *should* try to come closer to being unconditional parents. Nor is there much doubt about whether we *can* do so. Just because there will always be room for improvement doesn't mean that we can't do better than we're currently doing. We can and we should. The question is how.

Approaching Unconditionality

The first step is simply to be mindful of the whole issue of unconditional parenting. The more we're thinking along these lines, reflecting on whether the things we do and say to our kids could reasonably be interpreted as conditional affection (and, if so, why), the more likely we are to change what we do. Consider a parent who reports the following: "We were trying to figure out what to do with our son, who yelled something nasty and slammed his door after I asked him to tidy up his room. Should we give him a few minutes to calm down? How firm should we be? I'd never really thought about this before, but now I'm wondering whether the things we were thinking of doing will leave him feeling we don't love him when he's angry." My point is that merely considering that possibility is a move in the right direction, regardless of how this parent finally decides to handle the situation.

Second, we need to get in the habit of asking ourselves a very specific question: "If that comment I just made to my child had been made to me—or if what I just did had been done to me—would *I* feel unconditionally loved?" It's not terribly complicated to perform this sort of imaginative reversal, but to do so on a regular basis can be nothing short of transformative.

When the answer to that question is clearly no, it brings us up short. We might conclude that what we just did is something we shouldn't do again. We might be moved to offer an apology. But if we don't ask this question, it's easy to continue justifying anything we do. In fact, some parents, upon realizing that what they said or did had a negative effect, may even tell themselves that the child is just being too sensitive. Once we ask ourselves, "How would *I* have felt?" it's a lot harder to let ourselves off the hook.

As soon as a child is born, it's time to think about our parenting style, and specifically about the way we react when things don't go smoothly. Do we make sure that an infant feels loved and accepted even when she won't stop crying, even when she promptly messes the diaper we just finished putting on, even when she's not a "good sleeper"? Some people very quickly become fair-weather parents, supportive and attentive only when their children are easy to be with. But unconditional love matters most when they're not.

As they get older, kids can try our patience in new ways. Need we review the possibilities? They say hateful things sometimes. They act abominably. They do exactly what we just told them not to do, which particularly infuriates parents who, because of their own psychological issues, insist on absolute obedience. They conspicuously prefer one parent to the other, which doesn't feel especially warming when you're the other. They figure out where we're most vulnerable and use that to their own advantage. And through it all, we not only have to keep accepting them, we have to keep letting *them* know that we still accept them.

Somehow, in other words, we have to communicate that we love them even when we're not thrilled with what they're doing. However, the recommendation to make that distinction is sometimes tossed around a little too casually. The fact is that it's often hard even for an adult, much less a child, to make sense of it. "We accept you, but not how you act" is particularly unpersuasive if very few of the child's actions find favor with us. "What is this elusive 'me' you claim to love," the child may wonder, "when all I hear from you is disapproval?" As Thomas Gordon pointed out, "Parents who find unacceptable a great many things that their children do or say will inevitably foster in these children a deep feeling that they are unacceptable as persons."[2] That doesn't change just because the parents remember to say soothingly, "We love *you*, honey; we just hate almost everything you do."

At a minimum, it's necessary to realize that verbal reassurances are not free passes to be punitive or otherwise controlling. "Doing to" interventions are still bad news, and they're still likely to communicate conditional acceptance, even if we periodically utter some magic words.

What to Minimize

So, what are we supposed to do when children act in ways that are disturbing or inappropriate? Even when we disapprove of what they've done and want them to know it, our reactions should take account of the big picture—specifically, the imperative to make sure they feel loved, and lovable. The goal is to avoid crossing over into conditional parenting. Here's how.

LIMIT THE NUMBER OF YOUR CRITICISMS.

Bite your tongue and swallow a lot of your objections. For one thing, frequent negative responses are counterproductive. If kids feel we're impossible to please, they'll just stop trying. Being selective about what we object to or forbid makes the "no" count for more on those occasions when we really do have to say it (p. 135). But the main point is that too much criticism and disapproval may lead a child to feel unworthy.

LIMIT THE SCOPE OF EACH CRITICISM.

Focus on what's wrong with this specific action ("Your voice sounded really unkind just now when you were talking to your sister") rather than implying that there's something wrong with the child ("You're so mean to people").

LIMIT THE INTENSITY OF EACH CRITICISM.

It's not just how many times you react negatively that counts, but *how* negatively you react each time. Be as gentle as possible while making sure the message gets across. A little emotion goes a long way; the effect of what we say is magnified because of the power inherent in being a parent. Even when kids seem to tune us out, they are absorbing more of our negative reactions—and are more deeply affected by them—than they let on. In fact, we might end up having more of an impact precisely when our approach isn't heavy-handed. Be aware not only of what you're saying but also of your body language, your facial expression, your tone of voice. Any of these can communicate more disapproval, and less unconditional love, than you intended.

LOOK FOR ALTERNATIVES TO CRITICISM.

It may make sense not only to turn down the volume, so to speak, but to switch to a different station. When kids are careless or hurtful or obnoxious, try to see this as an opportunity to teach. Instead of "What's the matter with you? Didn't I just tell you not to do that?!"—or, for that matter, instead of "I'm disappointed in you when you do that"—try helping the child to see the effects of his action, how it might hurt other people's feelings or make their lives more difficult.

Explicit negative evaluations may not be necessary if we simply say what we see ("Jeremy looked kind of sad after you said that to him") and ask questions ("The next time you're feeling frustrated, what do you think you could do instead of pushing?"). This doesn't guarantee success, of course, but it markedly improves the chances that a child will develop a commitment to acting more reasonably. The odds improve further if you invite him to think about ways to make things better, to restore, repair, replace, clean up, or apologize, as the situation may dictate.

It may sound obvious, but we sometimes seem to forget that, even when kids do rotten things, our goal should not be to make them feel bad, nor to stamp a particular behavior out of existence. Rather, what we want is to influence the way they think and feel, to help them become the kind of people who wouldn't *want* to act cruelly. And, of course, our other goal is to avoid injuring our relationship with them in the process.

One very concrete way to make sure your interventions don't communicate conditional acceptance is to try hard never to hold a grudge. The exhortation to "be the parent!" usually is intended to mean that you should take control, put your foot down. But I use that phrase to mean that you should rise above the temptation of a childish quid pro quo: "Oh, yeah? Well, if you're not going to do your chores, then I'm not going to give you dessert! So there!" Many books actually encourage this sort of parental behavior (without the "Oh, yeah?" and "So there!" of course). Once you think about it, it's pretty obvious how unhelpful this sort of response really is.

I remember one day when my two-year-old son got tired of waiting for his six-year-old sister to finish with a toy so he could play with it. He attempted to wrest it away from her, leading her to protest angrily. After she had fended him off and reestablished possession, she announced, "Now I don't want to give it to him at all because he tried to grab it." She was going to teach him a lesson, and let him know that because he did something wrong he should be punished by having to forfeit his turn. The question is: Do we want to act with our children as though we, too, were six years old? An awful lot of what passes for discipline consists of tit-for-tat responses that merely give us the satisfaction of getting even.

To be the parent means you have certain obligations, and they're not always easy to meet. My wife is always reminding me, especially when yet another dinner we made for our children lies uneaten, that all we can do is prepare nutritious meals (taking their preferences into account whenever possible) and then hope for the best. Not only is that all we *can* do; it's what we *have to* keep doing, no matter how many of those meals end up in the garbage can.

So it is with unconditional love. You keep doing your best to provide it even if your efforts seem unappreciated and unreciprocated. Sometimes kids act toward us in a way that appears remarkably similar to love withdrawal. They may spit out, "Go away!" or "I don't love you!" when they feel betrayed or thwarted, even over something that seems trivial to us. But our job is to remain calm, to avoid acting the same way, and to understand this for what it is—a passing expression of frustration. They haven't really stopped loving us. Poignantly, even children who are abused continue to love their abusers. We must never forget the lack of symmetry here. This is not a relationship between two adults of equal power. Even the slightest indication that you are withholding love from your child has a far greater impact than a screamed "I hate you!" has (or ought to have) on you.

What to Maximize

We need to do less of whatever might send a message of conditional acceptance, but we also have to do more of whatever could send a message of unconditional acceptance. The first question here is so obvious that many of us never stop to think about it: What is my mood usually like when I'm with my kids? Of course, this isn't a concern for the kind of people whose sunny smiles never dim no matter what the circumstances. They can spend all day in a house full of noisy children and still respond patiently to each request, unruffled by an endless succession of demands. But what about the rest of us, who regard such chronically happy parents with a mixture of envy and incredulity? We can't just will ourselves to become more cheerful or patient people. But we can, and we should, invest the effort to be as positive as possible with our kids.

Rather than seeing differences in temperament or talent as fixed—some people are born this way while others are just naturally that way—I think it's more helpful to think in terms of how much effort each of us has to expend to get to the same place. My brother-in-law's spatial sense allows him to find his way around places he's never been before, without even paying attention. I, on the other hand, have to work really hard to get my bearings. So that's exactly what I do when I'm in an unfamiliar setting.

The same may be true of emotional states: Parents who aren't naturally upbeat and forgiving have an obligation to try to be more that way, at least around their children. The results of their efforts can help to determine whether, and how, those children feel loved. If our kids know that we're glad to see them, that's a start toward communicating something like unconditional acceptance. If, on the other hand, they often sense a negative judgment from us—a sour mood (which they may incorrectly assume is their fault); an eye-rolling, deep-sighing irritation—well, that can feel very *un*like unconditional love.

The more pressing question, of course, is how we can communicate our love after kids keep acting up even when we think they ought to know better. (We've certainly told them enough times!) Here it's common to assume that they're "testing limits." This is a very popular phrase in the discipline field and it's often used as a justification for parents to impose more, or tighter, limits. Sometimes the assumption that kids are testing us even becomes a rationalization for punishing them. But my suspicion is that, by misbehaving, children may be testing something else entirely—namely, the unconditionality of our love. Perhaps they're acting in unacceptable ways to see if we'll stop accepting them.

Our response has to be a stubborn refusal to take the bait. We must reassure them: "No matter what you do, no matter how frustrated I get, I will never, never, never stop loving you." It doesn't hurt to say that in so many words, but we have to say it through our actions, too. Unconditional parents offer reassurances on a regular basis, and particularly during periods of conflict, about how much their children matter to them. When a child acts in ways that are less than desirable, such parents may point out that this behavior is temporary and out of character; it doesn't really reflect the child they know and love. (Notice, by the way, that a reminder to emphasize the unconditionality of our affection is very different from the more conventional advice to alternate criticism with praise. Positive judgments don't cancel out negative judgments, because the problem is with judgment itself. More about this in a moment.)

These recommendations—like the whole idea of unconditional acceptance—are relevant to educators, too. Marilyn Watson, an educational psychologist who helps teachers transform their classrooms into caring communities, emphasizes how important it is for students to feel trusted and accepted. A teacher can make it clear that certain actions are wrong while still providing "a very deep kind of reassurance—the reassurance that she still care[s] about them and [is] not going to punish or desert them, even [if they do] something very bad." This posture allows "their best motives to surface," thus giving "space and support for them to reflect and to autonomously engage in the moral act of restitution"—that is, to figure out how to make things right after doing something wrong. "If we want our students to trust that we care for them," she concludes, "then we need to display our affection without demanding that they behave or perform in certain ways in return. It's not that we don't want and expect certain behaviors; we do. But our concern or affection does not depend on it."

Watson points out that it's easier to maintain this stance, even with kids who are frequently insulting or aggressive, by keeping in mind *why* they're acting that way. The idea is for the teacher to think about what these students need (emotionally speaking) and probably haven't received. That way, she can see "the vulnerable child behind the bothersome or menacing exterior."[3] Educators, like parents, may come to view provocations as a way for that child to test the adult to see whether his or her care will be withdrawn.

One teacher dealt with a particularly challenging student by sitting down with him and saying, "You know what[?] I really, really like you.

You can keep doing all this stuff and it's not going to change my mind. It seems to me that you are trying to get me to dislike you, but it's not going to work. I'm not ever going to do that." This teacher added: "It was soon after that, and I'm not saying immediately, that his disruptive behaviors started to decrease."[4] The moral is that unconditional acceptance is not only something all children deserve, but also a powerfully effective way to help them become nicer people. (Of course, it's important that we're sincere when we assure children that we love them no matter what. There's nothing worse than the hollow recital of a line learned from a book.)

Beyond Threats

It's not always easy to stop doing the things that subtly, and often unintentionally, give children the idea that they have to earn our approval. Ironically, though, some parents find it harder to give up the practices that are more heavy-handed, those that consist of using their love as leverage to make kids obey. A reliance on punishments (including time-out and other forms of love withdrawal) and rewards (including positive reinforcement) makes it much less likely that children will feel loved unconditionally.

Yet, for all the reasons outlined in chapter 6, it can be awfully hard to kick these habits. Like former smokers who must constantly restrain themselves from lighting up again, we're always susceptible to the pull of conditional parenting and the apparent convenience of bribes and threats. Even the various premises of behaviorism that underlie these techniques can be seductive. Now and then I still find myself wondering whether my children will view expressions of unconditional love as a reward for their misbehavior.

I know better, of course. As I've already indicated, my own experience has confirmed what I'd learned from watching exemplary parents: *Punishments and rewards are never advisable and never necessary.* Before conceding this, however, many people are inclined to ask,

"What's the alternative?" Such a question is more complicated than it seems because there isn't one particular practice that serves as a replacement for punishments and rewards. What I'm proposing is the creation of an entirely different dynamic between parent and child. The "alternative," in other words, doesn't consist of a specific technique; it consists of everything discussed in the latter half of this book.

Many discipline guides, as you may have noticed, offer suggestions for how to administer punishments and rewards more effectively, the goal being to make children back down and give in. I was thinking about that the other day in the supermarket when I heard a mother growl at her child, "If you ever want to come to the store again, *calm down!*" (Needless to say, her own tone was anything but calm.) It occurred to me that the typical discipline expert would point out, with some justification, that this threat was silly. For one thing, the prospect of not being dragged to the grocery store again is not exactly horrifying to most kids. And even if it were, there's virtually no chance that the mother would follow through and ban the child from the store forever. Particularly with kids too young to be left home alone, sometimes you have to take them along whether you want to or not. Hence the word from the experts: Make only those threats you'll actually carry out.

But telling parents this is rather like warning children that they shouldn't announce they're going to beat up a classmate after school unless they're confident they'll come out on top. The focus, in other words, is on getting better at doing something morally objectionable (and counterproductive) rather than on questioning whether it should be done at all. Unconditional parents want to know how to do something *other* than threaten and punish. They don't see their relationship with their children as adversarial, so their goal is to *avoid* battles, not win them. The use of punishments makes it much harder to achieve this goal, and being told how to punish more effectively makes it harder to understand that.

Consider the types of punishment that qualify as love withdrawal. To ignore a child when he does something inappropriate, to give him the silent treatment, is to employ a kind of temporary emotional abandonment. It's as if we're obliterating the child's very existence for as long as he displeases us. This assumes, in the usual behaviorist fashion, that our attention is just a "reinforcer" and its absence will make a child stop whatever he's doing. This is an incredibly simplistic analysis of why kids act the way they do, and it fails to address the underlying needs that are involved, to say nothing of the effects on our relationship.

The late psychologist Herbert Lovett once observed that if we ignore children when they misbehave, what we're saying to them is: "We don't know why you do this and we don't care." To justify such a response by insisting that children who act out are just doing it "for the attention," Lovett added, seems to imply that "wanting to be noticed [is] a mysterious or stupid need." It's as though someone ridiculed you for going out to dinner with your friends, explaining that you do this just because of your "need for companionship."[5]

There are times, to be sure, when a child may repeat a demand over and over. You explain why she can't have a brownie right before dinner; you smile sympathetically and agree that it's hard to resist something so yummy. She asks again, and again you explain the reason for saying no. With the umpteenth announcement of the news that she really, really wants a brownie right now, you can feel your patience ebbing. You point out calmly that asking another time isn't going to work, and you suggest an interesting activity that will occupy her until dinner. But if there is still no end in sight to brownie-related requests, I think it's appropriate to stop responding. The reason, however, is not to silence the child (or "extinguish the behavior," in the soulless language of behaviorists). Rather, you've stopped answering simply because there's not much more for you to say. And you do it as lovingly as you can, given that you're busy and fed up. You don't pretend she isn't there; you make it clear that you hear, you notice, you care. The child may still feel frustrated, but ideally she won't feel unloved.

Or take the other popular form of love withdrawal, the one called time-out. The point isn't to fine-tune it or do it more cleverly; the question isn't how long to isolate the child, or where, or for what offense. Rather, the issue is what nonpunitive strategies we can use instead. As

I mentioned earlier, it can be very helpful to offer a child the *choice* of retreating to a comfortable and comforting place when he's going berserk. This option should be discussed in advance, in part to make it clear that the child is not being incarcerated or isolated against his will. He's just deciding to take a breath in a quiet room, maybe vent a little without fear of repercussions, maybe spend a few minutes with a favorite book. At a time of crisis, the parent can gently ask him if he needs to do this. But even this suggestion probably should be our second step, the first having been to ask what's going on, to remind him that what he does has an impact on other people, to explain why some ways of acting just aren't acceptable, to problem-solve together, and so on.

And what if circumstances make such a discussion impossible at the moment? Or what if he's in such an agitated state that he simply can't be allowed to stay where he is, but he refuses your invitation to take some time by himself? In that case, the last resort is to gently remove him from the situation and the place where the problem is happening—*but not from you.* ("Let's go snuggle in the den.") Such an intervention may amount to imposing your will on him, making him do something he'd rather not do. That's why you should avoid this except in extraordinary cases. But even here you take care to do it in such a way that your love, your attention, your presence are not withheld.

I should also point out that there's nothing wrong with the *parent's* taking a time-out. When we've run out of patience, when we fear that we may do or say something that we'll regret, it makes sense to excuse ourselves and go cool off. Of course, we have to make it clear that this is because *we* need to calm down, not because we're pulling away from the child or requiring her to earn her way back into our good graces.

Beyond Bribes

What about the other version of conditional parenting, which consists of giving children what they need (or simply enjoy) only when they've obeyed or pleased us? The alternative is to give them things for no reason at all, now and then to offer a special treat or gift—the chance to do something fun, a book or toy of special interest—simply because you love them. In fact, it's rather disconcerting to realize how *unloving* it can be to give kids things as a reward for doing what we wanted. We can make only so many things conditional on a child's behavior before our love itself comes to be seen as conditional.

Of course, presents are sometimes offered for reasons that are less than ideal. Some parents, for example, buy things for their kids because they feel guilty about not spending enough time with them. And gift-giving can be overdone. We don't want to shower children with stuff, particularly when their rooms are already crammed nearly to the point of bursting.[6]

But my point here is that when we do give them things, there should be no strings attached. Presents should never be offered as an incentive for behaving well, getting good grades, or doing anything else. Once I bought tickets for a local children's theater production of *The Wizard of Oz*, which my daughter was wild about. The day before the show, she threw a temper tantrum about something and I had to fight down the impulse to threaten her with not going to see the play unless her behavior improved. I reminded myself that by giving in to such a temptation, I would be using the outing as an instrument of control rather than as an expression of love. We can't have it both ways.

While it may be possible to spoil kids with too many things, it isn't possible to spoil them with too much (unconditional) love. As one writer put it, the problem with children whom we would describe as spoiled is that they "get too much of what they want and too little of what they need."[7] Therefore, give them affection (which they need) without limit, without reservations, and without excuse. Pay as much attention to them as you can, regardless of mood or circumstance. Let them know you're delighted to be with them, that you care about them no matter what happens. This basic posture, as I've noted, is completely different from praise, which is doled out as a response to something a child does.

This doesn't mean that the feelings our children evoke in us must remain perfectly steady and uniform. How could they? Kids delight us and enrage us and perplex us. They bring tears to our eyes just because they're so adorable or vulnerable or suddenly so grown-up. They also make us cry because they're so infuriating. We may even find ourselves experiencing two contradictory emotions about them at the same time. And much of what we feel will leak out of our faces and our voices. We won't always be pleased, and they'll know it. That's why it's so important for us to strive to communicate in many different ways that *our basic acceptance of them is a given*, a rock-solid core beneath whatever we happen to be feeling, and they happen to be doing, today.

Likewise, I'm not saying you can't be proud of a particular accomplishment. Strangely, though, unconditional parents are just as proud even when their child doesn't succeed. This is a paradox I had trouble understanding before I had children of my own, and which I still find difficult to explain. You can take special delight when your child does something remarkable, but, again, not in a way that suggests your love hinges on such events. If you strike that balance correctly, children are less likely to grow up feeling they're worthwhile only when they succeed. They'll be able to fail without concluding that they themselves are failures.

The most destructive form of praise is the kind explicitly intended to reinforce what the child is doing. When we're advised to "catch children being good" (read: obedient) and then give them a verbal doggie biscuit, this is a calculated attempt to manipulate them with conditional love. But what if praise is just a spontaneous reaction of delight to something our children have done, with no attempt to "reinforce" a certain behavior?[8]

This is undeniably a big improvement with respect to our motives. But once again, what matters isn't the message you sent—or even the reason you sent it. What matters is the message the child received.

What's most striking about a positive judgment is not that it's positive. (If that were the case, the only real alternative to praise would be criticism.) No, what's most striking is that it's a judgment. Why do we feel the need to keep evaluating our children's actions, turning them into "jobs" that may, if they're lucky, be deemed "good"? From this perspective, it becomes clear that what we really ought to be looking for is a way of being positive that isn't couched as a judgment.

The happy news is that it's not necessary to evaluate kids in order to encourage them. The popularity of praise rests partly on the failure to distinguish between those two ideas. Just paying attention to what kids are doing and showing interest in their activities is a form of encouragement. In fact, it's more important than what we say immediately after kids do something marvelous. *When unconditional love and genuine enthusiasm are always present, "Good job!" isn't necessary; when they're absent, "Good job!" won't help.*

But in case you're still wondering what to say, there are several possibilities consistent with unconditional parenting. (Please see the chart on p. 157 for examples.) One option is to say nothing at all. Some people insist we must praise children when they do something helpful because, secretly or unconsciously, these people believe that the action was a fluke. If children are basically bad, then they have to be given an artificial reason to be nice (namely, to get a verbal reward); otherwise it will never happen again. But if that cynical assumption is unfounded, then praise would not be necessary.

At first, it can feel weird to hold back when you're used to offering these constant evaluations. ("Good drawing!" "Good drinking!" "Good drooling!") It may seem as though you're being unsupportive. But from observing many parents, including myself, I've become convinced that praise is less a function of what kids need to hear than of what we need to say. And whenever that's true, it's time for us to rethink what we've been doing.

On those occasions when we feel it would be appropriate to say something, we can simply point out what we've seen and allow the child to decide how to feel about it (rather than telling her how). A simple, evaluation-free statement lets a child know that you noticed. It also lets her take pride in what she did. When, in her second year, my daughter finally made it up the stairs under her own steam, I was thrilled, of course, but I didn't feel the need to subject her to my judgment. I just said, "You did it" so she would know that I saw and I cared, but also so she could feel proud of herself.

At other times, a more elaborate description may make sense, but even this need not be contaminated with evaluation. You can simply provide feedback about what you observed. If a child does something caring or generous, you might gently draw his attention to the effect of his action *on the other person*. This is completely different from praise, where the emphasis is on how *you* feel about his sharing.

Finally, even better than descriptions are questions. Why tell him what you thought of what he did when you can ask him what he thinks? That's likely to promote useful reflection about why it may be better to act one way than another. Questions you ask about something he wrote or drew or made, meanwhile, invite him to consider what he succeeded in doing and how he did it. This can spur further improvement and nourish his interest in the task itself. The research, remember, suggests that praise may have exactly the opposite effect, directing his attention away from the task and toward your reaction.

Recently, I found myself at a crafts activity sponsored by a local library in which children were invited to create snowflakes out of pipe cleaners and beads. A boy of about four or five sitting near me showed his mother what he had done, and immediately she gushed about how wonderful it was. Then, since I was the only other adult at the table, he held his snowflake out so I, too, could see it clearly. Instead of offering an evaluation, I asked him whether he liked it. "Not so much," he admitted. I asked why, and he began to explain, his tone suggesting genuine interest in figuring out other possible ways he might have used the materials. This is exactly the sort of elaboration and reflection that are stifled when we slather our kids with praise. They tend to stop thinking and talking about what they've done as soon as we pass judgment on it.

INSTEAD OF SAYING . . .	TRY . . .
"I like the way you . . ."	**saying nothing** (and just paying attention)
"Good drawing! I love those pictures!"	**describing, rather than evaluating, what you see:** "Hey, there's something new on the feet of those people you just drew. They've got toes."
"You're such a great helper!"	**explaining the effects of the child's action on other people:** "You set the table! Boy, that makes things a lot easier on me while I'm cooking."
"That was a great essay you wrote."	**inviting reflection:** "How did you come up with that way of grabbing the reader's attention right at the beginning?"
"Good sharing, Michael."	**asking, rather than judging:** "What made you decide to give some of your brownie to Deirdre when you didn't have to?"

All of the suggested responses in this chart avoid giving a message of conditional approval, a patronizing pat on the head for having lived up to *your* standards and met *your* expectations. At the same time, they do offer the acknowledgment, encouragement, and attention kids need. (Saying nothing doesn't, in itself, accomplish these goals, of course, but ideally we're providing those things all the time.)

Here's a strategy about which I have mixed feelings: If our goal is specifically to help children become generous people, one researcher proposes that we attribute generous inclinations to them. How we think of ourselves affects how we act, so the idea is to convince kids that their motives already are generous. We want them to see themselves as caring individuals rather than as people who do nice things only when they'll get something out of it. One study showed that after children imitated an adult who had acted generously, those who were informed that they had done so "because you're the kind of person who likes to help other people" were more generous later on than were children who were told they had donated because they were expected to do so.[9]

While this strategy is undoubtedly more effective than mere positive reinforcement, I'm not sure it's any less manipulative. We're not responding authentically and spontaneously to what a child has done; we're deliberately saying something (which may or may not be true) to produce a desired effect. Still, the general principle here seems worth taking seriously: Rather than using praise, which focuses on specific behaviors—and may lead children to feel that they are loved only under certain conditions—we need to help them think about the way they are and the way they want to be.

I'm often asked whether all of this means that we're not supposed to give compliments or say thank you. My response is that it depends on three things: why we're saying it, to whom we're saying it, and what the effects are of saying it.

Why: Is such a comment intended mostly to be nice, to make someone feel good ("What a cute shirt!" "I really appreciate your coming to visit")? Or is it just a different way of offering contingent reinforcement in order to control someone's future behavior? If the latter, then recasting praise as an expression of gratitude doesn't really change very much.

To whom: I'm much less concerned about thank-yous and even comments that sound very much like praise when they pass between two adults of equal status, especially if neither is especially dependent on the other for love and acceptance. If I thank my neighbor for loaning me her car or tell a fellow author how much I enjoyed his book, I'm not trying to manipulate these individuals, and I'd be unlikely to succeed even if that were my goal. Nor is there any concern that the unconditionality of my love for them will be compromised because we don't have that kind of relationship to begin with. We need to be a lot more careful with what we say (and how, and why) when we're talking to our children.

What effects: There are lots of gray areas in the case of praise, many examples where it's not absolutely clear whether a given comment is likely to be injurious or innocuous. My best advice here is to watch for the impact it has. If you're in the habit of saying something to your children that could be construed as praise, see if they then look to you for—and seem to need—such comments on a regular basis. Try to figure out whether their intrinsic motivation (their commitment to an action or their interest in a given activity) seems to have lessened as a result of these kinds of statements from you.

In short, I'm not suggesting that we stop saying positive things to our children. But I am saying that we should look at the underlying significance of what we say, and how it's heard, rather than just trying to use or avoid specific words. If children perceive that we're simply joining with them to celebrate their accomplishments, that's fine. But if they perceive that we're imposing our evaluations on them, this can easily crowd out their own instincts about when and why to feel proud of themselves. Pretty soon they may come to define the value of what they do in terms of whether it elicits our approval—or, later, the approval of other people in authority.

It's not easy to move away from this kind of conditional parenting. Instead of attempting to quit cold turkey, you might allow yourself a transitional period during which you continue to offer evaluations but *also* offer descriptions and questions. As you become more accustomed to providing these new responses, you may eventually find yourself able to break the habit of starting with a judgment.

At the same time, it makes sense to discuss what you're doing, and why, with your children. If they've been led to expect a "Good job!" for certain things they do, they will probably find it jarring to have the praise supply suddenly cut off. They may be inclined to view the absence of a positive judgment as tantamount to a negative one. Make it clear, therefore, that you're not proposing to be less positive, but to be *unconditionally* positive—to offer approval and affection freely rather than in response to specific behaviors of theirs that you deem worthy. (Then proceed to do just that.)

Also, consistent with the advice to talk less and ask more, invite children who are old enough to share *their* perceptions of being praised. Don't just ask whether they like it. Ask whether they feel they've become dependent on these verbal rewards. Or how they regard the activities that produce the praise. (Are these activities less appealing when there's no one offering positive reinforcement for engaging in them?) Or what ideas they may have for other ways you could offer encouragement.

On Success and Failure

Many children feel their parents' approval is based not just on being well behaved but on being successful, as I discussed in chapter 5. Thus, it's important for us to consider whether just such a dynamic already exists in our families. We need to observe, as through the eyes of an outsider, what we say to our kids about the importance of doing well at various things, how we react when they succeed and when they don't, and how they respond to our reactions. In some cases, it may make sense simply to ask our kids point-blank: "Do you sometimes feel as though I love you more when you get good grades [or do well in sports, or accomplish something I can brag about to my friends] than when you don't?" Naturally, this question is useful only if children believe they can be completely honest with us, which means, among other things, that they know we're able to hear whatever they say without becoming defensive or angry.

Part of the problem in many families is not just how conditional love makes its presence felt, but how much emphasis is placed on doing well. In a few years, no one will care (or perhaps even remember) who won that Little League game or what grade your child got in math. But the psychological effects of making her feel that she had to earn your affection will likely linger and fester. We need to evaluate our actions and our motives. We need to look in the mirror and ask whether it's possible that we're pushing our kids too hard—and, for that matter, whether their accomplishments are so important to us because of how they reflect on us. Even parents who readily agree with the statement "I just want my child to be happy" sometimes give a very different impression by their behavior.

Most of us are familiar with people who are (or were) successful in the conventional sense of that word but who lead frankly miserable lives. We may also know people who used to give the impression that they'd never amount to anything, but did. Plenty of brilliant and accomplished adults were mediocre students, while plenty of rising stars end up burning out. One researcher, after spending more than fifteen years following the careers of high school valedictorians, concluded that most of them simply "know how to do school. They are not the group to look for, for creative breakthroughs . . . or for becoming notable leaders in a particular area."[10] And even if they do become notable leaders, they may resent the parents who seemed to pay attention to them only when they made good.

In short, credential-happy people aren't always happy. Our obligation is to warn our children about the implications of becoming addicted to A's and dollars and trophies, not to serve as enablers of those addictions. We need to keep them—and ourselves—focused on the things that really matter. That means strengthening our relationship with them, making it clear that our love is absolutely unrelated to how well they perform. It means reconsidering how we respond to the thousand tiny triumphs and setbacks that fill a childhood.

Two conclusions emerge: First, it's when children fall short and feel incompetent that they most need our love—not our disappointment. Second, the dangers are just as great if, when they *do* succeed, we lavish positive reinforcement on them in such a way as to suggest that our love is based on what they've done, not on who they are—and that they'd better keep up the good work . . . or else.

To whatever extent it remains important to us to help our children excel, it's useful to remember that the people who are most thoughtful and creative tend to be those who get a kick out of what they're doing. As a rule, it's interest that drives excellence—and by that I mean interest in the task itself, not interest in being successful or in doing better than others.

A considerable body of evidence suggests that when children are led to become preoccupied with *how well* they're doing, they often take less pleasure from *what* they're doing.[11] That's a sad result in its own right, and often the cause of considerable stress, but it also has the paradoxical effect of holding them back from doing the best they can. When students are led to fret about the quality of their performance ("How good is this project? Have I met these standards? How much improvement have I shown?"), then learning tends to become a chore rather than an occasion for excitement. Now it's not stuff they want to figure out; it's stuff they have to get better at.

In place of pressure, therefore, we should offer support: gentle guidance, encouragement, trust in children's growing competence, and help when it seems necessary. In place of competitive activities, we should offer opportunities to have fun and learn in ways that don't require having to defeat someone else.

In place of an excessive focus on school achievement, we should take a lively interest in what the child is learning. "So, what's *your* opinion about how dinosaurs became extinct?" is a question that supports intellectual growth. "How come only a B-minus on that paper?" is not. If a child has written an essay, it makes sense to focus not on whether it's good enough but on its content (and on the process of crafting it). A parent might ask: "How did you come to choose what to write about? What did you learn from your research? Why did you save that important point for the end? Did your opinion about the topic change at all after you started to write?"

Again, the most effective (and least destructive) way to help a child succeed—whether she's writing or skiing, playing a trumpet or a computer game—is to do everything possible to help her fall in love with what she's doing, to pay less attention to how successful she was (or is likely to be) and show more interest in the task. That's just another way of saying that we need to encourage more, judge less, and love always.

Teachers and Parents Together

While some exceptional teachers (such as the one quoted on pp. 148–49) provide students with the unconditional support they need, the sad reality is that many classrooms are not set up to do so—or, for that matter, to honor the principles described in the preceding chapter. School environments are often distinguished by an array of punishments and rewards, with elaborate behavior-management systems, "recognition" for those who are obedient, and sanctions for those who aren't. Children aren't helped to become caring members of a community, or ethical decision-makers, or critical thinkers, so much as they're simply trained to follow directions. In the worst-case scenario, the encouragement of learning takes a back seat to the enforcement of order. These are environments that aren't healthy for children and other living things.

I often hear from parents who explain that they're struggling to create "working with" homes—only to realize at some point that they're sending off their children every morning to "doing to" schools. (Of course, I also hear from frustrated teachers who describe a mirror-image situation: "We hold democratic class meetings to solve problems together—and then the kids go home to be manipulated with star charts and time-outs!") Obviously, things work best when parents *and* teachers are helping kids to become good people—and, better yet, when they're actively supporting one another's efforts.

The first step for parents: Be aware of what's happening at your child's school.

- Is it a place whose primary agenda is to meet children's needs or to get compliance?

- Are troublesome behaviors seen as problems to be solved or as infractions to be punished?

- Do the teachers view their jobs as helping kids learn to make good decisions—or do they insist on making almost all of the decisions themselves?

- Are students encouraged to collaborate with one another, or are most assignments intended to be completed alone (or even in competition with their peers)?

- If *you* attended this school or sat in this classroom, would you feel unconditionally accepted? Would you want to be there?

If you don't like what you see and hear, you'll need all the skills of diplomacy you can muster to invite your child's teacher to rethink some of his or her practices. This might be accomplished by raising the question of long-term goals. After all, educators typically endorse the same sorts of goals that parents do; they want their students to be responsible, caring, moral, curious, lifelong learners, and so on. You might focus on the objectives for children that you share with the teacher, and then gently raise the possibility that there may be better ways of achieving those objectives than traditional discipline practices, which rarely help kids to become responsible decision-makers.

You should be prepared to introduce your children's teacher to articles, books, and videos that offer guidance in creating "working with" classrooms.[12] Do some research so that you can talk about how some of the teacher's colleagues have made progress in creating such places. This can be done either by suggesting classrooms to visit (and teachers to talk to) or by recommending written material that highlights success stories from real schools. It can be reassuring for both you and the teacher to realize that schools don't have to be "doing to" places. Indeed, there are schools all over the country that have shown how to create a respectful and appealing environment for learning in the absence of carrot-and-stick control.

However, if a teacher is unreceptive to feedback and advice, no matter how respectfully it's offered, then you'll need to decide whether the situation is so disturbing that it's worth the risks involved to take action. Also, how likely is it that your efforts will succeed? Is the problem mostly confined to a specific classroom? If so, perhaps you can have your child moved to another one. The strategy you choose may depend on whether the principal—or, perhaps, an administrator in the school district's central office—is sympathetic to your point of view or at least open to persuasion. You may want to find several other parents who share your concerns; the more people who object to a practice or policy, the less likely it is that the complaint will just be dismissed.

While all this is going on, and especially if you decide that the situation is unlikely to change anytime soon, it's vital to do everything you can to protect your child. Here's the tightrope you must walk: On the one hand, you don't want to encourage your child to ignore, or act disrespectfully toward, the teacher—even though the teacher may be acting disrespectfully toward children. On the other hand, you don't want to endorse actions that you believe are indefensible, or cause your child to feel as though adults always stick up for one another (and unite against kids) even without good reason. Your primary obligation is to do right by your child.

What you say, and how you say it, will naturally be influenced by your child's age as well as by whether you view what's happening at school as merely less than ideal or as absolutely egregious. Think of your goal as giving your child a kind of inoculation, providing him with the unconditional love, respect, trust, and sense of perspective that will serve to immunize him against the most destructive effects of an overcontrolling environment or an unreasonable authority figure. He should be encouraged to reflect on why some adults feel the need to use punishments and rewards, what they could have done instead, and whether his own actions, too, could have been different. At best, this not only helps to buffer the negative impact of dubious discipline policies but offers a chance for your child to learn.

Remember that kids also learn from watching how we respond to challenges: whether we've taken their concerns seriously (as opposed to automatically siding with the teacher) and whether we involve the child in coming up with solutions (as opposed to trying to deal with the problem unilaterally). Also, children will notice the extent to which we convey respect for the teacher even while expressing disagreement with some of her actions, and how willing we are to understand and acknowledge the teacher's or principal's perspective on these issues.

Because your child is watching, because it's the right thing to do, and because it's more likely to be effective, you should be clear with the teacher that you don't want an adversarial relationship. Your goal is to work together, to take everyone's needs into account—not just your child's, but those of all the children and also the adults. At the same time, you can remain firm about the unacceptability of coercing children with bribes and threats.

The result may continue to be that your child is treated one way at home and another way at school. Here, the focus is on reasons and values; there, on behaviors. Here, he's led to consider the consequences of his actions to others; there, the consequences to himself. Here, he's encouraged to think; there, to do what he's told. Here, he's appreciated for who he is; there, only for what he does. Inconsistency can be confusing for a child; it's never ideal. But it's better than having home and school work in perfect harmony to do bad things to children.

9

CHOICES FOR CHILDREN

One afternoon, the woman who was cutting my hair began to tell me about a problem she was having with her son. I wasn't anxious for this to turn into an extended consultation, so when she finished her story I simply suggested that she might invite the boy to propose some ways of dealing with the issue. To my surprise, she became so excited about this idea that I began to worry she would accidentally snip off part of my ear.

There's nothing brilliantly original about the notion that kids should be part of the problem-solving process when things go wrong, or, for that matter, that they should have some say about what happens to them on an ongoing basis. Yet I continue to be struck by how often parents fail to consider these possibilities, or neglect to act on them, or even angrily resist them. So perhaps it's worth spending some time reviewing why—and how—to let children participate in making decisions. Let's start with why.

The Benefits of Choosing

The first argument is a moral one: All people ought to have some control over their own lives. In the case of children, of course, there are limits to how much control and what kind; plenty of things have to be decided for them, particularly when they're young. But that doesn't negate the basic principle. I believe our default position ought to be to let kids make decisions about matters that concern them except when there is a compelling reason for us to override that right. We should be prepared to justify why, in each case, kids *shouldn't* be allowed to choose.

All of us have a basic need to be "origins" in our lives rather than "pawns," as one researcher put it. It's important to experience a sense of autonomy, a feeling that we are the initiators of much of what we do. In fact, the particular choices we make are often less significant than the act of choosing itself. I briefly forgot this one evening when my son, then three-and-a-half, asked me for a sticker book. I found a collection of them in the closet, selected one with a truck theme that I thought he would enjoy, and handed it to him. "No," he insisted. "*I* want to pick." I put back the book I had chosen and gave him the whole pile. Guess which one he ended up taking.

When our need for autonomy is chronically frustrated, the consequences can include not merely aggravation but depression and even physical illness.[1] As we saw in chapter 3, various undesirable effects tend to show up when kids feel they're overcontrolled by their parents. In the classroom, too, students tend not to think as deeply, or to be as interested, if they have little to say about what they're learning or about the circumstances in which they're learning it. (Sadly, traditional and "back to basics" styles of education are distinguished by just such an enforced passivity.) Adults in the workplace, meanwhile, are most likely to burn out not because they have too much to do but because they don't have enough choice about what it is they're doing.

The research doesn't merely show that people fail to flourish when they feel powerless. It also clearly demonstrates the benefits of *having* the chance to choose. For example, when parents not only avoid the temptation to rely on control but also go out of their way to help children experience a sense of autonomy,[2] these children are more likely to do what they're asked and less likely to misbehave. Teenagers who are able to participate in family decision-making are more apt to rely on their parents and to share many of their beliefs. They also end up feeling better about themselves, liking school more, and preferring more challenging assignments—and, if all that's not enough, they're also more likely to stay out of trouble. Finally, college students whose parents had encouraged them to be independent as children are more likely than their peers to feel confident about themselves and to persist in the face of difficulty or failure.[3]

When teachers give their students more choice about what they're doing, the results are equally impressive. According to one summary of the research, the advantages include "greater perceived competence, higher intrinsic motivation, more positive emotionality, enhanced creativity, a preference for optimal challenge over easy success, greater persistence in school (i.e., lower drop-out rates), greater conceptual understanding, and better academic performance."[4]

Thus, helping children to feel empowered makes sense at all ages, at home and at school, and with regard to both immediate outcomes and long-term goals. When you think about it, life provides us with an endless series of choices about issues that range from minuscule to monumental, and we want our kids to be able to deal with them in a thoughtful way. If I were to summarize the relevant research and real-life experience on this question in a single sentence, it would be this: *The way kids learn to make good decisions is by making decisions, not by following directions.*

At the same time, we have to concede that people aren't always permitted to participate in decision making. Democracy is noticeably absent from most American classrooms and workplaces, and some parents use that fact to rationalize their "because I said so" practices. But the best way to prepare children for experiences where they will be unnecessarily controlled is not to immerse them in similar experiences beforehand. That would be like saying that, because there are a lot of carcinogens in the environment, we should expose kids to as many cancer-causing agents as possible while they're young.

On the contrary, it makes sense to raise them with respect, to offer them unconditional support, and to give them choices on a regular basis. That foundation allows them to evaluate the controlling people and institutions they'll eventually face by applying the higher standard they encountered while growing up. It also means they'll be more likely to work for positive changes in our society rather than just accepting power-based arrangements as they are—or believing those arrangements are inevitable.

In short, empowered kids are in the best position to deal constructively with disempowering circumstances. And we, as parents, are in the best position to empower them—as long as we're willing to limit *our* use of power over them.

First Words and Last Words

Limiting our power doesn't necessarily mean that we must be silent about our preferences, but whenever possible we ought to leave the final decision in the child's hands.[5] For example, I might state in a matter-of-fact tone that I believe it would be appropriate for my child to apologize for something she did, but leave it up to her to decide whether that conclusion is right and whether she will act on it. (After all, the alternative is to compel her to say she's sorry when she isn't.)

Even when we're unwilling to give kids the last word, we can still give them the first word—that is, a chance to make their case. Thus, when children ask whether it's okay to do something, it often makes sense to respond with "Well, what do you think?" This lets them know that their viewpoint counts, and also invites them to play an active role in considering the implications of their request.

The question of whether, and how, to let children decide becomes somewhat more complicated in the case of sibling conflicts.[6] Many parents jump in prematurely and then make matters worse by siding with one child against the other, or unfairly condemning them both, or struggling to figure out who's to blame. In so doing, they short-circuit the process by which kids learn to negotiate their own solutions.

However, I'm not entirely comfortable with blanket advice to "let them work things out for themselves." First of all, a child who feels she has a legitimate grievance may get the idea that you don't care enough to get involved, that you're indifferent to her complaint. Second, your hands-off policy may leave the weaker child to the mercies of the one who is stronger or cleverer—and you may give the impression that any outcome, no matter how unfair, has your blessing.

Be clear that you're concerned and sympathetic; find out what's going on. If you then decide to have the children construct their own solution, make sure you know what it is. This is a learning process for all concerned. Talk to both children after the fact to help them hone their conflict-resolution skills, to reflect on issues of fairness, and to think about what they might do next time. But be careful: As one child psychologist points out, "Parental intervention does not guarantee fairness; it only brings into the conflict an even stronger participant whose word is final regardless of the facts."[7]

Even in the absence of a nasty disagreement, children may try to make decisions for their younger siblings, to tell them how they should be doing things. A doing-to style comes easily to children (as it does to adults); it's autonomy support that has to be learned. To provide that support for young children is to protect them from anyone who would try to control them unnecessarily.

Deciding Together

Even babies can be allowed to choose. They have very clear preferences for when they want to eat, how they prefer to be held, where they like to be tickled, which toy they'd rather play with, and so on. It's important that we tune in to what they're telling us and try to honor their requests whenever possible rather than insisting on a fixed schedule for eating and sleeping, or interacting with them in a way that entertains us but doesn't really please them.[8]

Toddlers are better able to communicate their desires, and they have more options for expressing displeasure if those desires are thwarted. Along with the ability to arrange things so they get more of what they want, of course, comes the potential for conflict. That's why we often have mixed feelings about our young children's growing mastery. It was great when my eighteen-month-old daughter figured out how to turn a toy on and off; I was proud of her competence and perhaps a bit relieved that she didn't need to call me as often. But the stage was then set for a clash of wills. I turned off a noisy device and she turned it right back on. At that point my options were pretty much limited to two: my way or her way. Either I let her keep the toy on or I didn't. (In this case, I did.)

As a child gets older, though, it becomes increasingly possible to explain and discuss. This is a real breakthrough: Rather than being forced to choose between either giving in or imposing our will, we now can take advantage of a third possibility, which is to work things out together. Notice that this is different from merely coming down somewhere between the extremes of absolute freedom, on the one hand, and excessive control, on the other. Sometimes the best alternative to black and white isn't gray but, let's say, orange. In other words, there may be a possibility outside the continuum that has defined our options. It's not just a matter of figuring out *how much* choice to give kids, what percentage of the decisions to leave to them, but how to become active—and interactive—in the *way* we help children decide.

An early study of parenting practices discovered that children became more "active, outgoing, and spontaneous" when they were given plenty of opportunities to make decisions. On closer inspection, however, it turned out that freedom wasn't enough. A "high level of interaction between the parent and child" was also required.[9] In a general sense, that means we have to proactively support kids' capacity to choose and help them feel that they are at least to some extent self-determining. Our job is to nourish their sense of autonomy and also to think together about ways of negotiating solutions for specific issues, such as bedtime, curfew, where to take a family vacation, and so on.

Consider a child who is spending what we believe is too much time in front of the TV or the computer. Recently I had separate conversations with two different parents about this issue. One was unhappy about excessive television watching in her household, but she shrugged and asked rhetorically, "What are you going to do? It's the times we live in." The other mother, by contrast, felt she had to take action— so she hid the remote control from her daughter.

Together, these responses define a classic false dichotomy. If we let kids do whatever they want, even when we disapprove, we risk sending the message that we really don't care, that we're washing our hands of responsibility. (In the case of TV, the do-nothing option may actually be more appealing to some parents because, despite their misgivings, they find it convenient to have their children occupied and quiet.) On the other hand, the second response is a doing-to solution. Never mind that hiding the remote is unlikely to work (at least for very long) and merely invites the child to find a way to work around it. What's more important is that this teaches children to use power—or sneakiness—to get their way.

What these two strategies share is that neither of them takes any time, any talent, any skill, any care, or any courage. As I noted earlier, a true working-with approach is more demanding than either "I'm the parent; I decide" *or* "Do whatever you want." A more constructive response would begin with listening—not only so that kids *feel* heard but so that you can learn more about what's really going on. TV programs and computer games are appealing in their own right, but children who spend inordinate amounts of time with them may be doing so because they're depressed or trying to avoid other activities (including social interaction) for specific reasons that need to be dealt with. In addition to listening, we need to be candid about our feelings and, ultimately, to look for solutions together: "Let's talk about what's fair to you but also what might address my concerns. Let's come up with some ideas and try them out."

In this case, that may mean agreeing on a reasonable limit to the time spent in front of the TV or PC, as well as specifying which programs or games are okay and which are not (and why). But that's just the beginning of the discussion. We may need to explore the underlying issues that explain why the television has become the child's best friend. And we may decide to spend more time with our kids—at activities they help to choose.

Here's another example: It's one thing to lock your car's rear door so that a young child can't accidentally open it while you're speeding down the highway. It's something else to lock the electric windows so that only you, the driver, can control them. That's another doing-to solution, a way of trying to make the problem go away by stripping children of power. Instead, we might just allow the kids to play with the windows, knowing that eventually the game will lose its novelty. If there really is a problem with what they're doing, however, we should take the time to explain *why* it's a problem and ask them to refrain from fooling with the buttons too much.

This general approach almost always works with my own children, and I hear from many other parents across the country who have the same experience. Kids really respond when they're treated with respect, involved in problem solving, and assumed to be well intentioned. By contrast, it's the children who are raised with more traditional disciplinary practices (and the corresponding assumptions) who tend to take advantage. "Give 'em an inch, they'll take a mile" turns out to be true primarily of children who have only been given inches in their lives.

In short, with each of the thousand-and-one problems that present themselves in family life, our choice is between controlling and teaching, between creating an atmosphere of distrust and one of trust, between setting an example of power and helping children to learn responsibility, between quick-fix parenting and the kind that's focused on long-term goals.

These alternatives are particularly salient for parents who struggle continuously with getting their children out of bed, dressed, fed, washed, and out the door in time for school—that is, most of us. Not long after our first child started preschool, my wife and I fell into the trap of nagging and relying on various coercive strategies. What we were doing in an increasingly desperate effort to get her going in the morning was tiresome for all of us, and we weren't acting like the parents we wanted to be. Finally, we sat down with our daughter at a time when none of us was feeling pressured, and calmly laid out the problem. Then, instead of lecturing, we listened. Instead of creating a "behavior plan" to be done to her (much as one might try to house-train a pet), we brainstormed together: What could we do that would make mornings more pleasant for all of us?

Abigail suggested that things might go a lot faster if she could just sleep in the clothes she was going to wear the following day. We couldn't think of any good reason not to try this, so we did. (She doesn't wear the kind of clothing that's apt to become wrinkled—and, even if that did happen, so what?) It worked. Mornings are still a struggle sometimes, but less so than if getting dressed were still part of the routine.

My point here is not necessarily to recommend the option of sleeping in one's clothes, you understand. The process matters more than the product, and it should be a process that encourages children to reason and plan and participate in figuring something out. What counts is that kids know their needs matter to us and that we're willing to take their ideas seriously. Anyone who wants to raise a clear-thinking, self-confident child—someone who *doesn't* grow into a troubled teen—should imagine the likely effect of years filled with examples of mutual problem-solving, then compare that to years of having the parent make all the important decisions. In fact, we don't have to speculate about the results. We have good data to show that children are more likely to control themselves if their parents are willing to negotiate and are open to changing their minds in response to children's arguments.[10]

Such openness often produces more questions and challenges, and that can become frustrating. Many of us jokingly long for the good old days when kids just did what they were told and knew better than to talk back. But, of course, *we* know better. The old days really weren't so good, whereas the process of talking things out and deciding things together produces benefits that repay our patience many times over.

Look at it this way: One option for parents of older children is to monitor and control them in a desperate effort to make sure they don't get into trouble—read their diaries and rifle through their backpacks when they're not looking, devise technical fixes to prevent them from watching inappropriate TV programs, maybe even install hidden cameras so we can keep an eye on them. The other option is to build a trusting relationship with them from the time they're small and involve them in making decisions. That way, the doing-to approach, which we already know to be offensive and counterproductive, proves to be unnecessary as well.

But are there enough hours in the day to talk over everything with our kids? I think we can offer four responses to this concern. First of all, while it's theoretically possible to spend too much time hashing things out, most parents have a long way to go before they have to worry about erring in this direction. The far more common mistake is to share decision-making authority too rarely. The vast majority of families suffer from too little democracy, not too much.

Second, I'm not suggesting that everything has to be negotiated, only that kids should know many issues *can* be negotiated. Paradoxically, they'll feel less need to challenge every decision when they're confident that it's possible for them to object (or suggest an alternative) on those occasions when they feel it's important to do so.

Third, children are much less likely to resist decisions that they helped to make. The top-down, "while you're living in my house, you'll do as I say" approach ends up taking a lot more time and energy than we realize because of the defiance it so often provokes. Even apart from the stress experienced by parents and children alike—and the damage to their relationship—the apparent efficiency of bypassing discussions by deciding things unilaterally turns out to be an illusion when you take the long view.

Finally, speaking of the long view, even if working things out with kids really did end up taking more time and effort than the traditional approach, it's one of the best ways parents can spend their time. To appreciate this, we have to look beyond the specific issue we're discussing and remember that this process provides incalculable benefits to our children's social, moral, and intellectual development.

Pseudochoice

Some parents talk about "choice" not in the context of allowing kids to have more say but rather as a way of blaming them for deliberately deciding to do something bad.[11] A sentence such as "You *chose* to break the rule" amounts to using this word almost like a bludgeon against children. It's also a way of trying to justify a punitive response, so it shouldn't be surprising to learn that people who talk this way are indeed more likely to use punishment and other power-based interventions.[12]

Adults who blithely insist that children choose to misbehave are rather like politicians who declare that people have only themselves to blame for being poor. In both cases, potentially relevant factors other than personal responsibility are ignored. A young child in particular may not have the fully developed capacity for rational decision-making or impulse control that is implicit in suggesting he made a choice. (Parents who take those limits into account are likely to try to help the child develop the relevant skills, rather than to punish and blame.) A second similarity between the attribution of choice by parents and politicians is that in both cases it's the very people claiming this who tend to benefit from such thinking. They have no need to reconsider their own decisions and demands. Parents, for example, can simply tell themselves that their children "chose" whatever happened.

Sometimes it's the idea of choice that's misused rather than just the word. We find this when parents pretend to let the child decide while actually keeping all the real decision-making authority to themselves. There are three common forms of "pseudochoice," all of which, sadly, can be found in discipline books as examples of what we're supposed to do.

In the first version, the parent asks a loaded question such as "Do you want to do the dishes now or would you rather do them while your favorite TV program is on?" The problem here isn't just that the options have been reduced to two. It's that no real choice is being offered at all. Obviously, the child doesn't want to miss her program. The parent is really saying "Wash the dishes now or else I'm not going to let you watch TV"—or, in generic terms, "Do what I tell you or you'll be punished." The language of choice is used to disguise what is basically just a threat.

The second kind of pseudochoice is different only in that the deception occurs *after* a child does something regarded as inappropriate. The parent announces that a punishment will be imposed, but describes it as something the child asked for—as in, "You've *chosen* a time-out." This phrase appeals to some parents because it seems to relieve them of any responsibility for what they're about to do, but it's fundamentally dishonest and manipulative. To the injury of punishment is added the insult of a kind of mind game whereby reality is redefined and children are told, in effect, that they wanted to be made to suffer. "You've chosen a time-out" is a lie; a truthful parent would have to say, "I've chosen to isolate you."

A slightly different version of this ploy consists of saying something like "Don't make me spank you!" (or ". . . send you to your room," or ". . . take away your allowance," or whatever)—in effect, pretending that the child is responsible for "making" the parent resort to punishment. It's interesting to observe how many people who piously declare that children must take responsibility for their own behavior—sometimes even before they're really old enough to do so—end up twisting reality so as to escape responsibility for *their* behavior. ("Don't look at me! My kid forced me to do bad things to her!")

The last version of pseudochoice occurs when parents go through the motions of letting the child choose but make it clear how the results must come out. Some options are acceptable and others are not, and the child is expected to figure out what the parent wants him to do—that is, if he ever wants to have the chance to "choose" again. ("I guess you're not mature enough to be allowed to decide these things for yourself" means "You didn't pick what I wanted you to.") Better just to tell a child "I'm going to pick for you," which at least is honest, than to go through this charade.

The Limits of Limits

Even parents who avoid these deceptions should reflect on whether they might be unnecessarily limiting their children's opportunities to choose. Although there are certain kinds of choices that adults have to make for their children—and even though the choices children can make for themselves often must be circumscribed—I become uneasy when parents (or people who advise parents) make emphatic, self-satisfied declarations about the need to "set limits." Too often this phrase is used to justify an approach that features far too much control.

This is particularly true when it's also asserted that we shouldn't feel bad about what we're doing because kids, despite their apparent resistance, actually want limits. As Thomas Gordon pointed out, that's a "dangerous half-truth." Children may *accept* limits and even acknowledge their value, but what they *need* is to be consulted rather than just constrained. Watch how differently kids react to "limits imposed by an adult and . . . limits they have a voice in determining." The question we ought to be asking, as Gordon saw it, isn't whether limits and rules are sometimes necessary. It's "who sets them: the adults alone or the adults and kids—together."[13]

Sometimes the limits parents impose take the form of allowing kids to make choices only about meaningless matters. I remember a mother telling me proudly that she makes a point of letting her child choose whenever she doesn't much care how things turn out. The advantages of autonomy that I described earlier require that children have a say about some issues where we *do* care what happens. Kids should be able to make some choices that have the potential to make us gulp a bit.

Naturally, the extent to which we give them those opportunities will depend partly on their ages: I'm not saying a three-year-old should decide whether to get vaccinated. But even at this age a child can have some input into matters more significant than which color sippy cup to use for lunch. It's also important to consider the type of question that's under discussion. In some realms, such as health and safety, children might be limited to peripheral choices, such as *when* to take a bath or which style of helmet to put on before getting on a bike or skateboard. But in other realms, such as how to furnish and decorate their bedrooms, they should have much more latitude to do things as they see fit. (Authoritarian parents, by contrast, not only offer minimal opportunities for their children to choose, but tend to treat matters of taste or personal style as if they were moral issues with a single right answer—an answer that must, of course, be provided by the parent.)

I won't try to specify exactly what a given child (whom I've never met) should be allowed to decide at a given age. But the challenge for all of us is to make sure that, if we're saying our child *shouldn't* have any choice about a certain issue, we're really doing so because it doesn't make sense, not just because we're unwilling to give up some control. Even the most effective parents often find it tough to relinquish some of their authority, but they do so anyway. And when they don't, they may smack their foreheads later and mutter, "Wait a minute! Why did *I* make that decision on my own? Why did I tell when I could have asked?"

One way to make sure that choices are real and meaningful is to do more than allow kids to select one option from a menu that you've constructed. ("Would you like to do *x, y,* or *z?*") That sort of limited choice may be all that a very young child can handle, but by the time children are five or six, they should have plenty of opportunities to *generate* different possibilities rather than merely picking one from among those that you've set before them. Try to ask more open-ended questions, such as "What would you like to do today?" It's fine to suggest some ideas if children seem stymied. But don't hem them in prematurely. Real autonomy comes from construction more than from selection.[14]

When They Have To, But Don't Want To

Even after we've challenged ourselves to think carefully about whether there's a reasonable justification for what we're asking children to do (or not to do), there will be some demands that really are nonnegotiable. There will be some occasions when compliance is vital, some times when we truly must say "You have to" or "You can't." What then?

The good news is that parents who haven't overplayed their hand by demanding obedience all the time are likely to find that their children will give them the benefit of the doubt and do what they're asked when the situation requires it. (This is similar to how children who know they can participate in making decisions won't feel they have to do so about every single issue.) Resistance is more common among children who feel powerless and are driven to assert their autonomy in exaggerated ways.

Still, there will be times when they resist what you tell them, however good your reasons are and however sparingly you invoke your authority. But even then, there are alternatives to rewarding and punishing and crudely laying down the law.

1. USE THE LEAST INTRUSIVE STRATEGY.

Be as gentle and kind as possible. Don't overwhelm a child with your power. If a child is in a foul temper, angrily resisting every suggestion you make, don't get pulled into a struggle. Discussion doesn't make sense when she's unable to reason, and of course hollering back never makes sense. Give her a few minutes to recover. The storm will pass.

This advice also makes sense when you're confronted with passive resistance. Suppose a young child ignores your request to put away a toy. He sits with his back to you and continues playing. The impulse is very strong here to insist, to use heavy-handed tactics and ratchet up the stakes. After all, your authority has been challenged! Kids can't be allowed to ignore their parents! But what if you took a breath, asked him to clean up when he's done playing, and then walked away?

By backing off a bit and giving him some space, you let him maintain his autonomy and his dignity.

In my experience, this kind of nonconfrontational approach really does produce better results—and, in the bargain, keeps the mood pleasant and the relationship relatively unscathed. (In fact, the same request-and-move-away strategy can be effective when used by classroom teachers.)[15] But it does require considerable self-restraint as well as plain old patience. Especially with younger children, we can't expect instant compliance on every occasion, no matter what our parenting style may be. We have to be prepared to repeat the request or prohibition (along with the reason for it) several times. We have to allow for bad days. It's unrealistic to expect that children will always obey, and it's destructive to think of these impasses as battles that we must always win. Remember, the traditional methods really don't work better in the long run, and they can do an awful lot of harm.

2. BE HONEST WITH THEM.

If what you're asking your child to do isn't much fun, acknowledge that fact. If you want him to be quiet just because you've had enough ruckus for one day, say so. Don't invent more-impressive-sounding justifications for your request, or pretend that something you're telling him to do will be enjoyable when that's unlikely to be true. Try to see things from his point of view (more about that in the following chapter), and capture that perspective in your words: "I know it's frustrating when you can't [name of desired activity], sweetie, and you probably wish I'd just leave you alone, huh? But . . ."

3. EXPLAIN THE RATIONALE.

"Because I said so" is not a reason at all; it's an appeal to brute force and a way of teaching children to rely on it themselves. It's better not only to avoid that phrase but to make a point of offering reasons. Most of our requests can be explained even to two-year-olds in words they can at least partly grasp. ("Your brother's waiting for us to pick him up at school; if we don't go get him now, he won't know where we are and he'll be sad.") Offering explanations doesn't guarantee that a child will cheerfully accept our demands—just as it wouldn't always work if someone were telling us we had to do this, or couldn't do that—but it makes acceptance a lot more likely. In any case, people of any age are entitled to a reason when someone is limiting their options.

4. TURN IT INTO A GAME.

Use your imagination to help children find some enjoyment in doing things that aren't intrinsically all that delightful. When young kids resist brushing their teeth, you can encourage them to listen for the sound of bristles on enamel, which provides instant evidence that they're succeeding in getting rid of yucky stuff. More elaborate games may include planes (disguised as toothbrushes) repeatedly taking off and landing in the mouth. Invent your own variations—or, better yet, ask the child to do so. Older kids, meanwhile, can be invited to think of various ways to do a given chore, or to calculate how much time it takes to do it this way versus that way.

5. SET AN EXAMPLE.

Adults don't have to follow all the same rules that children do, but most rules ought to apply to us, too. If we're asking them to clean up after themselves or turn off the light when they leave the room, if we're telling them not to interrupt or swear or use an insulting tone, then we should do likewise. Apart from simple fairness, it's easier to get kids to do something that we ourselves are willing to do.

6. GIVE THEM AS MUCH CHOICE AS POSSIBLE.

Within the constraints of what they have to do, ask them how they want to do it, or where, or when, or with whom. Once you start to think creatively about these issues—and, again, have your kids join you in doing so—it's amazing how much opportunity there is for decision making even when the bottom line is that something must be done.[16]

These half-dozen suggestions can often be used in combination. For example, suppose a child resists washing her hands before dinner. A parent might say, "Well, I know what you're doing right now is more fun than coming over to the sink, but your hands do have to be washed so that you don't get sick from eating dirt. If your hands aren't clean, then your mouth might be happy with what you eat, but your tummy will get upset. [Optional: Insert your impression of a tummy protesting in a funny voice.] So would you like to wash them here in the kitchen or in the bathroom?" Other choices can be provided, too: "Would you like to wash them by yourself, or would you like to wash them with me? (I always wash my hands before I eat, too.)" "Would you like to use the sink or swish them around in a big bowl with bubbles?" And so on.

On occasion children will do things that are absolutely unacceptable and we simply must thwart their intentions. They may experience our intervention as a punishment, which makes it harder to address the underlying issues calmly or to avoid damaging the relationship. For that reason, the use of outright coercion is a last resort, a strategy to be used reluctantly and rarely. When it is absolutely necessary, we should do everything possible to soften the blow and minimize the punitive impact of such a move. Our tone should be warm and regretful and also confident that we can eventually solve the problem together.

Furthermore, we should look for ways to help the child reclaim his dignity and a sense of potency. If we're not comfortable letting a twelve-year-old attend an unsupervised party, and if that decision provokes bitter resentment, perhaps there's another part of his life where we can offer him more control. We might let him have more say about his wardrobe, or his curfew, or his use of the computer. If you want a fancy name for this, call it "compensatory autonomy support."

When I was doing an errand one day with my three-year-old daughter, she refused to walk back to the car and held a sit-down strike right there on the sidewalk. Luckily, I wasn't in a hurry, so I remained pleasant and just waited her out. Eventually she stood up and stomped her way back, refusing to speak to me. I had avoided doing anything overtly coercive, but the reality was that I got my way, she didn't get hers, and she wasn't happy about it. When we pulled into the garage, she announced that she wanted to stay in the car and listen to music. Not only did I let her do so for longer than I ordinarily would have, but I visited her periodically to ask if she was ready to come in yet. My intent was to make sure she knew—and that she knew I knew—that it was her decision. Again, the idea is simple: When you must act in a way that diminishes a kid's sense of self-determination over here, make an effort to strengthen it over there.

The passive-aggressive response of a sit-down strike, of course, doesn't test us as intensely as does the active-aggressive response of a full-blown tantrum. Some thoughtful authors see tantrums as important for healthy development, while others regard them as a sign that children are frustrated with their parents' behavior—very likely for good reason—and don't know how else to express that frustration. Perhaps each of these views captures part of the truth; perhaps tantrums aren't inevitable or especially desirable, on the one hand, but aren't necessarily an indication of bad parenting, on the other. In any case, what matters is that if and when they do occur, we respond as constructively as possible.

Rule number one: If you're in public, ignore everyone around you. The more worried you are about how other people will judge your parenting skills, the greater the chance that you'll respond with too much control and too little love and patience. This is not about what people think of you; it's about what your child needs.

Rule number two: Imagine how this looks from her point of view. Someone having a tantrum is very likely afraid of her own rage, terrified of being out of control. Consequently, you do her no favors by ignoring her or by responding harshly. Use only the minimum control necessary to make sure that people (and, less importantly, property) aren't in danger. Focus on providing comfort and calm reassurance. Let the tantrum play itself out. Later, you can try to address the underlying causes together.

Trying It Out

One of my objectives in this chapter has been to make it clear just how often we exclude our children from making choices that they're capable of making, thereby missing opportunities to help them learn and to meet their need for autonomy. To that end, I've offered some real-life examples of letting children choose.

The trouble is that I have no way of knowing whether any of those examples are relevant to *your* life. If we were sitting in the same room, I'd be able to ask you about, and respond to, your specific concerns. Perhaps I could make some suggestions, based on your unique situation, for how to help your child participate more often or more significantly. This being a book and not a workshop, however, the best I can do is to turn the last part of this chapter over to you. In each of the following three activities, I'd recommend that you involve your spouse or partner, or maybe even a friend who is also a parent.

EXERCISE 1

To begin with, it may be helpful to come up with some responses to common scenarios. The point is to get in the habit of devising working-with strategies and to see how they differ from the more common doing-to responses.

Example A: Your child resists going to bed, first pretending not to hear you announce that it's bedtime, then begging for a few more minutes, then insisting that there's only one last little-bitty thing that needs to be finished, then arguing that it's not fair to have to go to bed so early, and finally just refusing in an angry voice.

List a few conventional doing-to responses:

Now try to think of a couple of working-with alternatives:

Example B: Lately, your child has begun to adopt an insulting tone in conversations with you—or, perhaps, with a sibling.

Again, list some doing-to responses:

And list some working-with alternatives:

EXERCISE 2

Now think of something that *your* child has been doing that bothers or worries you. It can be an issue discussed in this book or something I've neglected to mention.

First, describe the problem.

Let's assume that by now you have a pretty good idea of what not to do. Take as much time as you need—minutes, hours, even days—to invent a couple of ideas that might just be more successful. Jot them down here.

Circle or underline one idea on the list that you're actually going to try. Then go try it. After enough time has passed, make a note about how well it worked—and, perhaps, what you might do differently next time to improve its effectiveness.

Repeat this process one or two more times, if you find it useful.

EXERCISE 3

Now that you've read about working-with strategies, created some of your own, and finally created some in response to real problems you've been experiencing with your child, it's time for the last step—devising working-with strategies not only for your child but *with* your child.

If you'd like to do this with a problem other than the one you used in the last exercise, describe that new problem.

When the time is right, ask your child to think about what might be a good way to deal with this issue. Try to elicit two or three ideas and write them down.

1.

2.

3.

Together with your child, pick one of these ideas that seems especially promising. Then try it out.

Finally, write down how well it worked—and, again, what you and your child believe might be a better way of implementing the same idea next time.

10

———

THE CHILD'S PERSPECTIVE

How do we raise our children to be happy? That's an important question, but here's another one: How do we raise our children to be concerned about whether *other* people are happy?[1]

It's important that we don't allow the first issue to upstage the second—or, for that matter, that we don't spend more energy trying to get kids to be polite and well behaved than on trying to help them become genuinely compassionate and committed to doing the right thing. We need to focus on our children's moral development.

To do so is to recast various ideas that are discussed in other parenting books. For example, "boundaries" and "limits" are usually thought of as restrictions that adults impose on children. But shouldn't our goal be for the children to refrain from doing certain things not because we've forbidden them, but just because they're wrong? The limits on kids' behavior, in other words, should be experienced as intrinsic to the situation. We want them to ask "How will doing *x* make that other kid feel?"—not "Am I allowed to do *x*?" or "Will I get in trouble for doing *x*?"

This is an ambitious goal, but not an unrealistic one because we have good material to work with. Human beings are born with the capacity to care. Thus, parents hoping to raise a child who is responsive to the needs of others already have "an ally within the child," as Martin Hoffman once put it.

Of course, that doesn't mean that kids will automatically grow into ethical people if left to their own devices. They need our help. To begin with, they need us to stop doing things that interfere with moral growth, things like punishments and rewards, which are rooted in—and underscore a child's preoccupation with—self-interest. The elimination of these staples of traditional discipline is an important step toward helping children become attuned to the well-being of others. But it's only a single step. The subtraction of bad parenting practices must be accompanied by the addition of good ones.

Moral Kids

Quite a lot of research on this topic has been conducted by child development specialists, and particularly by those who focus on what's called "prosocial" behavior. If we sift through the data, it's possible to distill several key recommendations for promoting moral growth.[2] (And, by the way, it's not a coincidence that these items overlap substantially with some of the unconditional parenting principles presented in chapter 7.)

1. CARE ABOUT THEM.

The cornerstone of moral development is the connection between parent and child. All instruction and intervention must be nested in a relationship that feels warm, safe, and unconditionally loving to the child. The same words keep coming up in guidelines for raising a moral child that are offered by different experts: secure attachment, nurturance, respect, responsiveness, and empathy. These are basic needs that all human beings have. When these needs are met, a child is freed from having to be preoccupied with them and can be open to helping others. But if these needs are not met, they may continue to reverberate in the child's ears, with the result that he or she is deaf to other people's cries of distress.

Children who know they're loved feel safer and less defensive. Therefore, they tend to be bolder about reaching out to others—including people who are different from themselves. And there's a nice bonus: Children who are securely attached to their parents are not only more responsive to others; they're also more likely to be assertive and independent, to distinguish themselves as socially competent and psychologically healthy on a range of measures.

2. SHOW THEM HOW A MORAL PERSON LIVES.

Even before they're steady on their feet, children are soaking up your values. They're learning from you how to be a human being. If they see you nonchalantly walk by someone in trouble, they learn that other people's pain is no business of theirs. But if they see you showing concern, even for strangers, that teaches a powerful moral lesson. Studies have shown that children are more likely to donate to charity if they've watched someone else do so, even if it was a long time ago. The effect on children's behavior and beliefs is particularly pronounced if the example is set by people whom the child regards as warm and nurturing. Similarly, parents who want to teach the importance of honesty make it a practice never to lie to their children, even when it would be easier just to claim that there are no cookies left rather than to explain why they can't have another one.

We can also set an example by showing kids that not all ethical decisions are easy calls. It can be terribly difficult to grapple with a situation that seems to pit two values (say, honesty and compassion) against one another. It can also be hard to know how much weight to give another person's preferences when you'd rather do something else. Take children "backstage" and let them see how you think—and feel—your way through a dilemma. They may learn something about the process by which you try to live a moral life, but, more important, they'll figure out that morality is rarely cut-and-dried.

3. LET THEM PRACTICE.

As important as it is to watch, people also learn by doing. Therefore, it makes sense to give children plenty of opportunities to help. If kids are responsible for looking out for a younger sibling or taking care of a pet, they're provided with a living lesson in the effects of caring. They've not only heard about it and seen it—they've done it. This also leads them to define themselves as helpful people.

That's one reason the best teachers arrange their classrooms so that children frequently learn from one another. Literally hundreds of studies have shown that students think more deeply when they can pool their resources, put their heads together, and jointly devise problem-solving strategies. But they also learn something that goes far beyond academics: They learn to care about other people. Cooperation is an essentially humanizing experience that predisposes participants to a benevolent view of others. It encourages trust, sensitivity, open communication, and, ultimately, helpfulness. By contrast, raising or teaching children in a competitive or mostly individualistic environment not only deprives them of these benefits but is actually destructive. In fact, one group of researchers concluded that "competition may serve to suppress generosity to others to a greater extent than cooperation serves to enhance it."[3]

4. TALK WITH THEM.

For parents, there are two basic alternatives to the use of power: love and reason. The ideal is to provide some blend of the two, one drawing from the heart and the other from the head. Unconditional love, of course, has been a central theme of this book. But we also need to understand the importance of reason, and specifically its relevance to moral development. Because it's a bit more complicated than the previous three items, I want to linger on it a bit longer.

Parents who are serious about raising children to be decent people spend an awful lot of time guiding them and explaining things to them. It's not enough for us to have good values; these values must be

communicated directly and in a way that's fitted to the child's ability
to understand. If we fail to do this, our kids will still be influenced by
us, only not in the way we'd hoped. For example, to say nothing when
a child acts selfishly is to send a clear message, and that message has
more to do with the acceptability of selfishness than it does with the
virtues of nonintrusive parenting.

We need to establish clear moral guidelines, to be explicit about
what we expect, but in a way that minimizes coercion. Yes, there has
to be some force behind what we say to them (about how other people should, and shouldn't, be treated), but it's important that force
itself doesn't become the message. If it does, we create a climate of fear
that gets in the way of learning. If we lead kids to worry that doing
bad things will result in the withdrawal of our love, all we buy is temporary compliance without understanding or intrinsic motivation.

But let's take this a step further. Moral learning not only doesn't
come from yelling, it doesn't even come from telling. A simple prohibition ("Don't do that") isn't very helpful. In fact, it may make a child
more wary in general, less likely to reach out even to help.[4] A slightly
more specific sentence such as "We don't hit people!" isn't much better. To support moral development, our message can't be simply that
hitting is bad—or that sharing is good. What counts is helping kids to
understand *why* these things are true. When you don't explain why,
the default reason not to hit is that you'll be punished if you do.[5]

By patiently laying out reasons, we accomplish two things at once.
First, we let kids know what's important to us and why. Second, we
engage their minds, helping them to reflect on—indeed, to wrestle
with—moral questions. The use of reason promotes independent
thought and makes it clear that while we want to influence our children, we also want them to think for themselves. These effects have
been borne out by research: Once they've grown up, children whose
parents offered explanations rather than just demanding obedience
turn out to be more inclined to act altruistically when it really counts
(according to one study) and are more likely to become politically
active and involved in social service activities (according to another).[6]

So: Better than yelling is telling. Better than telling is explaining. Now let's add: Better than explaining—or better than *only* explaining—is discussing. Learning anything (say, math) is not mostly a matter of receiving information. People aren't passive receptacles into which knowledge is poured. We understand ideas by actively making sense of them from the inside out. What is true of math is true of values. To explain their importance, however eloquently, is unlikely to leave children with a commitment to any ideal. Kids have no reason to continue doing what's right if they haven't integrated what we're telling them into the way they think about the world. If we want them to become moral people, as opposed to people who merely do what they're told, then they have to be given the chance to construct such concepts as fairness or courage for themselves. They have to be able to reinvent them in light of their own experiences and questions, to figure out (with our help) what kind of person one ought to be.[7]

All of this is consistent, of course, with my earlier emphasis on supporting kids' autonomy. Here, my point is to emphasize the relevance of that idea to morality. Indeed, one study found that the most impressive moral growth took place in children (of various ages) whose parents didn't just talk at them but engaged in dialogues with them. The best results came when parents were supportive and encouraging by "eliciting the child's opinion, asking clarifying questions, paraphrasing, and checking for understanding." Other research has found, more broadly, that kids who are encouraged to become actively involved in decision making tend to exhibit higher-level moral reasoning.[8]

The process of supporting children's autonomy can take several forms. At a minimum, we want to make it clear that their opinions count by listening carefully and giving their views a respectful hearing. But Marilyn Watson, an expert on child development, also suggests that we refrain from "responding with the full force of our argument to justify our own positions, thereby overwhelming children with our logic." In fact, we should "help children develop reasons to support their own views, even if we don't agree with those views."

Watson offers the following example: Suppose your child wants to watch a TV program that you feel is inappropriate, and all she's able to say to support her preference is, "But all my friends watch it!" Sure, you could score debating points by using the old *reductio ad absurdum* argument—"And what if all your friends jumped off the roof . . . ?" But you know what she probably means (and is unable to express): "I'm afraid I'll be excluded from the culture of my peers because they'll all share an experience that I won't." So respond to what your child means—and if you aren't sure, check out your assumptions. "Help her to articulate her position," says Watson, "or even marshal the best argument you can think of from her perspective," even if ultimately it's not going to prevail—for example, because, as *you'll* argue, the program in question is simply too violent.

Remember—your ultimate goal isn't to get your way. Rather, you want to let your child know that she doesn't have to argue as well as you do in order to be taken seriously, and you want to help her learn how to frame her arguments more convincingly. We *want* kids to "talk back" to us, as long as they do so respectfully—and we want them to get better at it.[9]

The preceding section has been devoted to showing that the way we reason with our children matters. Now I want to add that, along with the style of our explanations, we need to pay attention to the content. I said earlier that it's not enough to tell kids it's wrong to hurt; we need to help them think about *why* it's wrong.

Okay, so why is it wrong?

One possible answer consists of an appeal to self-interest. As I've noted, that's the answer given by punishment, without our having to put it into words. Kids learn that the reason not to do something hurtful is that if they're caught, they'll be made to suffer. Some parents use explanations rather than heavy-handed threats, but the reasons they offer turn out to invoke the same basic motive. "If you're nasty with your classmates, no one's going to want to be your friend." "If you push other people, one of these days someone is going to push you back—or worse." Similarly, such parents may explain that the reason to help others is that the child will ultimately benefit: "If you give Marsha a turn on your scooter, maybe she'll let you play with her Legos later." In other words, people will treat you the way you treated them.

Can you see the problem here? This strategy doesn't promote genuine concern for others at all. It promotes self-regarding shrewdness. Some kids may be tempted to do hurtful things if they can figure out a way to avoid suffering any repercussions themselves—and they may wonder why they should bother helping others if they get nothing in return. That's why it's so important for parents not only to reason with children but to reason with them in a way that helps them to become moral individuals, not just individuals who always ask: "What's in it for me?"

In chapter 8, I suggested that praise for doing something generous gets kids focused on *our* approval of their behavior, and therefore that we might instead try to draw their attention to the effect of their action on the person they helped. ("When you give Marsha a turn on your scooter, she gets to have fun, too, and that makes her happy.") Exactly the same approach makes sense when kids do something hurtful: Rather than getting them focused on *our* disapproval, we should gently invite them to think about the effect on the person they hurt. We might say to a very young child: "Oh, no! Look at Max's face! He seems very unhappy, doesn't he? Remember how you fell down last week and you were crying because it hurt a lot? I'm afraid that's how you made Max feel. What do you think you could do to help him feel better now?"

"Use your words!" is a common instruction given to small children, sometimes even when they don't really have the right words. But the best way for us to use *our* words is to help kids see that the reason to help—and not to hurt—isn't what they'll get out of it, but the effects their actions have on others. To put it differently, I'm all in favor of teaching by "consequences," as long as the consequences we're stressing are those experienced by the people our children are interacting with rather than just those that they themselves experience.

Many researchers have followed Martin Hoffman in referring to this approach as "other-oriented" reasoning or "inductive" discipline (because children are induced to think about the effects of their actions on others). Hoffman discovered that children whose mothers consistently did this tended to show "advanced moral development." Subsequent research has confirmed that finding, and while some psychologists have argued that induction is most effective with older children, one study found that it helps preschoolers to be more cooperative, less aggressive, and popular with their peers. Another study discovered that even toddlers tended to respond to someone in distress with more care and sympathy if their mothers were in the habit of explaining to them "the consequences of [their] behavior for the victim."[10]

Other-oriented reasoning also may be useful in reframing the issue of politeness. Sometimes so much stress is placed on conforming to what are really just arbitrary social conventions—saying "Excuse me" at the proper moment or taking off one's hat in a certain place—that children come to believe these norms are more important than the things that really matter. Or, worse, they get the idea that human interaction is a matter of putting on an act: "Mind your manners" or "Be good now" (as parting words from a parent) is just a reminder to memorize and recite certain lines.

Long ago I vowed never to be the kind of parent who prompts his children with a parrotlike "Whaddaya say?" whenever they're given something, the idea being that they should respond with an equally mechanical "Thank you." Likewise, I told myself I would never badger my children by chirping "What's the magic word?" when they asked for something. (*Please* is only magic, of course, if we refuse to give kids what they want until they say it, which means we're just appealing to self-interest again.)

At home, it's easy enough for me to minimize these pleasantries in favor of more important values. But I had to face facts: Even if I don't care about such things, other people do. There's a cost to flouting social convention, and refusing on principle to be polite is not where I want to make my stand. More to the point, I don't want to make this stand at my children's expense. The reality is that they'll be judged and found wanting if they fail to sprinkle their conversations with the obligatory social niceties.

The solution for me came from thinking about *please* and *thank you* as ways to make people feel good rather than as politeness for its own sake. I remind my kids that saying these words is a nice thing to do because people like to hear them. Sure, there are more meaningful ways to help and please others, but why not do everything we can, big and small, toward that goal? Don't say thank you because you're afraid I'll get mad at you if you don't; that's a terrible reason. Don't say thank you because it's polite; that's not much of a reason at all. Say thank you because of its effect on the people you're thanking.

Perspective Taking

One day, at the age of three, my son, Asa, had a revelation about a friend of his. In a tone of wonder, he announced, "David stays at his house always!" Of course, he already knew that after we visit David, we go home without him. But now he was beginning to think about what happens after we leave, how David says good-bye to us and then continues to live in his house, just as we live in ours. Asa was making sense of the fact that David has a life that isn't dependent on him, one that unfolds parallel to his own.

To step outside one's own viewpoint, to consider how the world looks to another person, is, when you think about it, one of the most remarkable capabilities of the human mind. Psychologists call it "perspective taking," and it comes in three flavors. The first is spatial: I can imagine how you literally *see* the world, such that what's on my right is on your left when we're facing one another. In the second type, I can imagine how you *think* about things—for example, how you might have trouble solving a problem that's easy for me, or how you might hold beliefs about, say, raising children that are different from mine. The third kind consists of imagining how you *feel*, how something could upset you even if it doesn't have that effect on me. (This last type of perspective taking is sometimes confused with "empathy," which means that I share your feelings. To empathize isn't just to understand that you're angry but actually to feel angry along with you.)

Jean Piaget, who pioneered the study of perspective taking, believed it was something children couldn't do until they were about seven years old. Now, however, it appears that the measurement techniques he used were just too complicated for younger kids to show what they were capable of understanding. Even before kindergarten, a child may indeed be able to do a rudimentary form of perspective taking.[11] She knows that other people might be cold even though she's warm, or sad even though she's happy. She begins to recognize that Daddy doesn't know the words to that song because he wasn't in school when it was sung. She can sort of understand that even though she wants to play with that other kid's markers, he'll probably become upset if they're snatched away. True, she may not be able to do these things consistently—or to act on what she realizes in every instance. But quite early on we get these twinkling glimpses of a capability that will grow steadier with time.

Given that the ability to imagine other people's points of view is an act of the imagination, a way of thinking differently, you may not be surprised to learn that those who are adept at it are likely to be impressive thinkers in other ways, too. But my primary interest in perspective taking here is ethical rather than intellectual. What we're talking about, after all, is quite literally the opposite of self-centeredness, and therefore it offers a foundation for morality.

People who can—and do—think about how others experience the world are more likely to reach out and help those people—or, at a minimum, are less likely to harm them. Kafka once described war as a "monstrous failure of imagination." In order to kill, one must cease to see individual human beings and instead reduce them to abstractions such as "the enemy." One must fail to realize that each person underneath our bombs is the center of his universe just as you are the center of yours: He gets the flu, worries about his aged mother, likes sweets, falls in love—even though he lives half a world away and speaks a different language. To see things from his point of view is to recognize all the particulars that make him human, and ultimately it is to understand that his life is no less valuable than yours. Even in popular entertainments, we're not shown the bad guys at home with their children. One can cheer the death only of a caricature, not of a three-dimensional person.

Less dramatically, many of the social problems we encounter on a daily basis can be understood as a failure of perspective taking. People who litter, or block traffic by double-parking, or rip pages out of library books, seem to be locked into themselves, unable or unwilling to imagine how others will have to look at their garbage, or maneuver their cars around them, or fail to find a chapter they need.

To work on seeing things as others see them is to live a very different sort of life. You're sitting in a theater, craning your neck to see around the head of the person in front of you and growing increasingly irritated at this inconvenience. Suddenly, it dawns on you that the person in the row behind may regard you in exactly the same way: You are not only blocked but blocking.

Or consider a different kind of example. While many people dismiss those with whom they disagree ("How can she hold that position on abortion!"), those accustomed to perspective taking tend to turn an exclamation point into a question mark ("How *can* she hold that position on abortion? What experiences, assumptions, or underlying values have led her to a view so different from my own?"). That effort to step outside oneself is what we should try to cultivate in our kids.

There are different levels of perspective taking, of course, and more sophisticated versions may elude very young children. The best we may be able to hope for in the case of a four-year-old is the rather primitive ethics of the Golden Rule. We might say (in a tone that sounds like an invitation to reflect, rather than a reprimand), "I notice you finished all the juice and didn't leave any for Amy. How do you think you would feel if Amy had done that?" The premise of this question, probably correct, is that both kids like juice and would be disappointed to find none available.

But George Bernard Shaw reminded us that this sort of assumption doesn't always make sense. "Do *not* do unto others as you would have them do unto you," he advised. "Their tastes may not be the same"—or, we might add, their needs or values or backgrounds. Older children and adults can realize that it's not enough to imagine ourselves in someone else's situation: We have to imagine that person in that situation. We have to see with her eyes rather than just with our own. We have to—if I may switch metaphors—ask not just what it's like to be in her shoes, but what it's like to have her feet.

So how *can* we promote perspective taking in our children? How can we help them to develop an increasingly sophisticated understanding of how things look from points of view other than their own? One way, again, is by setting an example. A supermarket cashier says something rude, and the parent on the receiving end of his short temper comments to the child who has witnessed this: "Huh. He didn't seem to be in a very good mood today, did he? What do you think might have happened to that man that made him so grouchy? Do you think someone might have hurt his feelings?"

It is enormously powerful to say things like this to our kids, to teach them that we need not respond to an individual who acts unpleasantly by getting angry—or, for that matter, by blaming ourselves. Instead, we can attempt to enter the world of that other person. It's our choice: Every day our children can watch us as we imagine someone else's point of view—or they can watch us remain self-centered. Every day they can witness our effort to see strangers as human beings—or they can witness our failure to do so.

Besides setting an example, we can encourage perspective taking by discussing books and television shows with our kids in a way that highlights the characters' diverse perspectives. ("We're seeing all of this through the eyes of the doctor, aren't we? But what do you think the little girl is feeling about what just happened?") We can even use perspective taking as a tool to help siblings resolve their conflicts.

"Okay," we might say after a blowup. "Tell me what just happened, but pretend you're your brother and describe how things might have seemed to him."[12]

Finally, we can help younger children become more sensitive to others' emotions by gently directing their attention to someone's tone of voice, posture, or facial expression and inviting them to reflect on what that person might be thinking and how he or she might be feeling. The point is to build a skill (learning how to read other people), but also to promote a disposition (*wanting* to know how others are feeling, and being willing to figure it out). "I know Grandma said it would be okay to go on another walk with you, but I noticed that she paused a few seconds before agreeing. And did you see how tired she seemed when she sat down just now?"

The very act of teaching kids to pick up on such cues can help them to develop the habit of seeing more deeply into others. It encourages them to experience the world as another person does, and perhaps to get a feel for what it's like to *be* that other person. This is a major step toward wanting to help rather than to hurt—and, ultimately, toward becoming a better person oneself.

Through Your Child's Eyes

While perspective taking is something we want to communicate *to* our children, it's also vital that we take the perspective *of* our children. This is, in itself, a major shift of perspective. We can help a child learn to imagine another person's point of view, but as parents our first priority must be to imagine how things look from the child's point of view. That's not just a way to model this particular skill: It's a staple of good parenting, period.

Perspective taking is really a common denominator of many different points I've been making throughout this book. For example, the effects of punishment—such as causing children to focus mostly on not getting caught—become much more obvious once we see things through the eyes of the person being punished. So, too, for the impact of two parents presenting a unified front, or of positive reinforcement for behaviors that please us. The negative impact of these things is less surprising when we imagine how they seem to the child.

We're always teaching kids, but to find out *what* we're teaching, it helps to take the child's perspective. According to the research, remember, it's the message he or she receives—as opposed to the one we think we sent—that predicts the effects of our actions. Thus, what matters is whether kids *feel* unconditionally loved, whether *they* believe they have a chance to make decisions, and so on.[13] Or let's take a more concrete example. We may have the best of intentions when we tell a teenager who comes home late that he's missed dinner. We think the lesson here is: "Next time, maybe you'll be more prompt and considerate." But perhaps what the child hears is: *They don't care about the reasons this happened, or what's going on in my life. It would take two minutes to reheat my dinner, but they'd rather that I go hungry. Obviously their stupid rules matter more to them than my well-being. . . . Is it that I'm not worth caring about?*

Perspective taking is also threaded through the recommendations I've been offering in the last few chapters. To "take kids seriously" is to see them as people with distinctive points of view. To "talk less, ask more" is a way to learn about how they see things. And once we do so, once we realize that what we're demanding may seem a lot less reasonable from their perspective, we may need to "rethink our requests" rather than just trying to enforce them. I've also suggested that when we must insist on compliance, we should acknowledge (out loud) our understanding of how that feels to the child. And if all hell breaks loose, our response will again be a lot more effective if we take the child's perspective: What does it feel like to be out of control, and how can we be helpful in light of that?

Perspective taking helps parents attend to, and learn about, their children's needs. Researchers have found that parents who do so are less likely to define their relationship in terms of control, or to use punishment.[14] In fact, there's also more direct evidence regarding the effects of perspective taking. A group of Dutch researchers spent time with 125 families, interviewing the parents and watching as they played with their six-to-eleven-year-old kids. It turned out that one of the most important factors in predicting the quality of their parenting was how well they seemed to understand the unique interests and needs of their children, and how willing they were to consider that perspective as distinct from their own.

In 1997, the year that study was published, two other journals coincidentally published reports on the same topic. One found that Canadian parents who were better able to "accurately perceive their [teenage] children's thoughts and feelings during a disagreement" ended up having fewer conflicts with those children—or at least a more satisfactory resolution of the conflicts that did occur. The other was a U.S. study of families with toddlers, and it showed that parents who were "able to adopt the child's viewpoint" were more responsive to the child's needs as a result. That greater responsiveness, in turn, made it more likely that the child would adopt the parent's values and respond more positively to requests.

So: With children from two to fifteen years old, and in three different countries, we have confirmation that it really does help for parents to try to see things from the child's point of view.[15] Few things that parents do can equal the positive impact of trying to picture how our words and actions are experienced by our children. In fact, it's triply beneficial:

Perspective taking helps us figure out what's really going on, particularly when a child cannot or will not explain her motives to us, so we don't leap to an incorrect assumption—and, from there, to a punitive response. We acquire information that can help us go below the surface rather than just responding to behaviors. That way, we can devise a strategy for addressing the deeper meanings and underlying issues.

Perspective taking makes us more patient with children's moods. When we see the world as they see it, we're more likely to respond with kindness and respect than if we were just looking in from the outside. That, in turn, helps kids to feel good about themselves and to feel safe with us, connected to us, valued by us.

We set an example, encouraging the child, too, to do perspective taking.

The trouble is that many people find perspective taking hard to do. When an infant is crying, most of us will try to figure out what's bothering her. But we may be less willing to imaginatively enter the world of an older child who is yelling and stamping her feet. Here our first impulse may be to blame or control rather than to understand. Paradoxically, though, the situations in which we're least likely to do perspective taking are those where it's most important that we do so. If you can't escape your own point of view, then it's harder to listen, harder to acknowledge that there's another legitimate way of understanding what's going on, harder to recognize how the battle that's likely to erupt could have been avoided. The more you allow yourself to remain trapped in your own perspective, the more you'll be tempted to revert to coercion—and the worse things will get.

The absence of parental perspective taking assumes many forms. At its most disturbing, it can resemble—or lead to—an utter dismissal of what children are feeling or an attempt to impose our experience on theirs (as in the classic "I'm cold. Go put on a sweater."). More commonly, we simply fail to appreciate how different their worlds, and their worries, are from ours. One day when my daughter was five, she described to me at some length how concerned she was about the possibility that, if she wore a hooded costume for Halloween (which was still months away), she might not be able to see through the eyeholes well enough to make sure she didn't mistakenly eat a kind of candy she doesn't really like.

The last thing a child needs is to be informed that her anxieties are silly. This is especially true when a child is sobbing. To our way of thinking, little kids often cry over nothing, but to them, it's not nothing at all: What prompted the outburst matters a great deal. We feel

exasperated—and, if we're in public, embarrassed—by a child's outburst, but we seem to forget that the experience may be agonizing
rather than merely annoying for the child.

Sure, it's hard to be a parent. But it can be a lot harder to be a kid.

We don't mean to make them feel foolish or unsupported, but that's
just what happens when we trivialize their fears or their tears. We lose
patience with a preschooler: "Come *on*, honey! What difference does
it make whether your left sock goes on before your right one?" We
assume pitiless logic will resolve a teen's inner turmoil: "Well, just ask
her out if you like her. The worst that can happen is she says no, right?
You'll get over it."

Shouldn't we know better? After all, scientific research has proved
that most adults were children themselves at one time or another. Have
we just forgotten what it's like to have our world turned upside down
by things grown-ups don't understand—and, worse, what it's like to
have those feelings written off by the same grown-ups?

Some therapists have a provocative answer to these questions.
Alice Miller, for example, argues that there's nothing paradoxical
or particularly surprising about such behavior. She believes it's not
accurate to say that so many parents dismiss their children's fears, or
fail to see things from the child's point of view, *in spite of* having
gone through this themselves. Rather, they do so *because* they went
through this themselves. It's hard to adopt the perspective of a child
because it's even harder to adopt the perspective of oneself-as-a-child.
It hurts too much to acknowledge what was done to us once upon a
time.

"Disrespect is the weapon of the weak," Miller observes, and the disrespect so many parents show for their children's feelings is a function
of how weak they remain behind a thin façade of strength. First, adults
continue to have fears of their own, so it makes them feel powerful to
pooh-pooh the silly fears of a child. Second, some parents may be taking revenge "for their own earlier humiliation." That this pattern plays
out unconsciously makes perfect sense, given that it's too painful to
remember, let alone to relive, one's own powerlessness and pain.[16]

I honestly don't know how much of that theory is true, or how many people it describes. It may be that there are other reasons, more superficial and situational, for the fact that parents so often fail to imagine how things feel to their children. Maybe we're just too short of time or patience to ask, "How does my child make sense of what just happened?" Frankly, I'd like to think the explanation is that simple, because then we can solve the problem more easily. But either way, we ought to do our best to recall specific experiences of being a child so as to make more real for ourselves what our children are going through. There may even be value in trying to recapture experiences we've had as adults that are analogous to those of our children—for example, what it's like to be bossed around, or to have our preferences ignored, or to feel pressured to stop doing something fun.

These are just exercises, of course—preparations for the real event, which is imagining the child's perspective. That's something we need to begin doing from the start. When my daughter was only a few months old, she hated to have her diaper changed. At first, my response was, basically, "Sorry, honey, but it has to be done whether you like it or not." Then I noticed that she was particularly resistant when the changing happened as soon as she woke up. I tried to see it from her point of view: *Hey! I'm still half-asleep here and already I'm being whisked over to That Place Where They Do Things to My Butt!* I experimented with giving her ten or fifteen minutes to wake up fully before I changed her diaper, and sure enough, her reaction was far more positive.

Taking an infant's perspective is useful, in part to help us get in the habit of doing it later. We'll surely need to do it by the time they start to talk, if only to turn the usual clichés about childhood on their heads. For example: Two-year-olds are famous for saying no a lot. But from the child's perspective, the problem is that *we're* always saying no, preventing him from doing this, going there, playing with that really interesting thing on the kitchen counter.[17]

Children of different ages are frequently described as "manipulative." But, again, from the child's perspective, she may just be struggling to have some say over what happens to her. If anyone is trying to manipulate here, it's probably the grown-up. Perhaps kids would benefit from a helpful book called *How to Handle Your Difficult Parents*. Given how much time we spend judging and correcting them, it's entertaining to imagine their having regular opportunities to do the same to us—such as, say, a *Zagat for Tots* review of what we feed them:

> Diners give an enthusiastic thumbs-up to the "awesome" hot dogs and high-quality desserts ("if you're lucky enough to get one"), but caution that certain side dishes are "really gross"; hot cereals in particular are apt to "look like barf." Service is rated as inconsistent: There are high marks for personal attention, but at least one customer says he can do without "that lady who's always telling you to sit up straight and stop dawdling."

The use of humor is closely related to perspective taking because laughter is often a direct result of a shift in perspective. Humor can be a very effective strategy for defusing a stressful situation, or at least warming up a potentially chilly encounter. If you're sitting down with your child to discuss something about her behavior that you'd like to see changed, you might invite her to imitate how you typically sound when you're nagging her on that topic. This is a way of releasing tension, letting her feel empowered, and making it clear that you understand how things seem from her point of view—all at once.

Perspective taking is also important when you're spending time with someone else's child. It's remarkable how many adults barrel ahead with their own agenda, ignore strong nonverbal signals, and then pronounce the child who recoils from them "shy" (or worse). By contrast, adults who are said to "have a way with kids" usually display an intuitive feel for how things look to them. When they're introduced to a child, they don't expect instant effusiveness, just as they know their own normally bubbly kid probably won't act with a stranger the way he acts with them. They don't smother their new acquaintance with enthusiasm or start right in with a cross-examination ("How old are you? Where do you go to school?").

Rather, they keep their distance at first and let the child warm up to them, perhaps finding something he's interested in and asking him about that. Then they might try to find some activity they can do alongside the child. They take their cue from him regarding what he's interested in, whether he wants to talk or play, and so on.

It's easier to take one's cue from a child, whether someone else's or our own, if we can see the world as that child sees it. On an everyday basis, perspective taking makes for better parenting. Even when we can't honor children's preferences, it's terribly important that we do our best to understand and acknowledge their perspective ("I guess to you it seems as though . . ."). That helps them feel heard, cared about, and unconditionally loved.

Of course, it's not all or nothing. When we're talking about how often, and how well, parents try to imagine the way things look from a child's point of view, there are many gradations between "constantly" and "never"—or between "expertly" and "miserably." And so it is for all the issues discussed in this book. Few parents pursue strategies that are exclusively doing-to or working-with, or offer love that's purely conditional or unconditional. Most of us are somewhere in between. By the same token, I'm not suggesting that there's a switch we can flip that will instantly allow us to stop being this way and start being that way. Rather, we can think of ourselves as being on a journey such that we commit ourselves to making steady progress in the right direction.

Is it ever too late to begin that journey? I'm sometimes asked for assurances that it's possible to undo the damage that may have been done by years of conditional parenting and overcontrol. Of course, it's impossible to say for certain, but it takes tremendous courage to acknowledge that one may have been on the wrong course, and such courage is itself an excellent omen for what the future holds. There's reason to believe that, no matter how old one's children are, it's not too late to have a positive impact from this point forward. All of us have considerable room for improvement. To whatever extent, and for whatever reason, we may have been raising our kids in a way that hasn't been very constructive, this is as good a time as any to turn things around.

APPENDIX

Parenting Styles:
The Relevance of Culture, Class, and Race

In discussing any aspect of human behavior, there's always the possibility that one's descriptions (This is what it means to raise children. . . .) or evaluations (This is the way one ought to raise children. . . .) will be based on a worldview that isn't held universally. Much of what we take for granted about child development and other issues often turns out to be bounded by cultural assumptions. To that extent, they may be open to dispute. The content of this book is necessarily informed by the fact that I'm a white, middle-class American. How would, and how should, someone who doesn't share those characteristics regard what I've written?

Even if I were an expert on parenting beliefs and practices around the world, which I'm not, I wouldn't be able to do justice here to the vast research literature on this topic. There is enormous variation in the assumptions made about children and what it means to care for them properly, including how much, when, and under what circumstances parents punish, or reason with, their children. For example, one anthropologist describes how members of the Gusii tribe in southwestern Kenya were shocked to learn that American mothers would leave their babies crying even for a few seconds: "For them, the prevention of infant crying through continuous physical contact was not only a device of pragmatic value but also a morally mandated script for maternal behavior."[1]

Toddlers, too, are treated very differently from one culture to the next. As a result, some new research demonstrates that "the 'terrible twos' transition is not universal"; its existence seems to depend on how much "parents attempt to assert their authority"[2] and, perhaps, on what their ultimate goals are for their children. This is but one illustration of the larger point that culturally specific assumptions and practices produce different behaviors. Over and over, what we take to be simple facts about child development turn out not to be true everywhere.

It may not be surprising, then, that the central themes of this book are not immune to being challenged from a cross-cultural perspective. Fred Rothbaum at Tufts University suggests that unconditional parental love is less in doubt in some cultures than it is in ours. However, he adds, there are places where the very concept may seem to be beside the point. Unconditional acceptance may be predicated on valuing the individual self in a way that is by no means universal. We may believe that children have to be loved by their parents in order to accept themselves, but the idea of accepting oneself doesn't have the same significance everywhere and may even seem a bizarre idea in less individualistic cultures.

What's more, Rothbaum points out that uttering the phrase "I love you" to children implies the possibility of not loving them: If we're saying it, we're suggesting that it can't be taken for granted. If our love is unconditional, it's because we decide to feel that way, whereas in many cultures the connections between individuals—including parents and children—reflect roles and norms that are unquestioned. They're obligations one has, not commitments one makes.[3] Is this a different, even deeper, form of unconditional parenting—or is it less meaningful than love that's freely chosen? Regardless of what judgment we end up making, it may be necessary to rethink the very idea of unconditionality.

And speaking of "freely chosen": I've emphasized the importance of easing up on our control of children and helping them to experience a sense of autonomy. The benefits of doing so are well substantiated by research. But is that research applicable only in certain places? Do children benefit from the chance to have some say about their lives only in cultures that are relatively individualistic or less bound by tradition? *Our* children seem to be happier and more motivated when they can participate in making decisions than when authority figures tell them what to do, but is that true everywhere?[4]

The extent to which parents are inclined to control their children is unquestionably affected by where they live. However, that's "quite different from saying that controlling techniques are preferable" in any society, as Wendy Grolnick points out. She proceeds to cite research showing that "controlling parenting is associated with more negative outcomes for children across cultural contexts."[5] Similarly, Richard Ryan and Edward Deci point to data suggesting that "autonomy may indeed be universally important." One reason this contention has been challenged, they add, is a function of how the word is defined. Autonomy is often equated with independence and "resistance to influence, or self-assertion over and against others." Anyone who accepts that definition may well assume the concept is "relevant only to individualistic cultures." But autonomy understood as volition or "choicefulness" is a different story. In that sense, "people can just as readily be autonomously collectivistic as they can be autonomously individualistic."[6] Thus, easing up on control may be a good thing for children regardless of whether they're being raised in the West or the East, in a huge modern city or a tiny Third World village.

Needless to say, differences in discipline styles occur not only across cultures but among groups within a single culture, particularly when we're talking about a complex modern society such as the United States. Before mentioning a few of those differences, however, I should point out that we're trafficking here in statistical generalizations. Even if parents in group A treat their children in a particular way more than parents in group B do, that doesn't mean everyone in group A acts that way—or that no one in group B does.

With that in mind, we can begin by noting that researchers have routinely found differences related to families' socioeconomic status (SES), including the extent to which punitive discipline is used. Most studies have found that, as that status declines, "rates of parents' use of corporal punishment rise," according to one review of the available data. Another group of researchers concluded that, as a rule, "children in the lower socioeconomic classes are more likely than their peers to be the objects of harsh discipline, to [be] . . . raised by mothers who are relatively less warm in their behavior toward them . . . and who are more likely to hold values that aggression is an appropriate and effective means of solving problems."[7]

Those facts are explained partly by economic pressure: The more such stress parents are experiencing, the more likely it is that they will use coercive methods to get their children to obey.[8] Melvin Kohn famously showed that working-class parents are more likely to raise their children to conform to rules and respect authority—and to use punishment to achieve those goals—whereas middle-class, notably white-collar, parents are more likely to want their children to be self-directed and autonomous decision-makers. Kohn hypothesized that this, in turn, is related to the expectations the parents themselves face at work, which often vary by class. His general findings have been confirmed by other researchers, and they've been echoed by international data showing that physical punishment is more common in cultures that value conformity in children than it is in cultures that value self-reliance.[9]

Then there is the complex question of race. Within the United States, it appears that African Americans are "less likely than white parents to prefer autonomy in children and are more likely to prefer obedience," even after SES is held constant. African American mothers are more likely than white mothers to approve of their children's being aggressive with their peers.[10] As for the use of harsh disciplinary practices, including physical punishment, two conclusions emerge from the data: Class may have more of an impact than race, but race matters, too. When thousands of parents were asked (in 1990) whether they had spanked their children in the last week, about 70 percent of African Americans and 60 percent of whites said yes. The figures were 77 percent and 59 percent, respectively, in another study that asked parents (in 1995) whether they had spanked their children in the last year. The difference was still statistically significant, although somewhat reduced, once SES was taken into account.[11]

When parents were asked (in 1988) about their *attitudes* toward physical punishment, a little more than 22 percent of whites opposed the idea, as compared with less than 9 percent of African Americans. What's particularly striking is the disparity in how attitudes have changed over time. In 1968, spanking was endorsed by more than 90 percent of Americans in all ethnic groups. A series of surveys from that point until 1994 have found a steady and remarkably sharp decline in the number of whites who support spanking; approval has dropped by a third, in fact. But the decline was only 14 percent for African Americans over the same quarter-century.[12]

The evidence against the wisdom of using such punishment is quite compelling, but in the last few years an interesting argument has been put forth to the effect that a given practice doesn't necessarily have the same meaning across racial lines. Kirby Deater-Deckard, Kenneth Dodge, and two other researchers have attracted considerable attention in their field by contending that, because disciplining children with physical force is more widely accepted by African Americans, black kids may not experience being hit by their parents in the same way that white kids do, and therefore it won't have the same negative effects. Their study of 466 white children and 100 black children found that higher levels of physical punishment resulted in aggression and similar problems only among the white children. These researchers—all of whom are white, incidentally—speculated that African American children may not "view their parents' physical discipline as an indication of parental lack of warmth and concern"—provided that the punishment doesn't reach levels usually classified as abusive.[13]

This presents a provocative challenge to those of us who find the idea of deliberately hurting children objectionable no matter where it's done, or by whom, or why. It forces us to ask whether our objection is informed by a set of premises that can't be applied universally. Does a maxim such as "Never hit a child" simply reflect the familiar arrogance of a powerful group attempting to impose its ethics on a less powerful group? Or, on the contrary, can we declare that some things are just wrong and it's the attempt to *silence* judgment that's more offensive?

I've argued that psychological effects in general don't follow in mechanical stimulus-response fashion from the things that happen to us. Rather, what matters is the meaning we ascribe to what happens. It's not the act itself that predicts its impact; it's what the act signifies to individuals and communities.[14] But now that interpretive approach faces its ultimate challenge: Are there some behaviors, such as striking children and deliberately causing them pain, that can never be construed as innocuous (much less loving) regardless of the parent's intentions? We— or, more important, the child—may struggle desperately to regard an act of violence as an expression of caring but ultimately find it impossible to perform this act of emotional alchemy. And even if a child *could* reconcile these things, is a commingling of love and violence a good thing? Do we want children to grow up thinking that hurting people is a way of showing concern for them?

At least part of the reason for opposing physical punishment is practical rather than moral, of course. Researchers who regard the practice as problematic generally point to the effects it has. To that extent, the Deater-Deckard and Dodge (D-D & D) claim—that those effects don't occur in some children—is important to consider. But for several reasons, I'm not convinced it's true.

First of all, the argument (that black kids aren't adversely affected by physical punishment in the way white kids are) rests on the premise that physical punishment is much more pervasive in the African American community. That, as we've seen, is true. But it poses a problem for drawing conclusions about the effects of this punishment. Consider an analogy: If we wanted to study whether eating a lot of fish had certain beneficial health effects, it would be wise to look at a group of subjects that included some people who ate huge amounts of fish, some who ate less, and some who ate none at all. Then we could investigate whether there was a relationship between health and the amount of fish that was consumed, once other factors were taken into account. But if we studied a group of people almost all of whom regularly ate fish, it would be more difficult to assess the significance of how healthy they were. Thus, for a group of families who routinely rely on physical punishment, it's hard to isolate the effects of being subjected to it. The fact that there's less range or variability in how African Americans discipline their children might explain a lack of correlation between physical punishment and specific effects.[15]

In fact, with any group where the idea of discipline virtually *means* physical punishment—and where such punishment is supposed to be, as D-D & D argue, a marker for parental involvement and concern—its absence may signal a lack of just such involvement and concern. Thus, it wouldn't be surprising to find that kids who weren't punished didn't necessarily fare better than those who were.[16]

These considerations may also apply to a few other studies that have echoed D-D & D's findings. One discovered that, among teenagers who were African American—but not among those who were European

American, Asian American, or Hispanic American—"unilateral parental decision making was correlated with better adjustment: less involvement in deviance and higher academic competence." However, joint decision-making, where parents and teens worked things out together, also predicted lower rates of deviance for children of all ethnic backgrounds.[17]

A second study found "no association between corporal punishment and conduct problems in communities where corporal punishment was widely prevalent." But here, too, there was an important caveat: Even in these communities, such punishment was "not beneficial in preventing antisocial behavior . . . once the effects of caretaker monitoring and discipline [were] taken into account." Thus, even if there are variations in the *damage* caused by hitting children, that doesn't mean that hitting children is ever *useful.*[18]

More significant still is the fact that other research fails to support the D-D & D finding. A 1997 study found that the use of corporal punishment led to more antisocial behavior for both minority and white children, and the extent of that effect was directly related to the amount of punishment they had received earlier.[19] Three years later, another study confirmed that coercive discipline was associated with conduct problems in low-income African American children. The psychologists who reported this result pointedly noted that it "stands in contrast" to the D-D & D finding.[20]

The idea that hitting children doesn't harm them if they're part of a culture that accepts this practice as appropriate would seem to imply that the children themselves regard it as legitimate. Toddlers are too young to have formed such a judgment, which may in itself pose a problem for the whole theory. But one study asked older children (ages nine to sixteen) in the West Indies, where harsh physical punishment is widespread, what they thought about it. It turned out that such punishment had the same negative effects on kids who believed it was appropriate that it did on those who didn't believe this: "The psychological adjustment of youths who believe parents should punish them physically tends to be impaired to the same degree as the adjustment of youths who do not share this cultural belief."[21]

Finally, though, let's assume for the sake of the argument that specific negative outcomes, such as the presence of conduct disorders, really don't show up (at least right away) in African American kids who are subjected to corporal punishment. That hardly proves that such punishment is harmless. If I'm right about the insidious effects of leading children to equate love and violence, then researchers who examined a wider array of possible outcomes might well find negative impacts that cut across lines of race and class.

Again, parents who dictate to or hit their children may well be doing so in an attempt to teach them, and they may be doing so out of concern for their well-being, particularly in places where these have become the default ways of expressing that concern. Unfortunately, admirable intentions don't guarantee a positive outcome. Bad things done for good reasons aren't nearly as helpful as *good* things done for good reasons.

Nor are positive results assured even if the children themselves accept that this style of parenting really is an expression of love—or convince themselves of this once they're grown. We learn to take what we can get—say, if physical punishment appears to be the only alternative to indifference. But the question is why these are assumed to be the only two possibilities available. This is analogous to my earlier point about praise: If conditional acceptance is the only possibility, kids will drink it in and even say they wish they'd gotten more. But that's not a persuasive defense of praise. Not all forms of acceptance—or love, or motivation, or ways of getting children's attention when they've done something wrong—are the same, nor are they equally desirable.

There's another way that differences among groups are used to explain and justify a specific approach to raising children. It's sometimes said that physical punishment, along with a more authoritarian style of parenting in general, is a rational response to living in a dangerous neighborhood. The argument goes something like this: Maybe affluent families can afford the luxury of a more relaxed, progressive, or democratic approach to child rearing, but things are very different in the inner city. There, making sure that kids follow the rules—obey the law, toe the line, defer to authority figures even when what they're demanding may seem unjust—can literally determine whether these kids survive to adulthood. In this view, strict discipline is adaptive and perhaps even necessary. Michelle Kelley, a researcher at Old Dominion University, and her colleagues put it this way: "The consequences of disobedience in a low-income neighborhood . . . [where children] are at greater risk for involvement in anti-social activity (either as victims or as perpetrators) . . . may be much more serious [than in a middle-class neighborhood] and may require more forceful methods to prevent *any* level of involvement."[22]

This is an interesting theory, in part because it suggests that something about the environment, rather than something about the individuals living in that neighborhood (such as their race or class), accounts for the use of heavy-handed discipline. It's also a reminder to many suburban whites that they haven't a clue about the day-to-day reality faced by people of color in low-income, high-crime neighborhoods.

Nevertheless, there are several problems with this explanation. For one thing, it's not clear that the evidence supports it. Kelley herself hasn't consistently found that the way "lower-class black mothers or caregivers" raise their children is influenced by the extent to which they're worried about them.[23] Something other than an objective appraisal of danger may be responsible for their favoring a certain approach to discipline.

If the dangerous neighborhood theory were true, moreover, we might expect that the relation between how children are disciplined and whether they engage in antisocial behavior would vary depending on where they lived. But two large studies—the first conducted in 1996 with more than 3,000 teenagers from different ethnic backgrounds; and the second conducted in 2002 with 841 African American families—found that the effects of discipline style didn't change depending on the kind of community they lived in, including the prevalence of crime and delinquency.[24]

Empirical evidence aside, the dangerous neighborhood argument seems to be constructed on some of those familiar false dichotomies, such as "coerciveness versus permissiveness." Granted, children in some areas may need extra protection and closer monitoring, but that's not the same thing as saying they need—or would benefit from—authoritarian parenting or physical punishment.[25] They may benefit from structure, but that doesn't mean they would benefit from being controlled. They may require a strong parental presence, but not a demand for absolute, do-what-you're-told-or-else obedience. (By the same token, it's important not to caricature what I've been calling a working-with approach by confusing it with laissez-faire permissiveness. To point out the flaws of the latter isn't the same as making an argument against the former.)

Look again at the research demonstrating the effects of heavy-handed control and punishment, which I reviewed in chapters 3 and 4, respectively. Children raised in these ways are less likely to acquire a sophisticated moral framework. They may find it harder to develop a flexible understanding of the situations they face, and they may remain trapped by a preoccupation with self-interest.

These things matter. Moral sophistication, cognitive flexibility, and the capacity to care about others aren't luxuries. More to the point, they're not mutually exclusive with basic survival skills and street smarts. We want kids to have all these things. But traditional, punitive discipline may result in their having none of them. Even if obedience were our goal, this is not a particularly effective way to get it. Remember, children whose parents are controlling are often *less* compliant, especially when their parents aren't around. But ultimately it makes sense to question the goal of just getting kids to obey authority, which is very different from the goal of developing good judgment and responsibility.

I'd even go so far as to say that the approach I've described in the latter half of this book—unconditional love, a relationship based on respect and trust, the opportunity for children to participate in making decisions, and so on—may be *most* important for kids who are growing up in tough neighborhoods.[26] In any case, there aren't many real-world situations in which children end up doing better as a result of being led to fear their parents.

NOTES

INTRODUCTION

1. I've borrowed this thought experiment from Deborah Meier.
2. Cagan, pp. 45–46.
3. This figure is from Simpson, p. 11. At the time, in the mid-1990s, there were more than 1,500 parenting books in print.
4. Even some of the better books, whose approach is reasonably respectful of children, seem to invite parody. For example, they not only advise us to use "reflective listening" so that kids know they've been heard, but sell this technique as though it had magical powers to produce instant results.

   Child: That is so unfair! You always do this to me! I hate you!!! (bursts into tears)

   Parent: Hmmm. It sounds like you think what I've proposed isn't fair. That makes you feel angry, doesn't it?

   Child: Yes! (sniffs) But . . . well . . . I guess I can live with it. (pause) Gosh, thanks for taking the time to understand me! I feel all better now!
5. For example, see the research reviewed in Chapman and Zahn-Waxler, p. 90.
6. Washington, D.C., study: Kuczynski and Kochanska. (Quotations on pp. 404 and 398, respectively.) "Compulsive compliance": Crittenden and DiLalla. Psychotherapists: For example, see Juul. Psychologists who study parent-child attachment patterns note that a healthy toddler is not one "who automatically complies with whatever the mother tells him/her. Rather, it is the child who shows a certain amount of noncompliance when requested to stop playing and clean up the toys, but who gradually cooperates with the mother" (Matas et al., p. 554).
7. See the discussion of Edward Deci and Richard Ryan's research on control on pp. 57–58. I explored this issue in *Punished by Rewards* (Kohn 1999a, pp. 250–52), drawing from Deci and Ryan's very useful analysis of different types of internalization. The least constructive version is "introjection," in which someone swallows a rule or value whole and then feels pressured from the inside to act in accordance with it. This is exactly the sort of internalization that's promoted by the kinds of discipline I analyze throughout this book.

8. DeVries and Zan, p. 253.

9. Coloroso, p. 77.

CHAPTER 1: CONDITIONAL PARENTING

1. It turns out that this view of children is a prejudice rather than a conclusion supported by good evidence. In an earlier book, *The Brighter Side of Human Nature,* I reviewed hundreds of studies supporting the view that it is as natural to be caring and empathic as it is to be aggressive or self-centered. An abbreviated version of this review can be found in a 1991 article for educators entitled "Caring Kids" (Kohn 1991).

2. This is from a psychologist named Stephen Beltz, in a book titled *How to Make Johnny WANT to Obey,* p. 236.

3. Baumrind 1972, p. 278. She continues: "The parent who expresses love unconditionally is encouraging the child to be selfish and demanding"—suggesting that an economic model for human relationships may go hand-in-hand with a dim view of human nature.

4. Margaret Clark published several studies in the late 1970s and '80s to explore the differences between what she called "exchange" relationships and "communal" relationships. The specific finding about marriages is from a study by Murstein et al. For a broader investigation of the ways that economic models and metaphors have come to take over other domains of life, see Barry Schwartz's book *The Battle for Human Nature* as well as many of Erich Fromm's writings.

5. For example, see Rogers 1959.

6. See www.doh.ie/fulltext/Children_First/Chapter2.html. While web links come and go, I have at various times found this document on the sites of a sheriff's department in Illinois and an anti-abuse group (CAPSEA) in Pennsylvania, as well as a reference to its having been included with a proposed law in Missouri. It has also been cited on other sites in England and Canada.

7. For example, "parents generally reported that they included their children more in family decision making than the children perceived to be true" (Eccles et al., pp. 62–63).

8. Three studies are cited to support this claim in Kernis et al., p. 230. Even when there's no opportunity to compare the relative accuracy of these two accounts, other research has found that parental self-reports don't always jibe with what the experimenter has observed (e.g., Kochanska 1997; Ritchie).

9. Hoffman 1970a, esp. Table IV on p. 106. These results, and others pertaining to the use of love withdrawal, are discussed on pp. 29–30. For corroboration of the basic finding that "it is the child's own experience of [parenting] behavior that is likely to have the greatest impact on the child's subsequent development," see Morris et al.; quotation appears on p. 147.

10. Assor et al. The quotation appears on p. 60. It's not clear from this study why these parents treated their children the way they themselves had been treated, but I discuss some possible explanations for conditional parenting in chapter 6.

11. Harter et al. Moreover, this "sense of being loved contingently, only if one does

what someone else wants one to do, tends to erect barriers to communication . . . [thus making] it harder than ever to avoid contingent love. . . . It's a vicious circle of communicative barriers" (Newcomb, p. 53).

12. The quotation is from Harter 1999, p. 181. For research on the effects of unconditional support from parents and teachers, see, respectively, Forsman; and Makri-Botsari. The latter study also found that students who felt unconditionally accepted by their teachers were more likely to be genuinely interested in learning and apt to enjoy challenging academic tasks (as opposed to doing things just because they were assigned and preferring easier tasks at which they knew they would be successful).

13. The first sentence here is from the Love Withdrawal Scale developed by Brent Mallinckrodt at the University of Missouri and his colleagues. The second sentence (changed into the first-person) is from an instrument used by Michael Kernis and his colleagues at the University of Georgia.

CHAPTER 2: GIVING AND WITHHOLDING LOVE

1. Chamberlain and Patterson, p. 217.
2. Chapman and Zahn-Waxler; quotations appear on pp. 90 and 92.
3. Hoffman 1970b, pp. 285–86.
4. Hoffman 1970b, p. 300.
5. Dienstbier et al., p. 307.
6. Self-esteem: This finding from Stanley Coopersmith's classic study of fifth- and sixth-grade boys is described in Maccoby and Martin, p. 55. A third of a century later, it was replicated with both boys and girls; see Kernis et al. 2000. Emotional health and delinquency: Goldstein and Heaven—a recent study of Australian high school students. Depression: Barber—a study of 875 fifth-, eighth-, and tenth-grade students.
7. Maccoby and Martin, p. 55.
8. Unusually anxious: A 1966 study by Perdue and Spielberger is described in Hoffman 1970b, p. 302. Afraid to show anger: Hoffman 1970a, pp. 108–9. Fear of failure: Elliot and Thrash. (These authors illustrate the concept of love withdrawal by referring to "the widely endorsed 'time-out' technique.") Avoid attachment: Swanson and Mallinckrodt; the quotation appears on p. 467. (The extent to which the 125 undergraduates in this last study had experienced love withdrawal was a very significant predictor of their tendency to avoid intimacy, even after taking account of other features of their families of origin. A second study, this one with more than 400 undergraduates—Mallinckrodt and Wei—confirmed a relationship between love withdrawal, on the one hand, and insecurity and attachment difficulties, on the other.)
9. Hoffman 1970a; and 1970b, esp. pp. 339–40. I should mention that an earlier study (Sears et al.) found that kindergarten children whose mothers used love withdrawal *and* generally seemed warm with them were more likely than other children to admit that they broke a rule, or to act guilty, before they were caught. (As another writer [Becker, p. 185] later put it, it made sense that there was an

effect only with warm mothers because here there was "more love to lose.") However, subsequent research has rarely shown anything resembling a positive effect on moral development as a result of love withdrawal. Other studies, including the one described in the text, suggest that this approach to discipline is "an insufficient basis for the development of . . . a fully [formed] conscience" (Hoffman and Saltzstein, p. 56). Indeed, one might question whether the "positive" result in the Sears et al. study—a compulsion to confess—is really what we're looking for. There's a difference between a fear of being caught, on the one hand, and a growing sense—growing, not yet firmly established, in a five-year-old—that an action is wrong, on the other. According to psychologist Wendy Grolnick, this internal pressure is "antithetical to a feeling of autonomy, because the child cannot choose to risk noncompliance—the stakes are simply too high" when the parent's love might disappear (Grolnick, p. 47).

10. But only a bit, because the ideas described in the next few paragraphs, along with the evidence to support them, have already been laid out at some length in my book *Punished by Rewards* (Kohn 1999a).

11. See Kohn 1999a, chapter 5; and Deci et al. 1999—and the scores of studies summarized in each.

12. Efforts to determine the effects of praise on intrinsic motivation are complicated by the fact that different researchers have meant different things by "praise" (see Kohn 1999a, esp. pp. 99–101, 261). A recent review of the research found that, "although verbal rewards enhance intrinsic motivation for college students, they do not do so for children" (Deci et al. 1999, p. 638).

13. M. B. Rowe.

14. This apt phrase is from DeVries and Zan, p. 46.

15. Burhans and Dweck. The content of praise may also be relevant here. Researchers agree: Comments that make people feel accepted only conditionally are most likely to have a negative impact. But researchers disagree, at least judging by two recent studies, about which sorts of comments do that. One experiment with young adults (Schimel et al.) found that positive feedback didn't make them feel more secure if it referred to their accomplishments, but did if it referred to who the individuals really were, what they considered their "true inner qualities." By contrast, Kamins and Dweck discovered that "person-oriented" praise, the sort that offers children a global "evaluation of themselves, their traits, or their abilities," is the kind most likely to induce a contingent feeling of self-worth and, therefore, to cause them to fall apart when they encounter setbacks.

16. Sure you can. Go right ahead. I'll even say thanks. However, specific informational feedback—exactly what in the book you found helpful, or not helpful, and why—would be even more welcome than a judgment, be it positive or negative. In any case, much as I'm sure I'd enjoy meeting you, the reality is that I don't depend on you for unconditional love. Communications from one adult to another, especially when the two have no close preexisting relationship, just aren't analogous to what parents say to their children. Therefore, the fact that I smile gratefully when you tell me this book changed your life doesn't allow us

to conclude that using positive reinforcement on our kids really isn't so bad.

17. For a discussion of that review, as well as of the issues raised in the following two paragraphs, see Kohn 1994.

18. Are you starting to see a pattern here? We have to move beyond the "single entity" way of thinking about things, whether it's parental love (p. 10), motivation (p. 33), or self-esteem. In each case, it's a matter not just of how much but of what kind.

19. Deci and Ryan 1995, p. 33. The heuristic value of focusing not on the simple level of self-esteem, but rather on its contingency (along with other indicators of its security or fragility), is also laid out in Kernis 2003. And it was noticed by Alice Miller, who suggested that one is free from depression "only when self-esteem is based on the authenticity of one's own feelings and not on the possession of certain qualities" (p. 58). She maintained that this is not something we need from, or that it would be enough to get from, a therapist. Carl Rogers believed that one of the most important ways psychotherapy can heal is by providing the "unconditional positive regard" that ought to have been received years earlier. But Miller is less hopeful: "This is a childhood need," she says, "one that can never be fulfilled later in life" (p. 68).

20. The drinking study: Neighbors et al. Citations for research that confirms the other consequences listed here are provided by Crocker and Wolfe, pp. 606, 614–15. Ultimately, these two authors believe that "behavior is not a function of whether self-esteem is contingent or not but rather depends on the specific domains on which a person has staked self-worth" (p. 597)—that is, whether people feel good about themselves on the basis of other people's approval, being virtuous, doing good work, and so forth. In a later study, Crocker et al. cite some evidence to support this idea that "the domains on which self-worth is staked are more important than whether self-worth is, overall, contingent or not" (p. 905)—at least among that particular sample of college students.

21. How many of us actually get there is another question. After describing the ideal scenario—in which an individual experiences only unconditional positive regard so that "no conditions of worth would develop, self-regard would be unconditional, the needs for positive regard and self-regard would never be at variance with organismic evaluation, and the individual would continue to be psychologically adjusted, and would be fully functioning"—Carl Rogers conceded that, while "hypothetically possible," this "does not appear to occur in actuality" (p. 224). The psychologist Albert Ellis, who also emphasizes the importance of unconditional self-acceptance, likewise regards it as "a habit that can never be perfectly acquired" (Chamberlain and Haaga, p. 172). And two researchers who specialize in this subject write as follows: "We do not deny that such noncontingent people exist. We suspect that they are quite rare, however, at least in our North American culture that emphasizes the importance of self-esteem and the relative worth or value of one person over another based on their accomplishments, appearance, athletic skills, net worth, or good works" (Crocker and Wolfe, p. 616; also see Crocker et al.). After all, they go on to point out, people with high self-esteem may be mostly successful at meeting the conditions they've

set up for liking themselves, but that's not the same thing as liking themselves unconditionally.

22. Less likely to be anxious or depressed: Chamberlain and Haaga.

23. Ryan and Brown, p. 74. This point is also made by Crocker.

24. I made this case, albeit with a less nuanced view of self-esteem, in chapter 5 of the book *No Contest* (Kohn 1992); see Crocker's work for more recent evidence. Of course, it's possible that competitiveness, the need to triumph over others, is also a *symptom* of self-esteem that is already contingent and otherwise fragile. People who harbor fundamental doubts about their self-worth may be drawn to compete in a desperate but ultimately futile effort to prove to themselves, once and for all, that they're good. Paradoxically, it may require a healthier sense of self to collaborate with others than it does to try to defeat them.

CHAPTER 3: TOO MUCH CONTROL

1. See Ginott, pp. 101–2.

2. For example, see Grusec and Goodnow, p. 7.

3. One study found a significant "coherence in mothers' childrearing beliefs" such that those with an authoritarian approach tended to view everything their children did through that lens (Hastings and Rubin). And the more parents "ignore contextual factors," rigidly "compar[ing] specific acts with external standards of good or bad behavior, and act[ing] accordingly," the worse the outcome for the child (Hoffman 1970a, p. 113).

4. Adorno et al. Quotation appears on p. 385.

5. One psychologist asks us to imagine a mother who is playing peekaboo with her baby. At some point, perhaps when the game becomes a little too stimulating, the baby turns away and sucks his thumb. Rather than taking her cue from him and waiting until he's ready to resume playing, this mother "leans over into the infant's line of vision while clicking her tongue to attract [his] attention. The infant, however, ignores the mother and continues to look away. Undaunted, the mother persists and moves her head closer to the infant. The infant grimaces and . . . turns even further away. . . ." The mother's need to control the interaction—her fundamental lack of respect for the baby's clear preference—can have lasting effects. He may come to see himself as helpless to affect the world around him, and he may come to see his parent—perhaps others in general—as unresponsive and unreliable. Figuring out how to escape from unpleasant experiences and how to console himself become priorities, thus "potentially compromising cognitive development and distort[ing] the infant's interactions with other people" (Tronick, pp. 112, 117).

6. This point is made, with accompanying citations, by Kuczynski 1983, p. 133; and 1984, p. 1062.

7. Stayton et al. Quotation on p. 1061. This suggests, according to the authors, that "a disposition toward obedience emerges in a responsive, accommodating social environment without extensive training [or] discipline" (p. 1065). For a review of other research that also found obedience was more often related to

responsive parenting than to discipline or control, see Honig. One pair of researchers found that when mothers tended to impose their will on infants in the manner described in the Stayton study—that is, when they were more likely to "disrupt the baby's ongoing activity rather than adapting the timing and quality of [their] interventions and initiations to the baby's state, mood, and current interests"—the children were significantly more likely to be rated as hyperactive when they were five or six years old (Jacobvitz and Sroufe). Alas, there has been no subsequent investigation of this intriguing finding for the simple reason that virtually all of the available funding in the field of childhood disorders is reserved for neurobiologically oriented research rather than for investigation of the possible relevance of parenting.

8. Crockenberg and Litman, p. 970.

9. Parpal and Maccoby.

10. Kochanska 1997.

11. Committed compliance: Kochanska and Aksan. Compliance with another adult: Feldman and Klein.

12. This is particularly true when the goal is to compel children to adopt a certain attitude or feeling. In the short run, we can sometimes succeed in getting kids to act a particular way, but we can't make them *want* to do so—which is why it's silly to ask for advice about how to "motivate" our children. Efforts to exert control are also futile to the extent they're based on the assumption that parent-child relationships are one-way affairs. Researchers have come to realize that mothers and fathers don't simply act on their children. Like it or not, the relationship is reciprocal, with each influencing the other. "The emphasis on interaction has led us away from viewing parental behavior as something that is done *to* children or *for* children towards the view that it is done *with* children" (Maccoby and Martin, p. 78). I'm arguing that what is true is also desirable: Interacting with children is, in one sense, an accurate description of what does happen and, in another sense, a sensible prescription for what ought to happen.

13. Baldwin, esp. pp. 130–32.

14. Lamborn et al. 1991. Quotation appears on p. 1062. This is consistent with other research (see Buri et al.) showing that young adults, and particularly young women, who were raised by authoritarian parents are likely to think poorly of themselves as a result.

15. Samalin, p. 6.

16. This is a point that Martin Hoffman has made repeatedly in his writings. The same general phenomenon seems to take place when children are overcontrolled by adults other than their parents. For example, in a classic series of experiments in the 1930s (Lewin et al.), boys took part in clubs run by men who were deliberately either democratic or dictatorial in their leadership style. Some of the children in the latter groups did indeed react by becoming aggressive or competitive, but many others just seemed withdrawn and apathetic—until, that is, the leader left the room (or the boys were moved to a less tightly controlled group), at which point there was a sharp rise in aggressive behavior.

17. Hart et al.

18. Juul, p. 220. This is also the theme of an intriguing book published in the 1970s by a clinical psychologist and devout Christian named Sidney D. Craig: *Raising Your Child, Not by Force but by Love.* It represents a perspective strikingly different from that offered in most religiously oriented parenting guides I've seen. Craig also pointed out, obviously well before I did, that "the 'enemy' of the child is not permissiveness, but rather the fear of being permissive. It is this fear which drives good, middle-class American parents to behave toward their children in those callous, unsympathetic, insensitive ways which ultimately result in youthful delinquency" (p. 38).

19. Ryan and Deci 2003, p. 265.

20. Assor et al.

21. Ryan and Deci 2000, p. 47.

22. Johnson and Birch. Quotation appears on p. 660. Birch is the same researcher who conducted a study that I mentioned in the last chapter, the one showing that children who were rewarded or praised for drinking an unfamiliar beverage came to find it less tasty than did children who received no rewards or praise.

23. Maccoby and Martin, p. 44. For one study supporting that conclusion, see Hoffman and Saltzstein.

24. The infant study was first published in 1984 and is described in Grolnick, pp. 15–16; and also in Frodi et al. The second study (Deci et al. 1993) found, incidentally, that it was impossible to predict how controlling parents were just on the basis of how much they talked to their children during the play session. What mattered was what they said and how they said it.

25. Grolnick et al. 2002. An earlier study had found that six- and seven-year-olds painted less creatively—and enjoyed it less—when they were given controlling instructions about how they were supposed to handle the paints (Koestner et al.). Other research, meanwhile (e.g., Dornbusch et al. 1987), has found a negative relationship between authoritarian parenting and the grades of high school students. However, grades are not a good measure of—and may even be inversely related to—deep thinking, interest in learning, and a preference for challenging tasks. The fact that a student is chasing and obtaining those extrinsic rewards known as A's may be reason to worry, not to celebrate, as I explain in chapter 5.

26. Parental control, the authors speculated, "may tend to focus the children's attention quite narrowly," whereas "the children whose autonomy was supported actually achieved greater conceptual understanding of the task and were therefore more able to apply these concepts when they were alone" (Grolnick et al. 2002, p. 153).

27. See Flink et al.; and Deci et al. 1982.

28. Grolnick's summary comments appear on pp. 20 and 150. Effects irrespective of age: p. 30. (Similarly, Grusec and Goodnow [p. 11] found that "power assertion seems to have the same negative effect on moral development regardless of age." Brody and Shaffer extended this conclusion to the effects of love withdrawal.) Effects irrespective of race, class, or culture: see the Appendix.

29. Sometimes parents and teachers use words like *structure* and *limits* to justify their actions even though what they're actually doing to children could more accurately be described as control. Conversely, Grolnick points out that research studies claiming to show that control is good for kids often turn out to have offered some sort of reasonable structure but labeled it "control" (p. 149). She defines healthy structures as "the provision of guidelines and information that children need so they can be self-determining" (p. 17). Also relevant here: the distinction between *behavioral control* and *psychological control,* which was originated by Earl Schaefer, revived by Laurence Steinberg, and further developed by Brian Barber.

CHAPTER 4: PUNITIVE DAMAGES

1. In some cases, children—and, even more commonly, adults—may be punished without regard to whether the intervention is effective. The point may be not to change future behavior but to exact retribution. This evidently motivates some teachers to punish their students (Reyna and Weiner); it's unclear how many parents resort to punishment with the goal of changing how their children act and how many see punishment as a moral imperative (see pp. 101–2).
2. Sears et al., p. 484.
3. Toner, p. 31. Likewise, "punitive discipline emerged as a common or shared predictor of all the dimensions of child disruptive behaviors," reported the multiuniversity Conduct Problems Prevention Research Group in 2000 (Stormshak et al.; quotation on p. 24). And from another study, conducted in the Midwest: Punishment of various sorts "contributed more unique variance to predicting problem-behavior ratings than all demographic predictors combined" (Brenner and Fox; quotation on p. 253). Of course, the discovery that punishment is associated with children's misbehavior could be explained by the possibility that parents with tough kids are more likely to punish them; in other words, punishment may be "pulled" by the child's actions rather than causing those actions. Undoubtedly it's true that the causal arrows point in more than one direction, but by now there's enough evidence, from studies designed specifically to test this hypothesis, to justify the conclusion that punishment is a cause more than an effect. For example, see Hoffman 1960, p. 141; Kandel and Wu, p. 112; Cohen and Brook, p. 162; and, for the causative role played by corporal punishment in particular, Straus 2001, chapter 12. Similarly, while parents may respond more harshly to a toddler who is unusually aggressive, that response is driven in large part by the parent's preexisting attitudes about child rearing (Hastings and Rubin; see also Grusec and Mammone).
4. At this writing, the most ambitious summary of the existing research on corporal punishment is a monograph published by Gershoff in 2002. Of the studies she reviewed that looked at the effects on short-term compliance, three found a positive effect and two did not (p. 547). (Even those three didn't prove that corporal punishment was more effective than other methods.) More important, her meta-analysis of a whopping eighty-eight studies discovered that corporal pun-

ishment by parents is associated with "decreased moral internalization, increased child aggression, increased child delinquent and antisocial behavior, decreased quality of relationship between parent and child, decreased child mental health, increased risk of being a victim of physical abuse, increased adult aggression, increased adult criminal and antisocial behavior, decreased adult mental health, and increased risk of abusing own child or spouse" (p. 544). Also see the work of Murray Straus.

5. McCord 1991, pp. 175–6.
6. I offer a critique of some of the "New Discipline" programs, including "Discipline with Dignity," "Cooperative Discipline," "Discipline with Love and Logic," and the recommendations offered by Rudolf Dreikurs and his followers, in my 1996 book for teachers, *Beyond Discipline*. See especially chapter 4: "Punishment Lite: 'Consequences' and Pseudochoice."
7. Pieper and Pieper, p. 208. This is not to say that there is no such thing as a true natural consequence. If we stay up late, we'll likely be tired in the morning. If we don't go shopping, we'll eventually run out of food. But these scenarios are very different from, say, a parent's refusal to heat up dinner for a child who comes home late. Call that whatever you like: It's still a punishment, and one that feels particularly humiliating, at that. (An accompanying "I told you so" or "It serves you right" or "I hope you've learned your lesson" will only serve to make the child feel even worse.)
8. Hoffman 1960. Needless to say, this is hard to do. Research (e.g., Ritchie) confirms that parents are more likely to respond punitively during a conflict in which they and their children are locked in a battle of wills than after a single act of noncompliance.
9. Ginott, p. 151.
10. Hoffman 1970a, p. 114.
11. Gordon 1989, pp. 74, 7.
12. Hoffman and Saltzstein, p. 54.
13. For example, see Hoffman 1970a, p. 109. Straus 2001 (p. 101) makes the additional point that parents who spank but explain why they're doing so are "teaching the child just what to do and what to say when he or she hits another child."
14. For evidence that this is true of love withdrawal, see Hoffman 1970a, pp. 109, 115.
15. This same phenomenon shows up in schools with regard to better and worse forms of teaching, as I argued in an article called "Education's Rotten Apples" (Kohn 2002).

CHAPTER 5: PUSHED TO SUCCEED

1. Luthar and Becker.
2. Fromm, p. xvi.
3. Luthar and D'Avanzo. These authors, who conducted a study of nearly five hundred teenagers, some in a suburban high school and some in an inner-city high

school, note that, despite these data, teachers seem to think the former students are in better shape. The researchers speculate that "what is seen as problem behavior within an inner-city school may be viewed as creative self-expression by the suburban teachers and thus responded to with greater tolerance" (p. 861).

4. Norem-Hebeisen and Johnson. Quotation appears on p. 420.

5. In one of his stand-up routines, George Carlin asks: "What kind of empty people need to validate themselves through the achievements of their children? . . . Here's a bumper sticker I'd like to see: WE ARE THE PROUD PARENTS OF A CHILD WHOSE SELF-ESTEEM IS SUFFICIENT THAT HE DOESN'T NEED US PROMOTING HIS MINOR SCHOLASTIC ACHIEVEMENTS ON THE BACK OF OUR CAR."

6. The available research does not support the practice of delaying the start of kindergarten. Apparent academic benefits turn out to be largely illusory, a function of the socioeconomic characteristics of the children whose parents held them back, rather than being due to the practice itself. In other words, the children of affluent, highly educated parents would have done just as well regardless of when they started school. Any benefits that do turn out to be real tend to evaporate within a couple of years. And the data show no social benefits of redshirting; if anything, they hint of disadvantages that may show up later. (For details, along with a list of references, see Marshall.) Some parents may be tempted to engage in this practice because of how kindergartens are becoming increasingly academic—a trend almost universally deplored by experts in early-childhood education—but if more children begin kindergarten when they're older, that may exacerbate the acceleration of a focus on academic skills, thereby creating a vicious circle (Cosden et al., p. 210).

7. The research to support what follows—including an extended discussion of alternatives to traditional grades—can be found in my 1999 book *The Schools Our Children Deserve,* and also, to a more limited extent, in some of the essays about grading available at www.alfiekohn.org/teaching/articles.htm.

8. Ames and Archer.

9. Grolnick and Ryan.

10. The studies are, respectively, Gottfried et al. 1994; and Dornbusch et al. 1988. A third study, of fifth-grade children and their parents in Vermont, also found that rewards for good grades and punishment for bad grades "were associated with lower grades and poorer achievement scores" as well as "less motivation, pleasure, and persistence in doing their work in school" (Ginsburg and Bronstein; quotation appears on p. 1470). Here, however—unlike in the two studies described in the text—it wasn't as clear that the parental strategies *caused* those problems. It's possible that parents resorted to bribes and threats because their kids already had academic difficulties for other reasons. But at the very least these strategies didn't make things any better.

11. Borek. Frank McCourt, the author of *Angela's Ashes,* once remarked that, during eighteen years of teaching at a prestigious high school, only once did a parent ever ask him, "Is my child enjoying school?" All the other questions were about test scores, college applications, and getting the work done (cited in Merrow, p. 102).

12. "Often unrealistic standards": Harter 1999, p. 282. "Letting their parents down": personal communication with Lilian Katz in 1997. Fear of failure: Elliot and Thrash.

13. Grolnick, p. 98.

14. I describe noncompetitive ways to play, learn, and work in a book called *No Contest: The Case Against Competition* (Kohn 1992).

15. Schimel et al., p. 50. For citations to other theorists who defend the idea of conditional acceptance and conditional self-esteem, see Crocker and Wolfe, p. 614.

16. Numerous studies have confirmed that children are naturally inclined to try to make sense of the world, to push themselves to do things just beyond their current level. More broadly, the idea that it is natural to do as little as possible is a relic of "tension-reduction" or homeostatic models, which hold that organisms always seek a state of rest. Few models have been so thoroughly repudiated in modern psychology. Interested readers might look up the work of Gordon Allport as well as findings concerned with the fundamental human impetus to attain a sense of competence (Robert White), to be self-determining (Richard de Charms, Edward Deci, and others), to satisfy our curiosity (D. E. Berlyne), or to "actualize" our potential in various ways (Abraham Maslow).

17. For one of many studies showing that failure leads to an expectation of future failure, see Parsons and Ruble. For research showing that failure leads to a preference for easier tasks and to lower intrinsic motivation, see Wigfield; Harter 1992; and various publications of Deci and Ryan.

18. Crocker and Wolfe, pp. 614, 617.

CHAPTER 6: WHAT HOLDS US BACK?

1. See, for example, the 1997 and 1999 surveys entitled "Kids These Days" conducted by Public Agenda, a public opinion firm. (For details about the latter report: www.publicagenda.org/specials/kids/kids.htm.) The newspaper summary of the first of these reports appeared in the *New York Times* on June 26, 1997.

2. Grubb and Lazerson, pp. 56, 85.

3. These statistics are from the National Center for Children in Poverty at Columbia University and the Urban Institute, respectively.

4. Clayton.

5. For example, parents who do much of their children's homework for them make a tempting target for critics. But the more pressing question is how much of that homework is worth doing by anyone. If we confine the discussion to whether parents are too involved, too eager to make things easy for their children, we fail to challenge traditional forms of teaching that are doing even more harm (see Kohn 1999b). The structure is uncritically accepted and criticism is directed exclusively toward individuals. Similarly, every time we agonize over the proper degree of parental intervention when our children are victimized by their peers, we are distracted from thinking about which aspects of schools may unwittingly promote (or at least fail to discourage) that kind of victimization.

6. Dix et al. Quotations appear on pp. 1387 and 1374.

7. Cross-cultural evidence: Petersen et al. Relation between conformity and discipline: Luster et al.; and Gerris et al.

8. Holt, p. 21. Today, he continues, vengeance "goes under the more dignified name of retribution, which literally means 'paying back.' How the suffering inflicted on an offender compensates for his crime has never been clear, unless it is through the vindictive satisfaction it might bring to his victims and society. But is this justice?"

9. Greven, p. 65.

10. For example, one Christian minister recounts how his eighteen-month-old son was "defiantly challenging" his authority by refusing to hold his hand in a parking lot. What followed was a "series of repeated spankings (with explanation and abundant display of affection between each one), until he finally realized that Daddy always wins and *wins decisively!*" This approach is described as "loving correction." (Larry Tomczak's book is quoted in Greven, p. 69.)

11. See, for example, Leviticus, chapter 26; Deuteronomy, chapter 28; Proverbs, chapter 1; or Romans, chapter 1.

12. Quoted in Gordon 1989, p. xxvi.

13. Much depends on how the terms are defined and translated into research measures. For example, you'd want to distinguish between parents who can't be bothered to respond when their children do something wrong and parents who, with care and deliberation, choose a policy of minimal intervention. In any case, the extent to which children were punished in one study was a powerful predictor of how aggressive and antisocial they were eight years later, whereas neglect was not (Cohen et al.).

14. We've already seen that Baumrind is enamored of a reciprocity model for family relationships and that she thinks unconditional love will make children "selfish and demanding" (p. 223n3). She also assumes that "structure" in the family requires the use of extrinsic motivators and "contingent reinforcement," which she strongly supports. She approves of spanking, dismisses criticisms of punishment as "utopian," and declares that parents who don't use power to compel obedience will be seen as "indecisive" (Baumrind 1996).

Unfortunately, the research she cites to show that authoritative parenting works best doesn't support any of these positions. Her original findings were interpreted as proving that a combination of warmth and "firm control" (or "enforcement") was optimal. But another researcher who looked at the data carefully (Lewis 1981) discovered that the positive outcomes for children of authoritative parents didn't actually seem to be connected to the use of firm enforcement at all. Kids whose parents were warm but not controlling did just as well as kids whose parents were both—probably, she suggested, because control in the traditional sense isn't required to create structure and predictability as Baumrind (and many others) assumed.

By the same token, Baumrind seemed to blur the differences between "permissive" parents who were really just confused and those who were deliberately democratic. There were no problems with the children of the latter parents, suggesting, in the words of another psychologist, that "a close look at Baumrind's actual data may reveal significant support for child-centered parenting" (Crain, p. 18) even though Baumrind has created a very different impression because she personally opposes that style.

Subsequent research using Baumrind's formulation seems to support this view. A huge study of teenagers (Lamborn et al. 1991) did indeed find benefits from what was described as "authoritative" parenting, but that term was defined to mean that parents were aware of, and involved with, their children's lives, not that they were even the least bit punitive or controlling. Another study (Strage and Brandt) similarly cited Baumrind by way of suggesting that parents need to be both supportive and demanding, but it turned out that being demanding when their children were young was unrelated, or even negatively related, to various desirable outcomes. By contrast, the extent to which the parents had been supportive, and also the extent to which they had encouraged their children's independence, had a strong positive relationship to those same outcomes.

15. Grusec and Mammone, p. 60; also see Hastings and Rubin. Barber et al. commented that "the most powerful sources of psychological control will be the parent's own psychological status" (p. 276).

16. Miller, p. 41.

17. Hastings and Grusec 1998. However, it's not always easy to tell whose needs are really being given top priority. Some parents who conspicuously sacrifice everything for their children, whose very lives seem to revolve around them, actually turn out to be rather narcissistic. The giveaway is that they tend to have specific, rigid expectations for their children and are likely to be inordinately controlling. Everything must be just so; nothing can deviate from their plan. The family appears to be child-centered to a fault, yet the child is really being used to meet the parent's own needs.

18. This can be a fear that one is incompetent at raising a child, but it can also be a symptom of a more general fear of inadequacy. Recall that a parent's fear of failure is associated with the use of love withdrawal (see p. 85).

19. Grusec and Mammone, p. 62.

20. Bugental et al., p. 1298.

21. This quotation, used by Kunc in his presentations, also appears at www.normemma.com/hmsvouts.htm.

22. Abusive parents see themselves as victims: Bugental et al., p. 1298. Indeed, according to later research (see Bugental and Happaney), some parents even ascribe malevolent motives to *infants,* leading to a cycle of perceived powerlessness, anger, and abuse. Looking for negative motives in the child: Lieberman, p. 64.

23. See Hastings and Grusec 1998, p. 477; and a summary of Hastings's research by Grusec et al. 1997, p. 268.

24. The act of watching television is not, as some people believe, inherently mind-numbing. Apart from *what* one watches, what matters is *how* one watches. This is a thesis that I developed in an essay entitled "Television and Children: ReViewing the Evidence" (Kohn 1998).

25. Gordon 1989, p. 214.
26. See Luster et al., p. 143.

CHAPTER 7: PRINCIPLES OF UNCONDITIONAL PARENTING

1. The statistic is from Straus 2004, citing a 1996 study by Robert Larzelere and his colleagues. The quotation is from Straus 2001, p. 210.
2. For example, mothers in one study were asked to get their four-year-old children to do something that wasn't terribly interesting (sort plastic forks and spoons) even though toys in the same room provided a powerful distraction. Half of the mothers were told that they would be asked to leave the room at some point to see if their children would continue working on the task when they were by themselves. It turned out that those in this group, whose goal was to elicit compliance for a longer period and in the absence of an adult, were more likely than the other mothers (who were focused exclusively on the here-and-now) to reason with their children, to use different kinds of explanations, and to be more nurturing in their interactions. Furthermore, what they did worked: Even as judged by the results when the mothers were still present, children were more likely to stay on task if their mothers were using the kinds of strategies designed with long-range goals in mind (Kuczynski 1984).
3. One group of researchers put it this way: The first priority for parents shouldn't be to look for "situation-specific solutions" to problems they're having with their children, but to "get more insight [into] their own way of thinking and feeling about their relationship with their child" (Gerris et al., p. 845). The next step, of course, would be to *use* that insight to try to preserve and strengthen the relationship. This should be a priority even if it sometimes takes precedence over making kids do what we say.
4. Gordon 1975, p. 228.
5. Coloroso, pp. 62–63.
6. Lieberman, p. 49.
7. Here my focus is on expectations that are unrealistic just because of the child's age. But many children have special needs and limitations that similarly restrict their capacity to do what their parents expect—and it's equally pointless in such cases, even cruel, to press one's demands. For a good analysis of the challenges faced by some children that make traditional discipline techniques particularly counterproductive, see Greene.
8. See, e.g., Noddings, p. 25. She points out that this idea is derived from the philosopher Martin Buber's idea of "confirmation."
9. Lewis 1995, pp. 132–33.
10. Even in such a case, however, as Marilyn Watson points out, the child may have intended less harm than he actually caused. She also remarks that, even in an instance when the assumption of innocence may be unfounded, the effect may be to prompt the child to try to live up to the parent's positive image of her (personal communication, June 2004).
11. For example, see the studies cited in Dumas and LaFreniere, p. 9.

12. "No . . . no . . . no . . . no . . . no . . . well, okay, I guess" is the mirror image of another unhealthy pattern that I described earlier, in which a parent lets everything slide and then suddenly explodes: "Okay . . . okay . . . okay . . . okay . . . okay . . . *NO!!!*"—accompanied by punishment.

13. Miller, pp. 88–89. Also see Gordon 1975, pp. 21–22, 257–59.

CHAPTER 8: LOVE WITHOUT STRINGS ATTACHED

1. That doesn't mean, however, that happiness should be one's only goal. See p. 239n1.
2. Gordon 1975, p. 27.
3. Watson, pp. 142, 30.
4. Ibid., p. 2.
5. Lovett, pp. 36, 69, 104–105.
6. The idea that happiness depends on what one owns is not something we want to cultivate in our children. Plenty of adults act as though they believe this, even those who are familiar with the cycle in which a very short-lived burst of pleasure from acquiring yet another pair of shoes or fancy digital gadget is followed by a rapid return to the preexisting state of restlessness or boredom. What has aptly been called "commodity fetishism" is not especially healthy, even if it is enormously profitable to the corporations that strain to convince us we need each new-and-improved item they're selling.
7. Juul, p. 61.
8. For more on these issues, see *Punished by Rewards* (Kohn 1999), especially chapter 6 ("The Praise Problem") and the Afterword.
9. Grusec et al. 1978. In another study, the likelihood of children's being generous increased both when they were praised and when they were led to think of themselves as helpful people. But in a follow-up experiment, the latter group turned out to be more generous than those who had received verbal reinforcement. In other words, praise increased generosity in a given setting but ceased to be effective outside that setting, whereas children with a deeper reason to be generous continued to act on that motivation in other circumstances (Grusec and Redler).
10. Karen D. Arnold of Boston College, the author of *Lives of Promise,* is quoted in Rimer.
11. For more on the importance of this distinction, see Kohn 1999b, chapter 2.
12. I've taken a stab at this myself by writing a short book for teachers called *Beyond Discipline* (Kohn 1996). I also recommend a book called *Learning to Trust* (Watson), which describes two years in the life of a teacher in an inner-city school who, by meeting the children's needs, successfully steers clear of more coercive approaches to classroom management.

CHAPTER 9: CHOICES FOR CHILDREN

1. I reviewed some of the research on this topic in Kohn 1993. Interested readers should also look up the work of Edward Deci, Richard Ryan, and Wendy Grol-

nick, who have written extensively about the experience of autonomy in different domains of life. The terms "pawns" and "origins," incidentally, come from the psychologist Richard de Charms.

2. Note that these are not the same thing. "The fact that a parent does not apply psychological control to a child does not automatically mean that this parent is encouraging or fostering autonomy" (Barber et al., p. 271).

3. Children are more likely to do what they're asked: See pp. 51–53. More apt to rely on their parents: Several studies supporting this finding are cited in Chirkov et al., p. 98. Feeling better about themselves: Eccles et al., p. 62. More likely to stay out of trouble: Youths from all ethnic backgrounds whose parents included them in decision making were less likely to use drugs and alcohol, and less likely to be involved in school misconduct or antisocial behavior a year later (Lamborn et al. 1996). College students feel confident about themselves: Strage and Brandt. In most of the studies cited in this paragraph, the extent to which parents supported their children's autonomy was judged by what the children experienced, not by what the parents reported. Eccles showed that these accounts often differ, and, as I've noted, it's what the kids believe that matters.

4. Cai et al., p. 373. In the original quotation, each of these items is followed by one or more citations in parentheses.

5. We have to be very careful here, though, because the enormous power that parents possess can easily turn what looks like a mere observation or recommendation into a virtual demand. The tacit threat of love withdrawal must be avoided, and the final decision should rest with the child in those cases where we say it does. It may be frustrating when kids decide not to do what we've suggested, but we should view those instances as confirmation that we've managed to help them feel truly autonomous.

6. For practical suggestions for dealing with sibling conflict, see Faber and Mazlish 1987. Their other books are also well worth reading.

7. Lieberman, p. 169. She continues: "One can end up with a situation where the parent is inflicting on the older sibling the same kind of arbitrary power that the older sibling is trying to inflict on the younger one. The parent's action to stop the stronger sibling's power can give the message: Do as I say, not as I do."

8. For example, see the description on p. 227n5.

9. Baldwin, p. 135.

10. See the reanalysis of Baumrind's data in Lewis 1981, especially p. 562. Another study, meanwhile, found that when parents treat misbehavior as an infraction to be punished, kids learn to defy, but when parents treat misbehavior as a problem to be solved together, kids learn to negotiate (Kuczynski et al.).

11. This point, along with much of what comprises the following paragraphs, is adapted from Kohn 1996.

12. Scott-Little and Holloway.

13. Gordon 1989, p. 9.

14. For a recent experimental demonstration of this in a classroom setting, see Reeve et al.

15. Many teachers believe that it's necessary "to stand over noncompliant students"

until they do what they're told. But it often turns out that these students "much more willingly comply with a request or a command" if the teacher simply makes the request clearly "and then [leaves] the student to comply in his or her own good time" (Watson, p. 130).

16. Experimental support for a combination of items 2, 3, and 6 was offered by Deci et al. 1994.

CHAPTER 10: THE CHILD'S PERSPECTIVE

1. The addition of this second question reminds us that there is something conspicuously insufficient about saying that our primary goal is for our children to be happy. Personally, I wouldn't want my kids to be perpetually miserable social activists, but neither would I want them to be so focused on their own well-being that they were indifferent about other people's suffering. Neither would I want happiness to be purchased at the price of their being unreflective, shallow, or unable to become outraged about outrageous things. Edward Deci put it this way: "When people want only happiness, they can actually undermine their own development because the quest for happiness can lead them to suppress other aspects of their experience. . . . The true meaning of being alive is not just to feel happy, but to experience the full range of human emotions" (1995, p. 192; emphasis omitted). In sum, I don't think it's possible to give any answer other than "Yes, but . . ." to the question "Do you want your child to be happy?"

2. Interested readers might want to look up the work of such researchers as Nancy Eisenberg and the late Paul Mussen (who collaborated on a very useful book called *The Roots of Prosocial Behavior in Children*), Martin Hoffman, Ervin Staub, Marian Radke-Yarrow, and Carolyn Zahn-Waxler.

3. Barnett et al., p. 93. There is also evidence from the field of sports psychology that competition promotes lower-level forms of ethical reasoning and the development of a lower moral standard (Kohn 1992).

4. "Frequent use of 'no,' 'stop,' 'don't' in the absence of clarifying information may result in the learning of a generalized inhibition, that is, learning to stand back in the face of all kinds of distresses, thus minimizing altruistic as well as reparative efforts" (Zahn-Waxler et al., p. 326).

5. In the words of Leon Kuczynski (1983, p. 132), a developmental psychologist who has studied this issue extensively, "An unexplained prohibition [is] not empty of motivational information, because it implicitly carrie[s] the threat of some degree of external consequences."

6. The study demonstrating a link between parents' use of reasoning and the altruism of grown children was actually quite dramatic: It was an investigation of which individuals chose to rescue European Jews from the Nazis. The parents of rescuers "were significantly less likely to [have] emphasize[d] obedience" or to have used physical punishment. Instead they focused on "reasoning, suggestions of ways to remedy the harm done, persuasion, and advice," thereby communicating "a message of respect for and trust in [their] children" that helped these children feel "a sense of personal efficacy and warmth toward others"

(Oliner and Oliner, pp. 162, 179, 182). The second study examined the child-hoods of more than a thousand undergraduates and found that those students who were involved in community volunteer work, and who took a stand in favor of a cause in which they believed, were more likely to have been raised by parents who seemed respectful of them and to have relied on a rational rather than a punitive approach to discipline (Block et al.).

7. For more on how understanding of social and moral ideas must be "construct-ed" by, rather than simply transmitted to, the learner, see the work of Constance Kamii and Rheta DeVries. I discussed this issue while criticizing traditional school-based "character education" programs (Kohn 1997).

8. "Eliciting the child's opinion": Walker and Taylor; quotation appears on p. 280. Other research has found: Eisenberg, p. 161.

9. Personal communications with Marilyn Watson in 1989 and 1990.

10. Hoffman discovered: Hoffman and Saltzstein; quotation appears on p. 50. Sub-sequent research has confirmed: See, for example, Kuczynski 1983. Most effec-tive with older children: Brody and Shaffer. Induction helps preschoolers: Hart et al. Even toddlers tended to respond: Zahn-Waxler et al.; quotation appears on p. 323.

11. A precursor to empathy may begin even earlier. Newborns are more likely to cry—and likely to cry longer—when they are exposed to the sound of another infant's cry than when they hear other noises that are equally loud and sudden. In three sets of studies, with infants ranging in age from eighteen to seventy-two hours old, such crying seemed to be a spontaneous reaction rather than a mere vocal imitation. The implication is that we may be born with a predisposition to be distressed by others' distress. (These studies are cited in Kohn 1990, as is a great deal of other research on perspective taking and empathy. Some of the dis-cussion that follows in the text is also drawn from that book.)

12. A variation on this, proposed by Coloroso, pp. 136–38, is to ask two siblings to explain what happened but only after they're able to agree on a single account.

13. This is why I suggested earlier that parents might ask themselves, "If someone had said that to me, would *I* feel unconditionally loved?" But such an imagina-tive reversal may not be enough for the simple reason that your child isn't you. It isn't hard to think of a scenario in which you could honestly answer that ques-tion in the affirmative, but your child most definitely would not feel uncondi-tionally loved.

14. See the study by Hastings and Grusec mentioned on p. 107. Such parents are also more likely to teach a constructive approach to resolving conflicts. (Author-itarian parents, by contrast, are more likely to see conflict—especially between themselves and their children—as something to be eliminated. They fail to dis-tinguish between different kinds of conflict or between better and worse ways of handling the conflicts that will inevitably arise.) Another study, meanwhile, found that when parents discussed things with their children, their tendency to use "self-oriented" arguments (intended to defend their own position) as opposed to "other-oriented" arguments (that took account of the other person's interests in an effort to find a compromise) had a measurable effect on the way

that the children dealt with their peers three years later. The researchers remarked that it may not be enough to teach conflict-resolution skills to children; we also have to consider the child's "first-hand exposure" to conflicts at home (Herrera and Dunn; quotation on p. 879).

15. Dutch study: Gerris et al. Canadian study: Hastings and Grusec 1997. U.S. study: Kochanska.

16. Miller, pp. 89–91. These arguments form the core of her entire body of work—and also that of many other therapists who write about raising children.

17. Recall that research supports the perception that parents are constantly stepping in to interrupt, thwart, and prevent. See pp. 133, 236n11.

APPENDIX: PARENTING STYLES

1. Levine.

2. Mosier and Rogoff; quotations on pp. 1057–58.

3. Rothbaum, personal correspondence, January 2002.

4. One group of researchers raises the intriguing possibility that a culture less focused on choice may provide a distinct advantage even if children have fewer opportunities to make decisions. Recall that authoritarian parents are more likely than nonauthoritarian parents to attribute negative motives to children. They tend to assume that a child acting in a way they don't like is being deliberately defiant or aggressive or malicious—and this may provoke them to respond with more coercion and power-based interventions, which sets a vicious circle into motion. But in some cultures, even parents who act in a way we would view as authoritarian may be less likely to make such assumptions about their children's motives because people aren't seen as independent, decision-making agents. Hence, there is less conflict in the relationship. (See Grusec et al. 1997, p. 272.)

5. Grolnick, pp. 75, 79. Barber and Harmon also report preliminary data from a study of nine different cultures, including two that are relatively collectivist, showing a consistent relationship between psychological control by parents and both depression and antisocial behavior in children.

6. Ryan and Deci 2003, pp. 265–67. For a different view of these issues—and a more detailed analysis of cross-cultural differences in "autonomy" and "relatedness"—see Rothbaum and Trommsdorff.

7. "Rates of parents' use": This conclusion by Gershoff, p. 562, is followed by fifteen citations. "Children in the lower socioeconomic classes": Dodge et al., p. 662. Also see Sears et al.; and Simons et al. 1991. Gershoff notes, however, that some studies have failed to find the same relationship. This may be related to the specific aspect of socioeconomic status that's being investigated. For example, the use of physical punishment may be more consistently (negatively) related to parents' level of education than to their income or occupation.

8. See Conger et al.; and also the evidence reviewed in Grolnick, pp. 83–87.

9. Melvin Kohn's results: M. Kohn. (No relation, in case you were wondering.) Kohn's findings confirmed by others: See, for example, Schaefer and Edgerton; Pinderhughes et al.; and Gerris et al. International data: Petersen et al.

10. Less likely to prefer autonomy: Alwin (p. 362) cites five studies to support this conclusion. More likely to approve of aggression: Dodge et al.

11. Class may have more of an impact than race: Pinderhughes et al. This same study, however, found that race remains relevant, as did Deater-Deckard et al.; Giles-Sims et al. (the study conducted in 1990); and Straus and Stewart (the study conducted in 1995). McLeod et al. (p. 586), relying on a huge national data set from 1988, also reported that "white mothers reported spanking their children less often" during the preceding week than did black mothers, but she added that this may have been at least partly because the latter in this sample were more likely than the former to be poor.

12. Opposition by 22 versus 9 percent: Flynn. Declining approval over 26 years: Straus and Mathur.

13. Deater-Deckard et al. That last qualification is very important: "There appears to be a boundary for the extremity of harsh physical discipline past which the effects are deleterious, and equally deleterious, for all children" (Deater-Deckard and Dodge, p. 168).

14. Of course, this point has been made by many other theorists, including Erik Erikson and—more relevant to this discussion—Deater-Deckard and Dodge, who argue: "Apparently similar parental behavior (such as spanking) may have different meaning and consequences in different cultural milieus" (p. 168).

15. This point was made by the late Hugh Lytton (p. 213), an eminent researcher in human development, and by D. C. Rowe (p. 221). Rowe also questions D-D & D's finding on the grounds that the measure of parenting practices may not have had equal reliability for whites and blacks, or equal validity (if, say, black mothers had reason to mistrust the interviewers).

16. This point is made by Straus 2005.

17. Lamborn et al. 1996. Quotation on p. 293.

18. Simons et al. 2002.

19. Straus et al.

20. Kilgore et al.

21. Rohner et al. Quotation appears on p. 691.

22. Kelley et al., p. 574.

23. "Maternal fears about child victimization were unrelated to parenting orientation" in the study reported in Kelley et al. (p. 579), although in an unpublished dissertation Kelley previously reported having found such a relation.

24. Lamborn et al. 1996; and Simons et al. 2002, respectively.

25. This point is also made by Straus et al. in the context of their finding that physical punishment has damaging effects on children of all races.

26. Grolnick made much the same point. In tough neighborhoods, "the development of self-regulation and responsibility—both outcomes of autonomy supportive parenting—are just as necessary, if not more so, than they are for children of advantage" (Grolnick, p. 74).

REFERENCES

Adorno, T. W., Else Frenkel-Brunswik, Daniel J. Levinson, and R. Nevitt Sanford. *The Authoritarian Personality.* New York: Harper & Brothers, 1950.

Alwin, Duane F. "Trends in Parental Socialization Values: Detroit, 1958–1983." *American Journal of Sociology* 90 (1984): 359–82.

Ames, Carole, and Jennifer Archer. "Mothers' Beliefs About the Role of Ability and Effort in School Learning." *Journal of Educational Psychology* 79 (1987): 409–14.

Assor, Avi, Guy Roth, and Edward L. Deci. "The Emotional Costs of Parents' Conditional Regard: A Self-Determination Theory Analysis." *Journal of Personality* 72 (2004): 47–89.

Baldwin, Alfred L. "Socialization and the Parent-Child Relationship." *Child Development* 19 (1948): 127–36.

Barber, Brian K. "Parental Psychological Control: Revisiting a Neglected Construct." *Child Development* 67 (1996): 3296–3319.

Barber, Brian K., Roy L. Bean, and Lance D. Erickson. "Expanding the Study and Understanding of Psychological Control." In *Intrusive Parenting: How Psychological Control Affects Children and Adolescents,* edited by Brian K. Barber. Washington, D.C.: American Psychological Association, 2002.

Barber, Brian K., and Elizabeth Lovelady Harmon. "Violating the Self: Parental Psychological Control of Children and Adolescents." In *Intrusive Parenting: How Psychological Control Affects Children and Adolescents,* edited by Brian K. Barber. Washington, D.C.: American Psychological Association, 2002.

Barnett, Mark A., Karen A. Matthews, and Charles B. Corbin. "The Effect of Competitive and Cooperative Instructional Sets on Children's Generosity." *Personality and Social Psychology Bulletin* 5 (1979): 91–94.

Baumrind, Diana. "Some Thoughts About Childrearing." In *Influences on Human Development,* edited by Urie Bronfenbrenner. Hinsdale, IL: Dryden Press, 1972.

———. "The Discipline Controversy Revisited." *Family Relations* 45 (1996): 405–14.

Becker, Wesley C. "Consequences of Different Kinds of Parental Discipline." *Review of Child Development Research,* vol. 1, edited by Martin L. Hoffman and Lois Wladis Hoffman. New York: Russell Sage Foundation, 1964.

Beltz, Stephen E. *How to Make Johnny WANT to Obey.* Englewood Cliffs, NJ: Prentice-Hall, 1971.

Block, Jeanne H., Norma Haan, and M. Brewster Smith. "Socialization Correlates of Student Activism." *Journal of Social Issues* 25 (1969): 143–77.

Borek, Jennifer Gerdes. "Why the Rush?" *Education Week,* May 23, 2001: 38.

Brenner, Viktor, and Robert A. Fox. "Parental Discipline and Behavior Problems in Young Children." *Journal of Genetic Psychology* 159 (1998): 251–56.

Brody, Gene H., and David R. Shaffer. "Contributions of Parents and Peers to Children's Moral Socialization." *Developmental Review* 2 (1982): 31–75.

Bugental, Daphne Blunt, and Keith Happaney. "Predicting Infant Maltreatment in Low-Income Families." *Developmental Psychology* 40 (2004): 234–43.

Bugental, Daphne Blunt, Judith E. Lyon, Jennifer Krantz, and Victoria Cortez. "Who's the Boss? Differential Accessibility of Dominance Ideation in Parent-Child Relationships." *Journal of Personality and Social Psychology* 72 (1997): 1297–1309.

Burhans, Karen Klein, and Carol S. Dweck. "Helplessness in Early Childhood: The Role of Contingent Worth." *Child Development* 66 (1995): 1719–38.

Buri, John R., Peggy A. Louiselle, Thomas M. Misukanis, and Rebecca A. Mueller. "Effects of Parental Authoritarianism and Authoritativeness on Self-Esteem." *Personality and Social Psychology Bulletin* 14 (1988): 271–82.

Cagan, Elizabeth. "The Positive Parent: Raising Children the Scientific Way." *Social Policy,* January/Februrary 1980: 41–48.

Cai, Yi, Johnmarshall Reeve, and Dawn T. Robinson. "Home Schooling and Teaching Style: Comparing the Motivating Styles of Home School and Public School Teachers." *Journal of Educational Psychology* 94 (2002): 372–80.

Chamberlain, John M., and David A. F. Haaga. "Unconditional Self-Acceptance and Psychological Health." *Journal of Rational-Emotive and Cognitive-Behavior Therapy* 19 (2001): 163–76.

Chamberlain, Patricia, and Gerald R. Patterson. "Discipline and Child Compliance in Parenting." In Marc H. Bornstein, ed., *Handbook of Parenting,* vol. 4, *Applied and Practical Parenting.* Mahwah, NJ: Erlbaum, 1995.

Chapman, Michael, and Carolyn Zahn-Waxler. "Young Children's Compliance and Noncompliance to Parental Discipline in a Natural Setting." *International Journal of Behavioral Development* 5 (1982): 81–94.

Chirkov, Valery, Richard M. Ryan, Youngmee Kim, and Ulas Kaplan. "Differentiating Autonomy from Individualism and Independence." *Journal of Personality and Social Psychology* 84 (2003): 97–110.

Clayton, Lawrence O. "The Impact upon Child-Rearing Attitudes, of Parental Views of the Nature of Humankind." *Journal of Psychology and Christianity* 4, 3 (1985): 49–55.

Cohen, Patricia, and Judith S. Brook. "The Reciprocal Influence of Punishment and Child Behavior Disorder." In *Coercion and Punishment in Long-Term Perspectives,* edited by Joan McCord. Cambridge, England: Cambridge University Press, 1998.

Cohen, Patricia, Judith S. Brook, Jacob Cohen, C. Noemi Velez, and Marc Garcia. "Common and Uncommon Pathways to Adolescent Psychopathology and Problem Behavior." In *Straight and Devious Pathways from Childhood to Adulthood*, edited by Lee N. Robins and Michael Rutter. Cambridge, England: Cambridge University Press, 1990.

Coloroso, Barbara. *Kids Are Worth It!* New York: Avon, 1994.

Conger, Rand D., Xiaojia Ge, Glen H. Elder, Jr., Frederick O. Lorenz, and Ronald L. Simons. "Economic Stress, Coercive Family Processes, and Developmental Problems of Adolescents." *Child Development* 65 (1994): 541–61.

Cosden, Merith, Jules Zimmer, and Paul Tuss. "The Impact of Age, Sex, and Ethnicity on Kindergarten Entry and Retention Decisions." *Educational Evaluation and Policy Analysis* 15 (1993): 209–22.

Craig, Sidney D. *Raising Your Child, Not by Force but by Love*. Philadelphia: Westminster Press, 1973.

Crain, William. *Reclaiming Childhood*. New York: Times Books, 2003.

Crittenden, Patricia M., and David L. DiLalla. "Compulsive Compliance: The Development of an Inhibitory Coping Strategy in Infancy." *Journal of Abnormal Child Psychology* 16 (1988): 585–99.

Crockenberg, Susan, and Cindy Litman. "Autonomy as Competence in 2-Year-Olds: Maternal Correlates of Child Defiance, Compliance, and Self-Assertion." *Developmental Psychology* 26 (1990): 961–71.

Crocker, Jennifer. "The Costs of Seeking Self-Esteem." *Journal of Social Issues* 58 (2002): 597–615.

Crocker, Jennifer, Riia K. Luhtanen, M. Lynne Cooper, and Alexandra Bouvrette. "Contingencies of Self-Worth in College Students: Theory and Measurement." *Journal of Personality and Social Psychology* 85 (2003): 894–908.

Crocker, Jennifer, and Connie T. Wolfe. "Contingencies of Self-Worth." *Psychological Review* 108 (2001): 593–623.

Deater-Deckard, Kirby, and Kenneth A. Dodge. "Externalizing Behavior Problems and Discipline Revisited." *Psychological Inquiry* 8 (1997): 161–75.

Deater-Deckard, Kirby, Kenneth A. Dodge, John E. Bates, and Gregory S. Petit. "Physical Discipline Among African American and European American Mothers: Links to Children's Externalizing Behaviors." *Developmental Psychology* 32 (1996): 1065–72.

Deci, Edward L. *Why We Do What We Do: The Dynamics of Personal Autonomy*. With Richard Flaste. New York: Grosset/Putnam, 1995.

Deci, Edward L., Robert E. Driver, Lucinda Hotchkiss, Robert J. Robbins, and Ilona McDougal Wilson. "The Relation of Mothers' Controlling Vocalizations to Children's Intrinsic Motivation." *Journal of Experimental Child Psychology* 55 (1993): 151–62.

Deci, Edward L., Haleh Eghrari, Brian C. Patrick, and Dean R. Leone. "Facilitating Internalization: The Self-Determination Theory Perspective." *Journal of Personality* 62 (1994): 119–42.

Deci, Edward L., Richard Koestner, and Richard M. Ryan. "A Meta-Analytic Review of Experiments Examining the Effects of Extrinsic Rewards on Intrinsic Motivation." *Psychological Bulletin* 125 (1999): 627–68.

Deci, Edward L., and Richard M. Ryan. "Human Autonomy: The Basis for True Self-Esteem." In *Efficacy, Agency, and Self-Esteem*, edited by Michael H. Kernis. New York: Plenum, 1995.

Deci, Edward L., Nancy H. Spiegel, Richard M. Ryan, Richard Koestner, and Manette Kauffman. "Effects of Performance Standards on Teaching Styles: Behavior of Controlling Teachers." *Journal of Educational Psychology* 74 (1982): 852–59.

DeVries, Rheta, and Betty Zan. *Moral Classrooms, Moral Children*. New York: Teachers College Press, 1994.

Dienstbier, Richard A., Donald Hillman, John Lehnhoff, Judith Hillman, and Maureen C. Valkenaar. "An Emotion-Attribution Approach to Moral Behavior." *Psychological Review* 82 (1975): 299–315.

Dix, Theodore, Diane N. Ruble, and Robert J. Zambarano. "Mothers' Implicit Theories of Discipline: Child Effects, Parent Effects, and the Attribution Process." *Child Development* 60 (1989): 1373–91.

Dodge, Kenneth A., Gregory S. Petit, and John E. Bates. "Socialization Mediators of the Relation Between Socioeconomic Status and Child Conduct Problems." *Child Development* 65 (1994): 649–65.

Dornbusch, Sanford M., Julie T. Elworth, and Philip L. Ritter. "Parental Reaction to Grades: A Field Test of the Overjustification Approach." Unpublished manuscript, Stanford University, 1988.

Dornbusch, Sanford M., Philip L. Ritter, P. Herbert Leiderman, Donald F. Roberts, and Michael J. Fraleigh. "The Relation of Parenting Style to Adolescent School Performance." *Child Development* 58 (1987): 1244–57.

Dumas, Jean E., and Peter J. LaFreniere. "Relationships as Context." In *Coercion and Punishment in Long-Term Perspectives*, edited by Joan McCord. Cambridge, England: Cambridge University Press, 1998.

Eccles, Jacquelynne S., Christy M. Buchanan, Constance Flanagan, Andrew Fuligni, Carol Midgley, and Doris Yee. "Control Versus Autonomy During Early Adolescence." *Journal of Social Issues* 47, 4 (1991): 53–68.

Eisenberg, Nancy. *Altruistic Emotion, Cognition, and Behavior*. Hillsdale, NJ: Erlbaum, 1986.

Elliot, Andrew J., and Todd M. Thrash. "The Intergenerational Transmission of Fear of Failure." *Personality and Social Psychology Bulletin* 30 (2004): 957–71.

Faber, Adele, and Elaine Mazlish. *Siblings Without Rivalry*. New York: Norton, 1987.

Feldman, Ruth, and Pnina S. Klein. "Toddlers' Self-Regulated Compliance to Mothers, Caregivers, and Fathers." *Developmental Psychology* 39 (2003): 680–92.

Flink, Cheryl, Ann K. Boggiano, and Marty Barrett. "Controlling Teacher Strategies: Undermining Children's Self-Determination and Performance." *Journal of Personality and Social Psychology* 59 (1990): 916–24.

Flynn, Clifton P. "Regional Differences in Attitudes Toward Corporal Punishment." *Journal of Marriage and the Family* 56 (1994): 314–24.

Forsman, Lennart. "Parent-Child Gender Interaction in the Relation Between Retrospective Self-Reports on Parental Love and Current Self-Esteem." *Scandinavian Journal of Psychology* 30 (1989): 275–83.

Frodi, Ann, Lisa Bridges, and Wendy Grolnick. "Correlates of Mastery-related

Behavior: A Short-Term Longitudinal Study of Infants in Their Second Year." *Child Development* 56 (1985): 1291–98.

Fromm, Erich. Foreword to *Summerhill: A Radical Approach to Child Rearing* by A. S. Neill. New York: Hart, 1960.

Gerris, Jan R. M., Maja Deković, and Jan M.A.M. Janssens. "The Relationship Between Social Class and Childrearing Behaviors: Parents' Perspective Taking and Value Orientations." *Journal of Marriage and the Family* 59 (1997): 834–47.

Gershoff, Elizabeth Thompson. "Corporal Punishment by Parents and Associated Child Behaviors and Experiences: A Meta-Analysis and Theoretical Review." *Psychological Bulletin* 128 (2002): 539–79.

Giles-Sims, Jean, Murray A. Straus, and David B. Sugarman. "Child, Maternal, and Family Characteristics Associated with Spanking." *Family Relations* 44 (1995): 170–76.

Ginott, Haim G. *Teacher and Child*. New York: Macmillan, 1972.

Ginsburg, Golda S., and Phyllis Bronstein. "Family Factors Related to Children's Intrinsic/Extrinsic Motivational Orientation and Academic Performance." *Child Development* 64 (1993): 1461–74.

Goldstein, Mandy, and Patrick C. L. Heaven. "Perceptions of the Family, Delinquency, and Emotional Adjustment Among Youth." *Personality and Individual Differences* 29 (2000): 1169–78.

Gordon, Thomas. *P.E.T.—Parent Effectiveness Training*. New York: Plume, 1975.

———. *Teaching Children Self-Discipline . . . At Home and at School*. New York: Times Books, 1989.

Gottfried, Adele Eskeles, James S. Fleming, and Allen W. Gottfried. "Role of Parental Motivational Practices in Children's Academic Intrinsic Motivation and Achievement." *Journal of Educational Psychology* 86 (1994): 104–13.

Greene, Ross W. *The Explosive Child*. New York: HarperCollins, 1998.

Greven, Philip. *Spare the Child: The Religious Roots of Punishment and the Psychological Impact of Physical Abuse*. New York: Vintage, 1992.

Grolnick, Wendy S. *The Psychology of Parental Control: How Well-Meant Parenting Backfires*. Mahwah, NJ: Erlbaum, 2003.

Grolnick, Wendy S., Suzanne T. Gurland, Wendy DeCourcey, and Karen Jacob. "Antecedents and Consequences of Mothers' Autonomy Support." *Developmental Psychology* 38 (2002): 143–55.

Grolnick, Wendy S., and Richard M. Ryan. "Parent Styles Associated with Children's Self-Regulation and Competence in School." *Journal of Educational Psychology* 81 (1989): 143–54.

Grubb, W. Norton, and Marvin Lazerson. *Broken Promises: How Americans Fail Their Children*. New York: Basic, 1982.

Grusec, Joan E., and Jacqueline J. Goodnow. "Impact of Parental Discipline Methods on the Child's Internalization of Values." *Developmental Psychology* 30 (1994): 4–19.

Grusec, Joan E., Leon Kuczynski, J. Philippe Rushton, and Zita M. Simuti. "Modeling, Direct Instruction, and Attributions: Effects on Altruism." *Developmental Psychology* 14 (1978): 51–57.

Grusec, Joan E., and Norma Mammone. "Features and Sources of Parents' Attributions About Themselves and Their Children." In *Review of Personality and Social Psychology* 15 (1995): *Social Development,* edited by Nancy Eisenberg.

Grusec, Joan E., and Erica Redler. "Attribution, Reinforcement, and Altruism: A Developmental Analysis." *Developmental Psychology* 16 (1980): 525–34.

Grusec, Joan E., Duane Rudy, and Tanya Martini. "Parenting Cognitions and Child Outcomes." In *Parenting and Children's Internalization of Values,* edited by Joan E. Grusec and Leon Kuczynski. New York: Wiley, 1997.

Hart, Craig H., D. Michele DeWolf, Patricia Wozniak, and Diane C. Burts. "Maternal and Paternal Disciplinary Styles: Relations with Preschoolers' Playground Behavioral Orientations and Peer Status." *Child Development* 63 (1992): 879–92.

Harter, Susan. "The Relationship Between Perceived Competence, Affect, and Motivational Orientation Within the Classroom." In *Achievement and Motivation: A Social-Developmental Perspective,* edited by Ann K. Boggiano and Thane S. Pittman. Cambridge, England: Cambridge University Press, 1992.

———. *The Construction of the Self: A Developmental Perspective.* New York: Guilford, 1999.

Harter, Susan, Donna B. Marold, Nancy R. Whitesell, and Gabrielle Cobbs. "A Model of the Effects of Perceived Parent and Peer Support on Adolescent False Self Behavior." *Child Development* 67 (1996): 360–74.

Hastings, Paul D., and Joan E. Grusec. "Conflict Outcome as a Function of Parental Accuracy in Perceiving Child Cognitions and Affect." *Social Development* 6 (1997): 76–90.

———. "Parenting Goals as Organizers of Responses to Parent-Child Disagreement." *Developmental Psychology* 34 (1998): 465–79.

Hastings, Paul D., and Kenneth H. Rubin. "Predicting Mothers' Beliefs About Preschool-Aged Children's Social Behavior." *Child Development* 70 (1999): 722–41.

Herrera, Carla, and Judy Dunn. "Early Experiences with Family Conflict: Implications for Arguments with a Close Friend." *Developmental Psychology* 33 (1997): 869–81.

Hoffman, Martin. "Power Assertion by the Parent and Its Impact on the Child." *Child Development* 31 (1960): 129–43.

———. "Conscience, Personality, and Socialization Techniques." *Human Development* 13 (1970a): 90–126.

———. "Moral Development." In *Carmichael's Manual of Child Psychology,* 3rd ed., vol. 2, edited by Paul H. Mussen. New York: Wiley, 1970b.

Hoffman, Martin, and Herbert D. Saltzstein. "Parent Discipline and the Child's Moral Development." *Journal of Personality and Social Psychology* 5 (1967): 45–57.

Holt, Jim. "Decarcerate?" *New York Times Magazine,* August 15, 2004: 20–21.

Honig, Alice Sterling. "Compliance, Control, and Discipline." *Young Children,* January 1985: 50–58.

Jacobvitz, Deborah, and L. Alan Sroufe. "The Early Caregiver-Child Relationship and Attention-Deficit Disorder with Hyperactivity in Kindergarten: A Prospective Study." *Child Development* 58 (1987): 1488–95.

Johnson, Susan L., and Leann L. Birch. "Parents' and Children's Adiposity and Eating Style." *Pediatrics* 94 (1994): 653–61.

Juul, Jesper. *Your Competent Child: Toward New Basic Values for the Family.* New York: Farrar, Straus, and Giroux, 2001.

Kamins, Melissa L., and Carol S. Dweck. "Person Versus Process Praise and Criticism: Implications for Contingent Self-Worth and Coping." *Developmental Psychology* 35 (1999): 835–47.

Kandel, Denise B., and Ping Wu. "Disentangling Mother-Child Effects in the Development of Antisocial Behavior." In *Coercion and Punishment in Long-Term Perspectives,* edited by Joan McCord. Cambridge, England: Cambridge University Press, 1998.

Kelley, Michelle L., Thomas G. Power, and Dawn D. Wimbush. "Determinants of Disciplinary Practices in Low-Income Black Mothers." *Child Development* 63 (1992): 573–82.

Kernis, Michael H. "Toward a Conceptualization of Optimal Self-Esteem." *Psychological Inquiry* 14 (2003): 1–26.

Kernis, Michael H., Anita C. Brown, and Gene H. Brody. "Fragile Self-Esteem in Children and Its Associations with Perceived Patterns of Parent-Child Communication." *Journal of Personality* 68 (2000): 225–52.

Kilgore, Kim, James Snyder, and Chris Lentz. "The Contribution of Parental Discipline, Parental Monitoring, and School Risk to Early-Onset Conduct Problems in African American Boys and Girls." *Developmental Psychology* 36 (2000): 835–45.

Kochanska, Grazyna. "Mutually Responsive Orientation Between Mothers and Their Young Children: Implications for Early Socialization." *Child Development* 68 (1997): 94–112.

Kochanska, Grazyna, and Nazan Aksan. "Mother-Child Mutually Positive Affect, the Quality of Child Compliance to Requests and Prohibitions, and Maternal Control as Correlates of Early Internalization." *Child Development* 66 (1995): 236–54.

Koestner, Richard, Richard M. Ryan, Frank Bernieri, and Kathleen Holt. "Setting Limits on Children's Behavior: The Differential Effects of Controlling vs. Informational Styles on Intrinsic Motivation and Creativity." *Journal of Personality* 52 (1984): 233–48.

Kohn, Alfie. *The Brighter Side of Human Nature: Altruism and Empathy in Everyday Life.* New York: Basic Books, 1990.

———. "Caring Kids: The Role of the Schools." *Phi Delta Kappan,* March 1991: 496–506. Available at www.alfiekohn.org/teaching/cktrots.htm.

———. *No Contest: The Case Against Competition.* Rev. ed. Boston: Houghton Mifflin, 1992.

———. "Choices for Children: Why and How to Let Children Decide." *Phi Delta Kappan,* September 1993: 8–20. Available at www.alfiekohn.org/teaching/cfc.htm.

———. "The Truth About Self-Esteem." *Phi Delta Kappan,* December 1994: 272–83. Available at www.alfiekohn.org/teaching/tase.htm.

———. *Beyond Discipline: From Compliance to Community.* Alexandria, VA: Association for Supervision and Curriculum Development, 1996.

———. "How Not to Teach Values: A Critical Look at Character Education." *Phi Delta Kappan,* February 1997: 429–39. Available at www.alfiekohn.org/teaching/hnttv.htm.

———. "Television and Children: ReViewing the Evidence." In *What to Look for in a Classroom . . . and Other Essays.* San Francisco: Jossey-Bass, 1998.

———. *Punished by Rewards: The Trouble with Gold Stars, Incentive Plans, A's, Praise, and Other Bribes.* Rev. ed. Boston: Houghton Mifflin, 1999a.

———. *The Schools Our Children Deserve: Moving Beyond Traditional Classrooms and "Tougher Standards."* Boston: Houghton Mifflin, 1999b.

———. "Education's Rotten Apples: From Math Instruction to State Assessments, Bad Practices Can Undermine the Good." *Education Week,* September 18, 2002: 48, 36, 37. Available at www.alfiekohn.org/teaching/edweek/rotten.htm.

Kohn, Melvin L. *Class and Conformity.* 2nd ed. Chicago: University of Chicago Press, 1977.

Kuczynski, Leon. "Reasoning, Prohibitions, and Motivations for Compliance." *Developmental Psychology* 19 (1983): 126–34.

———. "Socialization Goals and Mother-Child Interaction: Strategies for Long-Term and Short-Term Compliance." *Developmental Psychology* 20 (1984): 1061–73.

Kuczynski, Leon, and Grazyna Kochanska. "Development of Children's Noncompliance Strategies from Toddlerhood to Age 5." *Developmental Psychology* 26 (1990): 398–408.

Kuczynski, Leon, Grazyna Kochanska, Marian Radke-Yarrow, and Ona Girnius-Brown. "A Developmental Interpretation of Young Children's Noncompliance." *Developmental Psychology* 23 (1987): 799–806.

Lamborn, Susie D., Sanford M. Dornbusch, and Laurence Steinberg. "Ethnicity and Community Context as Moderators of the Relations Between Family Decision Making and Adolescent Adjustment." *Child Development* 67 (1996): 283–301.

Lamborn, Susie D., Nina S. Mounts, Laurence Steinberg, and Sanford M. Dornbusch. "Patterns of Competence and Adjustment Among Adolescents from Authoritative, Authoritarian, Indulgent, and Neglectful Families." *Child Development* 62 (1991): 1049–65.

Levine, Robert A. "Challenging Expert Knowledge: Findings from an African Study of Infant Care and Development." In *Childhood and Adolescence: Cross-Cultural Perspectives and Applications,* edited by Uwe P. Gielen and Jaipaul Roopnarine. Westport, CT: Praeger, 2004.

Lewin, Kurt, Ronald Lippitt, and Ralph K. White. "Patterns of Aggressive Behavior in Experimentally Created 'Social Climates.'" *Journal of Social Psychology* 10 (1939): 271–99.

Lewis, Catherine C. "The Effects of Parental Firm Control: A Reinterpretation of Findings." *Psychological Bulletin* 90 (1981): 547–63.

———. *Educating Hearts and Minds: Reflections on Japanese Preschool and Elementary Education.* Cambridge, England: Cambridge University Press, 1995.

Lieberman, Alicia F. *The Emotional Life of the Toddler.* New York: Free Press, 1993.

Lovett, Herbert. *Cognitive Counseling and Persons with Special Needs: Adapting Behavioral Approaches to the Social Context.* New York: Praeger, 1985.

Luster, Tom, Kelly Rhoades, and Bruce Haas. "The Relation Between Parental Values and Parenting Behavior: A Test of the Kohn Hypothesis." *Journal of Marriage and the Family* 51 (1989): 139–47.

Luthar, Suniya S., and Bronwyn E. Becker. "Privileged but Pressured?: A Study of Affluent Youth." *Child Development* 73 (2002): 1593–1610.

Luthar, Suniya S., and Karen D'Avanzo. "Contextual Factors in Substance Use: A Study of Suburban and Inner-City Adolescents." *Development and Psychopathology* 11 (1999): 845–67.

Lytton, Hugh. "Physical Punishment Is a Problem, Whether Conduct Disorder Is Endogenous or Not." *Psychological Inquiry* 8 (1997): 211–14.

Maccoby, Eleanor E., and John A. Martin. "Socialization in the Context of the Family: Parent-Child Interaction." In *Handbook of Child Psychology*, 4th ed., vol. 4, edited by Paul H. Mussen. New York: Wiley, 1983.

Makri-Botsari, E. "Causal Links Between Academic Intrinsic Motivation, Self-Esteem, and Unconditional Acceptance by Teachers in High School Students." In *International Perspectives on Individual Differences*, vol. 2: *Self Perception*, edited by Richard J. Riding and Stephen G. Rayner. Westport, CT: Ablex, 2001.

Mallinckrodt, Brent, and Mei-Fen Wei. "Attachment, Social Competencies, Interpersonal Problems, and Psychological Distress." Paper presented at the annual conference of the American Psychological Association, Toronto, August 2003.

Marshall, Hermine H. "An Updated Look at Delaying Kindergarten Entry." *Young Children*, September 2003: 84–93.

Matas, Leah, Richard A. Arend, and L. Alan Sroufe. "Continuity of Adaptation in the Second Year: The Relationship Between Quality of Attachment and Later Competence." *Child Development* 49 (1978): 547–56.

McCord, Joan. "Questioning the Value of Punishment." *Social Problems* 38 (1991): 167–79.

———. "On Discipline." *Psychological Inquiry* 8 (1997): 215–17.

McLeod, Jane D., Candace Kruttschnitt, and Maude Dornfeld. "Does Parenting Explain the Effects of Structural Conditions on Children's Antisocial Behavior?" *Social Forces* 73 (1994): 575–604.

Merrow, John. *Choosing Excellence*. Lanham, MD: Scarecrow Press, 2001.

Miller, Alice. *The Drama of the Gifted Child*. Rev. ed. New York: Basic, 1994.

Morris, Amanda Sheffield, Laurence Steinberg, Frances M. Sessa, Shelli Avenevoli, Jennifer S. Silk, and Marilyn J. Essex. "Measuring Children's Perceptions of Psychological Control." In *Intrusive Parenting: How Psychological Control Affects Children and Adolescents,* edited by Brian K. Barber. Washington, D.C.: American Psychological Association, 2002.

Mosier, Christine E., and Barbara Rogoff. "Privileged Treatment of Toddlers: Cultural Aspects of Individual Choice and Responsibility." *Developmental Psychology* 39 (2003): 1047–60.

Murstein, Bernard I., Mary Cerreto, and Marcia G. MacDonald. "A Theory and Investigation of the Effect of Exchange-Orientation on Marriage and Friendship." *Journal of Marriage and the Family* 39 (1977): 543–48.

Neighbors, Clayton, Mary E. Larimer, Irene Markman Geisner, and C. Raymond

Knee. "Feeling Controlled and Drinking Motives Among College Students." *Self and Identity* 3 (2004): 207–224.

Newcomb, Theod[o]re H. "The Family in 1955." *Merrill-Palmer Quarterly* 2 (1956): 50–54.

Noddings, Nel. *The Challenge to Care in Schools: An Alternative Approach to Education.* New York: Teachers College Press, 1992.

Norem-Hebeisen, Ardyth A., and David W. Johnson. "The Relationship Between Cooperative, Competitive, and Individualistic Attitudes and Differentiated Aspects of Self-Esteem." *Journal of Personality* 49 (1981): 415–26.

Oliner, Samuel P., and Pearl M. Oliner. *The Altruistic Personality: Rescuers of Jews in Nazi Europe.* New York: Free Press, 1988.

Parpal, Mary, and Eleanor E. Maccoby. "Maternal Responsiveness and Subsequent Child Compliance." *Child Development* 56 (1985): 1326–34.

Parsons, Jacquelynne E., and Diane N. Ruble. "The Development of Achievement-Related Expectancies." *Child Development* 48 (1977): 1075–79.

Petersen, Larry R., Gary R. Lee, and Godfrey J. Ellis. "Social Structure, Socialization Values, and Disciplinary Techniques: A Cross-Cultural Analysis." *Journal of Marriage and the Family* 44 (1982): 131–42.

Pieper, Martha Heinemann, and William J. Pieper. *Smart Love.* Boston: Harvard Common Press, 1999.

Pinderhughes, Ellen E., Kenneth A. Dodge, John E. Bates, Gregory S. Pettit, and Arnaldo Zelli. "Discipline Responses: Influences of Parents' Socioeconomic Status, Ethnicity, Beliefs About Parenting, Stress, and Cognitive-Emotional Processes." *Journal of Family Psychology* 14 (2000): 380–400.

Reeve, Johnmarshall, Glen Nix, and Diane Hamm. "Testing Models of the Experience of Self-Determination in Intrinsic Motivation and the Conundrum of Choice." *Journal of Educational Psychology* 95 (2003): 375–92.

Reyna, Christine, and Bernard Weiner. "Justice and Utility in the Classroom: An Attributional Analysis of the Goals of Teachers' Punishment and Intervention Strategies." *Journal of Educational Psychology* 93 (2001): 309–19.

Rimer, Sara. "Schools Moving to Curb Wrangling Over Rankings." *New York Times,* March 9, 2003: A16.

Ritchie, Kathy L. "Maternal Behaviors and Cognitions During Discipline Episodes." *Developmental Psychology* 35 (1999): 580–89.

Rogers, Carl R. "A Theory of Therapy, Personality, and Interpersonal Relationships, As Developed in the Client-Centered Framework." In *Psychology: A Study of a Science.* Study I: Conceptual and Systematic, vol. 3, edited by Sigmund Koch. New York: McGraw-Hill, 1959.

Rohner, Ronald P., Kevin J. Kean, and David E. Cournoyer. "Effects of Corporal Punishment, Perceived Caretaker Warmth, and Cultural Beliefs on the Psychological Adjustment of Children in St. Kitts, West Indies." *Journal of Marriage and the Family* 53 (1991): 681–93.

Rothbaum, Fred, and Gisela Trommsdorff. "Do Roots and Wings Complement or Oppose One Another?: The Socialization of Relatedness and Autonomy in Cultural Context." In *Handbook of Socialization,* edited by Joan E. Grusec and Paul D. Hastings. New York: Guilford, in press.

Rowe, David C. "Group Differences in Developmental Processes: The Exception or the Rule?" *Psychological Inquiry* 8 (1997): 218–22.

Rowe, Mary Budd. "Relation of Wait-Time and Rewards to the Development of Language, Logic, and Fate Control: Part II—Rewards." *Journal of Research in Science Teaching* 11 (1974): 291–308.

Ryan, Richard M., and Kirk Warren Brown. "Why We Don't Need Self-Esteem." *Psychological Inquiry* 14 (2003): 71–76.

Ryan, Richard M., and Edward L. Deci. "When Rewards Compete with Nature: The Undermining of Intrinsic Motivation and Self-Regulation." In *Intrinsic and Extrinsic Motivation: The Search for Optimal Motivation and Performance,* edited by Carol Sansone and Judith M. Harackiewicz. San Diego: Academic Press, 2000.

———. "On Assimilating Identities to the Self." In *Handbook of Self and Identity,* edited by Mark R. Leary and June Price Tangney. New York: Guilford, 2003.

Samalin, Nancy, with Martha Moraghan Jablow. *Loving Your Child Is Not Enough.* New York: Penguin, 1988.

Schaefer, Earl S., and Marianna Edgerton. "Parent and Child Correlates of Parental Modernity." In *Parental Belief Systems: The Psychological Consequences for Children,* edited by Irving E. Sigel. Hillsdale, NJ: Erlbaum, 1985.

Schimel, Jeff, Jamie Arndt, Tom Pyszczynski, and Jeff Greenberg. "Being Accepted for Who We Are." *Journal of Personality and Social Psychology* 80 (2001): 35–52.

Schwartz, Barry. *The Battle for Human Nature: Science, Morality, and Modern Life.* New York: Norton, 1986.

Scott-Little, M. Catherine, and Susan D. Holloway. "Child Care Providers' Reasoning About Misbehaviors." *Early Childhood Research Quarterly* 7 (1992): 595–606.

Sears, Robert R., Eleanor E. Maccoby, and Harry Levin. *Patterns of Child Rearing.* Evanston, IL: Row, Peterson, 1957.

Simons, Ronald L., Kuei-Hsiu Lin, Leslie C. Gordon, Gene H. Brody, and Rand D. Conger. "Community Differences in the Association Between Parenting Practices and Child Conduct Problems." *Journal of Marriage and the Family* 64 (2002): 331–45.

Simons, Ronald L., Les B. Whitbeck, Rand D. Conger, and Wu Chyi-In. "Intergenerational Transmission of Harsh Parenting." *Developmental Psychology* 27 (1991): 159–71.

Simpson, A. Rae. *The Role of the Mass Media in Parenting Education.* Boston: Center for Health Communication, Harvard School of Public Health, 1997.

Stayton, Donelda J., Robert Hogan, and Mary D. Salter Ainsworth. "Infant Obedience and Maternal Behavior." *Child Development* 42 (1971): 1057–69.

Stormshak, Elizabeth A., Karen L. Bierman, Robert J. McMahon, and Liliana J. Lengua. "Parenting Practices and Child Disruptive Behavior Problems in Early Elementary School." *Journal of Clinical Child Psychology* 29 (2000): 17–29.

Strage, Amy, and Tamara Swanson Brandt. "Authoritative Parenting and College Students' Academic Adjustment and Success." *Journal of Educational Psychology* 91 (1999): 146–56.

Straus, Murray A. *Beating the Devil Out of Them: Corporal Punishment in American Families and Its Effects on Children.* 2nd ed. New Brunswick, NJ: Transaction, 2001.

———. "Children Should Never, Ever, Be Spanked, No Matter What the Circumstances." In *Current Controversies on Family Violence,* 2nd ed., edited by Donileen R. Loseke, Richard J. Gelles, and Mary M. Cavanaugh. London: Sage, 2004.

———. *Primordial Violence: Corporal Punishment by Parents.* Walnut Creek, CA: AltaMira Press, 2005.

Straus, Murray A., and Anita K. Mathur. "Social Change and the Trends in Approval of Corporal Punishment by Parents from 1968 to 1994." In *Family Violence Against Children,* edited by Detlev Frehsee, Wiebke Horn, and Kai-D. Bussmann. New York: Walter de Gruyter, 1996.

Straus, Murray A., and Julie H. Stewart. "Corporal Punishment by American Parents: National Data on Prevalence, Chronicity, Severity, and Duration, in Relation to Child and Family Characteristics." *Clinical Child and Family Psychology Review* 2 (1999): 55–70.

Straus, Murray A., David B. Sugarman, and Jean Giles-Sims. "Spanking by Parents and Subsequent Antisocial Behavior of Children." *Archives of Pediatrics and Adolescent Medicine* 151 (1997): 761–67.

Swanson, Ben, and Brent Mallinckrodt. "Family Environment, Love Withdrawal, Childhood Sexual Abuse, and Adult Attachment." *Psychotherapy Research* 11 (2001): 455–72.

Toner, Ignatius J. "Punitive and Non-Punitive Discipline and Subsequent Rule-Following in Young Children." *Child Care Quarterly* 15 (1986): 27–37.

Tronick, Edward Z. "Emotions and Emotional Communication in Infants." *American Psychologist* 44 (1989): 112–19.

Walker, Lawrence J., and John H. Taylor. "Family Interactions and the Development of Moral Reasoning." *Child Development* 62 (1991): 264–83.

Watson, Marilyn. *Learning to Trust: Transforming Difficult Elementary Classrooms Through Developmental Discipline.* San Francisco: Jossey-Bass, 2003.

Wigfield, Allan. "Children's Attributions for Success and Failure." *Journal of Educational Psychology* 80 (1988): 76–81.

Zahn-Waxler, Carolyn, Marian Radke-Yarrow, and Robert A. King. "Child Rearing and Children's Prosocial Initiations Toward Victims of Distress." *Child Development* 50 (1979): 319–30.

ACKNOWLEDGMENTS

Without Abigail and Asa, whom you've met in these pages, my thoughts about raising children would be both less substantive and less interesting—and so would my life. Even apart from the stories I've told about them, my sense of what it means to be a parent is informed in every particular by being *their* parent. Similarly, my thinking—and, again, my life—has been immeasurably enriched by their other parent, my wife, Alisa. She, too, makes an appearance in these pages from time to time, but those references can't begin to capture how much I owe her. Her extraordinary insight and patience, her consistent focus on doing what's best for our children, inspire me and improve me and invite me to examine my own parenting choices. (So does the fact that she occasionally says to me, only half in jest, "Hmmmm. Now, what would Alfie Kohn say about what you just did?")

Alisa was invaluable to this book in another, more specific way. She read every single chapter and offered suggestions that reliably improved the argument and the tone. Remarkably, Marilyn Watson, to whom I'm not even related, performed a similar service, bringing her considerable wisdom, erudition, and life experience to bear on what I had written. I've known Marilyn for a good while now, and, as I explained in the foreword I was thrilled to write for her own book a couple of years ago, her thinking on child development has influenced me as much as that of anyone else in the field. But don't hold her—or, for that matter, Alisa—responsible for everything on these pages; just give them credit for the parts that make sense to you.

While I'm at it, there are other people who likewise should not be held responsible, and to whom I'm grateful for reading portions of the book and responding with useful comments, large and small: Wendy Grolnick, Rich Ryan, David Altshuler, Fred Rothbaum, and Ed Deci.

Of course, there might not have been a book for these people to improve if it weren't for the expertise and interest of Gail Ross and Tracy Behar, agent and editor extraordinaire, respectively. I'm indebted to both of them for—and gratified by—their dedication to this project.

INDEX

achievement
  effects on:
    of conditional vs. unconditional
      acceptance, 89–92, 224n12
    of fear of failure, 91–92
    of parental control, 82–83
    of rewards, 32
  pressures on children related to,
    74–79, 80, 82–87, 92, 160–62
  vs. enjoyment and well-being, 75, 84,
    86, 232n11
  vs. learning, 162
  See also control of children; grades
apologies
  offered to children, 126
  required from children, 14
assertiveness, 6–7
athletics. *See* sports
authenticity, 125–27
authoritarian parenting, 50–51, 103–4,
  180, 219, 240n14
authoritative parenting, 104–5,
  234–35n14
autonomy
  as basic human need, 57–58, 168–70
  cultural differences in attitudes
    toward, 213–15
  difficulty of supporting, 110
  lack of, as expressed in defiance, 55
  strategies for supporting, 184–85,
    196–97
  support for, as more than absence of
    control, 238n2
  See also choices for children
autoparent, 136

Baumrind, Diana, 17–18, 104–5,
  234–35n14

behaviorism, 13–16, 26, 35, 150–51
Bowlby, John, 106–7
bragging about children, 77–78

Cagan, Elizabeth, 4
children
  attitude toward, in U.S., 97–99
  conditional vs. unconditional love of,
    10–19
  described as manipulative, 209
  developmental limitations of,
    100–101, 129–30, 131–32
  difficulty of raising, 1–2
  dismissing, vs. taking seriously, 119,
    207–208
  excessive control of, 46–62
  frustrations experienced by, 99, 135
  goals for, of parents and teachers,
    2–4, 7–8, 118–19, 122–23, 164
  meeting other people's, 210–11
  motives attributed to, 110, 130–33,
    157–58, 174, 241n4
  nature of, 14–17, 191–92
  parenting practices as experienced by,
    20–22, 205
  pressures on, 74–77, 112–14 (*see also*
    achievement: pressures on children
    related to)
  relationships between parents and,
    68–69, 123, 125–27, 228n12
  respect for, 49, 98, 124–25
  taking the perspective of, 204–11
  with special needs, 113, 236n7
  See also choices for children; control
    of children; love of children; needs
    of children
choices for children
  benefits of providing, 167–70, 196

choices for children (*continued*)
  as generated by children vs. adults,
    180
  limits to, 167–68, 179–80
  meaningful, 179–80
  and parents' demands, 183–84
  and participation in decision-making,
    172–77, 218
  reasons given for failure to provide,
    180
  strategies for providing, 170–90
  vs. pseudochoice, 177–79
coercion
  explanations for parents' use of, 112,
    138, 207, 215
  falsely contrasted with permissive-
    ness, 102, 173, 220
  limited effectiveness of, 51, 96–97
  moral guidelines without relying on,
    70–71, 195
  parent's perceived powerlessness as
    related to use of, 109
  and school achievement, 83
  strategies for minimizing impact of,
    184–85
  See also control of children
college preparation, 74–75
Coloroso, Barbara, 7, 129
commodity fetishism, 237n6
competition
  among parents, 114
  effects of:
    on achievement, 88
    on generosity and moral develop-
      ment, 194, 239n3
    on parent-child relationships, 100
    on self-esteem, 45, 76–77, 227n24
  in sports, 86–88
  vs. cooperation, 88, 194
compliance
  alleged importance of, in dangerous
    neighborhoods, 219–21
  attempting to elicit, vs.:
    meeting children's needs, 118–19,
      127–28, 163
    promoting judgment and responsi-
      bility, 221
    rethinking one's requests, 121–22,
      138
  effects on, of control vs. choice,
    51–53, 168, 181

excessive, 6, 54
  as primary goal:
    of parenting guides, 4–5, 121
    of parents, 2
    of schools, 163–66
  strategies for eliciting, 181–84
compliments, 158–59. *See also* praise
conditional acceptance
  appeal of, for parents, 12
  and assumptions about human
    nature, 14–17, 90, 155
  basic examples of, 24
  and behaviorism, 13–16
  and control, 48
  despite assurances of love, 142–43
  and economic view of relationships,
    17–19, 101–2
  effects of, 15–16, 20–23, 45, 89–90
  as emotional abuse, 20
  experience of, by children, 20–22, 27,
    154
  as inherited, 22–23
  praise as example of, 36–41, 153
  and pressure on children to succeed,
    78, 84–85, 160–62
  reasons for, 93–115
  and religion, 102–3
  vs. unconditional acceptance, 10–19
  See also love withdrawal; praise;
    rewards; unconditional acceptance
conflict
  between siblings, 170–71, 203–204
  construed as problem with child, 110
  eliminating vs. resolving, 240–41n14
  unconditional support during, 23
  and use of perspective taking,
    203–204, 206
  See also negotiation
conformity, 101, 215. *See also* compli-
    ance
consequences
  as euphemism for punishment, 65
  as justification for punishment, 70
  "natural," 66, 231n7
  to self vs. others, 70–71, 191, 198
  as type of punishment, 65–66
consistency
  between home and school, 163,
    166
  between two parents, 137
  excessive emphasis on, 136–37

control of children
  attempts to secure, by means of:
    authoritarian measures, 51
    guilt, 49
    love, 24
    praise, 36, 40, 58, 154
    time-outs, 26–27
  and beliefs about human nature, 98,
    155
  conditional acceptance as related to,
    48
  difficulty of securing, 53
  effects of:
    on compliance, 51–53
    across cultures, 214
    in general, 61, 168
    on interest and skills, 59–61
    on relationships and emotional
      health, 54–57
    on self-regulation, 58–59
  explanations for parents' desire for,
    51, 93–115, 180
  fear of permissiveness and, 49, 114–15
  and internalization, 57–58, 84
  pervasiveness of, 46–48, 99
  in public, 111–12, 138
  rationalized by invoking "real
    world," 71, 135, 169, 219–21
  rationalized by invoking safety, 112,
    134
  regarding food, 47, 58–59
  regarding grades, 82–83
  and religion, 102–3
  as time-consuming, 176
  vs. participation of child in decision
    making, 172–77, 218
  vs. structure, 61, 220, 230n29
  See also choices for children; coer-
    cion; discipline; love withdrawal
corporal punishment
  compared to love withdrawal, 29–30,
    65–66
  declining acceptance of, 215–16
  effects of, 64, 118, 230–31n4
  and love, 72, 216–17, 219
  possible racial differences in effects
    of, 216–19
  relevance of race to prevalence of,
    215–16
  relevance of socioeconomic status to
    prevalence of, 214–15

  use of, in dangerous neighborhoods,
    219–21
criticism, 143–45
cultural differences in approach to parenting, 50, 61, 212–14

"dangerous neighborhood" theory,
  219–21
Deater-Deckard, Kirby, 216–19
Deci, Edward, 21–23, 44, 57–58, 60,
  214
decision making. See choices for children; control of children
defiance, 52, 55–57
dichotomies, false, 103–4, 173, 220
disabilities, children with, 113, 236n7
discipline
  authoritarian, 50–51, 103–4, 180,
    219, 240n14
  authoritative, 103–4, 234–35n14
  in dangerous neighborhoods, 219–21
  differences in, by class and race,
    214–19
  explanations for differences in
    approach to, 50, 106, 220, 230n3
  inductive, 198–99
  limited effectiveness of, 118
  by love withdrawal, 24–31, 42
  power- vs. love-based, 24, 29
  vs. changing child's environment,
    139
  See also conditional acceptance; con-
    trol of children; parenting
distraction (as technique), 129
Dobson, James, 102
Dodge, Kenneth, 216–19
Dweck, Carol, 40

eating, 47, 58–59
economic view of relationships, 17–19,
  101–2
education. See learning; school; teachers
either-or thinking. See dichotomies,
  false
empathy, 200–201, 240n11. See also
  perspective taking
ethics. See moral development
explanation
  of moral principles, 194–200
  of reasons for requests, 182–83
  vs. discussion, 196

explanation (*continued*)
  vs. questions, 127–29
  while punishing, 72

failure
  effects of, 91
  fear of, 85, 91–92
false self, 23
fear
  of babying children, 114–16
  for children's safety, 112
  of failure, 85, 91–92
  of incompetence as a parent, 108–9
  of judgment, 111–12
  of loss of parent's love, 30
  of permissiveness, 49, 114–15
  of powerlessness and vulnerability,
    109–10, 126, 208
  of spoiling children, 49, 95
Fromm, Erich, 75
Frost, Robert, 94

generosity, 35, 157–58, 198, 237n9
gifts, 153
Ginott, Haim, 49, 65, 67
Glasser, William, 65
goals for children, 2–4, 7–8, 118–19,
    122–23, 164
Golden Rule, 201–202
Gordon, Thomas, 53, 65, 68, 114,
    124–25, 143, 179
grades
  effects of, 32, 79–81, 161
  elimination of, 81–82
  parental pressure regarding, 82–83
Grolnick, Wendy, 60, 61, 86, 214
guilt
  control by means of, 49
  as explanation for spending money
    on children, 153
  as result of conditional parenting,
    57–58

happiness, 75, 140–41, 191, 239n1
Hein, Piet, 120–21
Hoffman, Martin, 29, 31, 192, 198–99
homework, 60–61, 233n5
honesty
  effects on, of punishment, 70
  lack of, in compulsory apologies, 14
  lack of, in pseudochoice, 178
  with one's children, 182, 193

with oneself, 120–21
human nature, beliefs about, 14–17,
    90, 98, 155, 191–92
humor, 210
hyperactivity, 228n7

ignoring (as technique), 25, 150–51
incentives. *See* rewards
infants
  fear of spoiling, 95, 114
  incipient empathy in, 240n11
  negative motives ascribed to, 235n22
  parental responsiveness to, in other
    cultures, 212
  parental will imposed on, 227n5,
    228n7
  preferences of, 171
  taking perspective of, 209
  unconditional acceptance of, 142
interest (in learning and other tasks)
  effects on:
    of fear of failure, 91
    of grades, 79–80
    of parental control, 59–60,
      82–84
    of rewards, 33–34
    of unconditional acceptance,
      224n12
  importance of, 161–62
internalization of values, 6, 57–58, 84,
    222n7

Kafka, Franz, 201
Katz, Lilian, 85
Kelley, Michelle, 219–20
kindergarten, delaying entrance to,
    77–78, 232n6
Kohn, Melvin, 215
Kunc, Norman, 110

learning
  as active meaning-making, 196
  effects on:
    of fear of failure, 91
    of grades, 79–81
    of parental control, 82–83
    of rewards, 32
    of unconditional acceptance,
      224n12
  focus on, vs. on achievement, 162
Lewis, Catherine, 132, 234n14
Lieberman, Alicia, 129

limits
  imposed on children vs. intrinsic to
    situation, 191
  setting, 179
  "testing," 132, 147
listening, 127–29, 173. See also reflec-
    tive listening
love of children
  in cross-cultural perspective, 213
  types of, 10
  and use of punishment, 72, 216–17,
    219
  vs. of their actions, 142–43
  See also conditional acceptance;
    unconditional acceptance
love withdrawal
  effects of, 27–31, 42, 85
  examples of, 25–27, 85, 150–52
  See also conditional parenting;
    time-outs
Lovett, Herbert, 151
lying. See honesty

manners. See politeness
McCord, Joan, 64
Miller, Alice, 10, 106, 137, 208
modeling. See setting an example
moral development
  effect on:
    of competition, 194, 239n3
    of love withdrawal, 31
    of parental control, 59
    of participation in decision mak-
      ing, 196
    of perspective taking, 201–203
    of punishment, 70–71, 192
  focus on, vs. on child's being well-
    behaved, 2, 191
  strategies for promoting, 192–200
morning, parenting challenges in the,
    174–75
motivation
  impossibility of creating in others,
    228n12
  intrinsic vs. extrinsic, 33–34, 36,
    79
  intrinsic vs. internal, 84
  as natural, 233n16
motives, beliefs about children's, 110,
    130–33, 157–58, 174, 241n4

"natural consequences," 66, 231n7

needs of children
  determining, through perspective tak-
    ing, 205–206
  effects of responding to, 192–93
  examples of:
    attention, 151
    autonomy, 57–58, 168–70
    parental approval, 40
    secure attachment, 192–93
    structure, 61
    unconditional love, 10–11
  as focus of parenting efforts:
    vs. compliance, 118–19, 163
    vs. parent's convenience, 5
    vs. parent's needs, 107, 235n17,
      240–41n14
    vs. wants, 134, 153
  importance of determining, 127–28
negotiation
  benefits of, 175
  between parent and child, 172–77,
    218
  between siblings, 170–71
  promoting children's skill at, 238n10
  time required for, 176–77
"no," saying, to children. See prohibi-
    tions
Noddings, Nel, 130–33

obedience. See compliance

parenting
  and attempts to win vs. avoid battles,
    150
  authoritarian, 50–51, 103–4, 180,
    219, 240n14
  authoritative, 104–5, 234–35n14
  beliefs about, as related to practices,
    114
  books and articles about, 4–5, 14,
    96, 121, 222n4
  cultural differences in, 50, 61, 212–14
  difficulty of, 1–2, 106
  "doing to" vs. "working with," 8,
    19, 72–73, 96, 110, 118, 163, 173
  excessive vs. poor, 77–79
  explanations for problematic
    approaches to, 93–115
  flexibility in, 136–37
  mindful, 136
  perceptions of, by children, 20–22,
    27, 154

parenting (*continued*)
  prevalence of control-based approach
    to, 46–48, 99
  reconsidering one's approach to,
    115–16, 120–21, 211
  relevance to, of one's own childhood,
    22–23, 94, 105–7, 109, 126,
    130–31, 208–209
  research on, 5, 21
  societal views about, 94–96, 99,
    111–12
  use of perspective taking in, 204–11
pediatricians, 95
permissiveness, 49, 99, 103–5, 114–15,
    220, 234n14
perspective taking
  absence of, 207–208
  and age of child, 201, 202
  barriers to, 207–209
  effects of, 201–203, 205–206
  and humor, 210
  moral significance of, 201–203
  by parents, 204–11
  strategies for promoting, 203–204
  variations of, 200–201
Piaget, Jean, v, 201
politeness, 111, 191, 199–200
positive reinforcement. *See* praise
praise
  alternatives to, 155–60
  asking children about, 160
  as conditional love, 36–41, 153
  effects of:
    on achievement, 34
    on generosity, 35, 237n9
    on intrinsic motivation, 35
    on self-image, 39–40
  as instrument of control, 36, 40, 58,
    154
  as judgment, 36, 148, 155–56
  motivated by parent's vs. child's
    needs, 155
  and preoccupation with behavior, 35
    (*see also* behaviorism)
  spontaneous vs. calculated, 154
  vs. encouragement, 155
  See also conditional acceptance;
    rewards
predictability, 137
pressure on children
  to achieve, 74–79, 80, 82–87, 92,
    160–62

to grow up faster, 112–14
  See also conditional acceptance; con-
    trol of children
prohibitions
  frequency of, 133, 209
  inadequacy of, without accompany-
    ing reasons, 195
  unnecessary, 133–36, 143
pseudochoice, 177–79
punishment
  adults' memories of, 130–31
  definition of, 63
  effects of, 63–72, 136–37, 230n3
  falsely contrasted with neglect, 103–4
  fine-tuning vs. eliminating, 150
  implications of, for moral develop-
    ment, 70–71, 192, 197
  justifications offered for, 71–72, 147,
    177
  by means of love withdrawal, 24–31
  and love, 72, 216–17, 219
  for poor grades, 82–83
  purposes of, 63, 101–2, 145, 230n1
  in schools, 163–66
  and use of explanations, 72
  vicious circle created by, 66–67
  vs. problem-solving, 124, 137,
    238n10
  See also consequences; corporal pun-
    ishment; time-outs

questions, 127–29
  vs. criticisms, 144
  vs. praise, 156–57

race, relevance of, to parenting,
    215–19
raising children. *See* parenting
reading
  love of, vs. pressure to master, 84
  motivation for, 33
reasoning
  importance of, for moral develop-
    ment, 194–99
  self- vs. other-oriented, 197–200
  supporting children's, 196–97
  through discussion, 196
  vs. dictating, 195
  vs. punishing, 68, 71
reciprocity, 18. *See also* economic view
    of relationships; self-interest
redshirting, 78–79

reflective listening
  appropriate use of, 182, 211
  exaggerated benefits claimed for,
    222n4
reinforcement. *See* rewards
religion, 102–3
report cards. *See* grades
research, parenting
  compliance as primary goal in, 5
  as rarely cited in parenting guides, 5
  techniques of, 21
respect for children, 49, 98, 124–25
retribution, 101–2, 145, 230n1
rewards
  and behaviorism, 13
  effects of, 32–34, 73, 192
  for good grades, 82–83
  popularity of, 31–32
  in schools, 163–66
  similarity of, to punishment, 73, 104
  as unloving, 153
  vs. gifts, 153
  See also behaviorism; grades; praise
Rogers, Carl, 20, 23
Rothbaum, Fred, 213
Rowe, Mary Budd, 39
Ryan, Richard, 44, 57–58, 60, 214

safety
  emotional, 128
  physical, 112, 133–34
Samalin, Nancy, 55
school
  cooperative learning in, 194
  delaying entrance to, 77–78, 232n6
  effects of giving students more choices
    in, 169
  control-based practices in, 163–66,
    168
  parents' efforts to improve, 164–66
  unconditional acceptance in, 138–39
  See also grades; learning; teachers
self-centeredness
  error of attributing, to human nature,
    223n1
  vs. perspective taking, 201–203
  See also self-interest
self-discipline, 6
self-esteem
  contingent vs. unconditional, 43–45,
    88–92, 140, 226–27n21
  contrasting views on, 42–43

effects on:
  of competition, 77, 227n24
  of conditional acceptance, 23, 45
  of praise, 39–40
self-handicapping, 85, 90
self-interest
  as misguided rationale for helping,
    197–99
  as promoted by punishments and
    rewards, 70–71, 192, 221
  vs. other goals for children, 239n1
setting an example
  by apologizing, 126
  by engaging in perspective taking,
    203, 207
  by following one's own rules, 183
  by moral reflection and action, 193
  by punishing, 67–68
Shaw, George Bernard, 203
siblings
  caring for, 194
  conflicts between, 170–71
Skinner, B.F., 13, 26
socioeconomic status
  relevance of, to parenting, 214–15
  relevance of, to pressure on children
    to excel, 75–76
spanking. *See* corporal punishment
special needs, children with, 113,
    236n7
spoiling
  fear of, 49, 95
  vs. unconditional parenting, 141
  with things vs. with love, 153
sports, 85–88
standards, excessively high, 85, 101,
    130
stress, 74. *See also* achievement: pres-
    sures on children related to

teachers
  effects on, of control, 61
  unconditional acceptance by, 148–49
  See also school
television, 113–14, 172–74, 203,
    235n24
temper tantrums, 185–86
"terrible twos," 213
thank-yous
  from children, 111, 199–200
  as similar to praise, 158–59
threats. *See* punishment

time-outs, 25–27, 65–66, 69, 151–52
    See also love withdrawal
trust, 56–57, 65, 98, 123, 176

unconditional acceptance
  alleged drawbacks of, 88–92
  assumptions about human nature
    underlying, 14–17, 90
  benefits of, 11, 15, 224n12 (*see also*
    conditional acceptance: effects of)
  change in perceptions involved with,
    124
  as consistent with pride and frustra-
    tion, 154

  in cross-cultural perspective, 213
  difficulty of providing, 140–42,
    147–49
  rarity of, 11, 141
  relevance to, of one's own childhood,
    107
  strategies for providing, 141–66
  by teachers, 148–49, 224n12
  vs. conditional acceptance, 10–19
  See also conditional acceptance

Watson, Marilyn, 148, 196–97
well-behaved children. *See* compliance